Arguing About Abortion

D1124862

Arguing
About Abortion

Lewis M. Schwartz

Lehman College

Wadsworth Publishing Company
Belmont, California
A Division of Wadsworth, Inc.

Philosophy Editor: Ken King
Editorial Assistant: Gay Meixel
Production Editor: Angela Mann
Managing Designer: Carolyn Deacy
Print Buyer: Diana Spence
Permissions Editor: Jeanne Bosschart
Designer: Detta Penna
Copy Editor: Holly Wunder
Cover Design: Cassandra Chu Design
Cover Photograph: © 1992 Rick Reinhard, IMPACT VISUALS
Signing Representative: Constance Jirovsky
Compositor: Weimer Incorporated
Printer: Malloy Lithographing

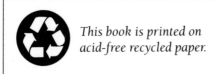 This book is printed on acid-free recycled paper.

Printed in the United States of America
1 2 3 4 5 6 7 8 9 10—97 96 95 94 93

Library of Congress Cataloging in Publication Data

Schwartz, Lewis M.
    Arguing about abortion / Lewis M. Schwartz.
       p. cm.
    Includes bibliographical references.
    ISBN 0-534-19542-3
    1. Abortion—United States.   2. Debates and debating—United
States.   I. Title.
HQ767.5.US39   1992
363.4'6'0973—dc20   92–14970

Socrates: . . . Some things I have said of which I am not altogether confident. But that we shall be better and braver and less helpless if we think that we ought to inquire than we should have been if we indulged in the idle fancy that there is no knowing and no use in seeking to know what we do not know—that is a theme upon which I am ready to fight, in word and deed, to the utmost of my power.

Plato, *Meno*

To my wife, Eileen,
who is the source of many arguments.

Contents

Part II:
Model Argument Reconstructions
53

Part III:
Supplementary Essays
173

Preface

Arguing About Abortion came into being as a result of my effort to find appropriate materials for a large section of a course in contemporary ethical issues. For me, the thought of 140 students arguing about abortion, or, for that matter, any other moral issue, was too much to bear given my previous experiences with such courses—albeit with smaller sections. Despite lively discussions, I had too often come away from these courses with the realization that I had not overcome the "bottom-line" syndrome: too few students had gone beyond mere reaction to the authors' conclusions. The vast majority of them had not come to appreciate the bases on which the authors had built their conclusions.

In short, my judgement was that I had regrettably missed two opportunities. The first was the opportunity to provide students with the wherewithal to analyze effectively any arguments they may encounter, either written or spoken, whatever the subject. I was not in need of the many reports that bemoan our students' lack of this skill. Certainly, the majority of students at my college, a typical urban, comprehensive college, simply do not deal adequately with argumentative discourse. The second was the opportunity to provide a sufficient basis for students to reconsider their initially held beliefs about the nature and worth of ethical argument. Predominantly, or so it seems to me, students tend to hold either that ethical considerations are "just matters of opinion" and therefore neither worthy of study in their own right nor of serious importance in making practical choices, or that ethical principles are of theological origin and so not corrigible.

In *Arguing About Abortion*, I have sought to provide material that will enable instructors to remedy these defects. As to developing the skills of analyzing arguments, the text provides not only a concise discussion of how to analyze argumentative discourse and how to evaluate it systematically, but it also introduces a format that students can use to reconstruct such discourse. The form is that of a linear map; it requires students to identify the main conclusion of an essay and to formulate the premisses on which that main conclusion rests, to identify the basis on which each premiss of that argument is introduced, and, in those cases in which a premiss of the main argument is itself a conclusion based on other premisses, to identify those other premisses.

This book also contains twelve essays in which the authors present reasoned arguments about abortion. For the first three essays, I have provided extensive discussion and presented students with a methodology for creating a map of the arguments contained in those essays. I have also provided model outlines of these essays and the three additional essays that appear in Part II. Then in Part III I have presented six other essays that help round out the argumentative landscape of the abortion issue and provide material students can use to practice the analytical and evaluative skills they have learned.

As to encouraging students to challenge their own beliefs about the foundations of ethics, an advantage of studying a series of essays in which the authors often comment extensively on one another's arguments is that even if students concentrate single-mindedly on the task of reconstructing the arguments contained in a particular essay, they nevertheless come to engage actively in the process of evaluating the arguments. They simply cannot reconstruct the arguments of a given author without appreciating the arguments of the author being criticized. By limiting the topics covered in a course to not more than two—I think of this text as providing material for slightly more than one-half of one semester—I have found that students can be helped to see the incompleteness of, and sometimes the inconsistency in, their own thinking about ethics.

A number of people have helped me with this text, but none more than those at Wadsworth, especially Angela Mann, who oversaw the production of the text. My thanks also to the reviewers Arthur F. Moeller, University of Pittsburgh, Greensburg; and Lynn Pasquerella, University of Rhode Island, for their helpful comments.

Arguing About Abortion

Part I

Analyzing Arguments

Reconstructing Argumentative Discourse

Introduction

This book has two purposes. One purpose is to introduce readers to serious philosophical discussion about the issue of abortion. At least an equally important purpose is to help readers develop a disciplined method for analyzing and evaluating discussions about a wide range of moral topics, whether the discussions concern abortion or any other question of personal or public choice.

The abortion issue, like almost every other difficult moral issue, elicits widely divergent opinions. With respect to just one important dimension of it—the question of when, if ever, abortion is morally permissible—the answers are almost inexhaustible. At one extreme, there are those who say that abortion is never morally permissible, even to save the woman's life. Others think abortion is never morally permissible except to save the woman's life. Still others include cases of forcible rape among the exceptions, and others include cases of fetal malformation. At the other extreme, there are those who maintain that even infanticide is sometimes morally permissible, and may be performed at will. Others take intermediate positions between these two extremes. Some believe that abortion is morally permissible only until the fetus's brain activity becomes detectable; others draw the line at the fetus's first movement, at the point that the fetus begins to resemble a person, or when the fetus is viable; and some allow for abortion at any time until birth. Nor are these the only positions taken.

Often the people who hold these various positions on the abortion issue do battle with one another; indeed, sometimes they do physical battle. But sometimes even people who do physical battle try to put forward their reasons for adopting their positions. They try to explain why they believe what they believe and why they do what they do. In the terms of this book, we say that people sometimes *argue* for their beliefs. We apply the term *argument* to all cases in which an individual cites something that he or she believes as reason for believing something or as reason for choosing to perform a particular action. Here are some examples of arguments that might appear in a discussion of abortion:

> Because a fetus is an organism conceived by human parents, it is a person and so it must not be killed.

> A woman may make any decision with regard to an early fetus because the fetus cannot live apart from the womb and so is merely a part of her body.

> Since we accept moral constraints on our conduct toward animals, the fact that a fetus is not a person does not mean that there are no constraints as to how we treat it.

The speaker in the first example argues to the conclusion that a fetus must not be killed. The reason given for adopting this conclusion consists of two claims: that because a fetus is an organism conceived by human parents it is a person and persons may not be killed. In the second case, the speaker argues to the conclusion that a woman may make any decision she pleases with regard to an early fetus, citing the claims that such a fetus cannot live apart from the woman's body and must therefore be considered to be part of her body. Note that whereas in the first example, the conclusion is stated last, in the second example it is stated first. The third example is slightly more complicated. Here the speaker argues to the conclusion that a different argument is unsatisfactory. The speaker says that it is unsatisfactory to argue from the claim that a fetus is not a person to the claim that we are not constrained as to how we treat the fetus. The reason cited for rejecting this argument is that we accept moral constraints even on our conduct toward animals.

As we read the various essays contained in this book, we will concentrate on identifying and laying bare the arguments within them. Our immediate task will be to reformulate each essay into a form that makes the conclusions the authors reach and the reasons they cite for adopting those conclusions as clear and precise as possible. For simplicity, we will call such reconstructions *argument outlines,* or *argument maps.*

Part I of this book presents, in some detail, methods for developing an argument outline. We shall discuss how to identify the parts of an argument—its premises and conclusions—and we shall discuss how to reconstruct an argumentative passage into an outline that clearly exhibits the interconnections among these parts. Part II contains six essays that present a wide variety of positions on the issue of abortion. We will discuss three of these essays paragraph by paragraph so that we can create an outline of their arguments step by step. The other three essays will be presented with outlines included at the end. Readers will get the most benefit from this section if they prepare their own argument outlines and then compare them to the models. Part III contains several other essays for which argument outlines have not been included. These essays round out the discussion of abortion and permit readers to have further practice in developing argument outlines on their own.

The purpose of learning to construct argument outlines is to enable readers to evaluate such essays more thoroughly. Unfortunately, not all arguments are good ones. Sometimes the reasons people give for what they believe and do fail to justify their conclusions. Although Part I of this book also discusses procedures and principles for evaluating arguments systematically and thoroughly, Part II concentrates on laying out the arguments for inspection. Readers will not, except incidentally, evaluate the essays in this section and will not be asked to decide which arguments have the most merit.

Despite the single-minded focus on reconstructing arguments, however, readers will have plenty of opportunity to study the processes of evaluation and to consider the merits of the various arguments presented. For one thing, the process of interpreting an author's arguments will sometimes require readers to consider which interpretation would give the author's argument the greatest strength and perhaps select a particular interpretation for just that reason. Also, because the authors of these essays often criticize arguments developed by other authors, reconstructing a particular argument will sometimes require comparative evaluation. Nonetheless, our principal task will be to present the authors' arguments as thoroughly as we can. Readers will thus be left to reach final evaluations of the arguments on their own.

Why Argue?

Most often people argue to persuade others to adopt their conclusions. Or, adding the plausible assumption that our beliefs influence our conduct, people may argue to persuade others to adopt a given course of conduct. But sometimes people put forward their reasons just for—or also for—the sake of having the argument criticized by others. One assumption underlying such a practice is the belief that because we sometimes make mistakes it often makes practical sense to lay out our arguments for others to examine. For example, someone might say, "Here are my reasons for having an abortion. Are they good ones?" Once we have presented our reasons, others might spot mistakes in our reasoning or identify assumptions that are questionable or simply false. They might also provide us with additional information or point to alternatives that we were unaware of and so lead us to a different, and perhaps more prudent, course of conduct.

Moreover, whenever our conduct significantly affects other people, it verges on a moral obligation to open our reasoning to criticism. Thus a policymaker might say, "Here are my reasons for permitting abortions in particular cases. Are they good ones?" Participants in the abortion controversy often believe their opponents are acting in ways that cause serious detriment to others. People who support the right to abortion believe that those who constrain that right do serious harm to the women who would seek an abortion. And people who oppose abortion believe that supporters of abortion are, at a minimum, allowing serious harm to human fetuses. Whenever people's beliefs and actions grounded in those beliefs affect others, it seems appropriate to expect them to put their reasons forward for criticism by others, especially those others who disagree with their conclusions.

It also makes both practical and moral sense to learn how to analyze and evaluate arguments put forward by others. Although we shall assume that the authors of the essays we examine seek only to persuade readers on the basis of arguments they believe to be sound, we know perfectly well that there are many whose argumentative goals are to persuade others regardless of the worth of their arguments or the correctness of their conclusions. We have all had experience with unscrupulous people, from misleading advertisers to demagogic politicians to con-men to unabashed scoundrels. Being able to reconstruct another's arguments so that we can thoroughly inspect them is the best protection against such deceivers. Even those who knowingly mislead others can profit by such discipline, for they, too, do not want to be misled by others.

This, then, is the spirit in which we will reconstruct the arguments presented here. We shall assume that the authors of the essays we read present their arguments not only to persuade others but also for the sake of having their views criticized by others. That is, we shall assume that the authors would not want to persuade us on the basis of ill-founded reasoning and would, therefore, welcome sound criticism of their arguments. In doing so, we take the notion of an essay literally, which means that we approach one as an attempt to put ideas to the test.

Although the authors of the essays presented in this book come to competing conclusions, all the essays share the quality of representing serious efforts to contribute to our understanding of the issues surrounding the abortion controversy. Indeed, good readers will often be able to feel the authors' struggles to make their own ideas clear, sometimes with more and sometimes with less success. This intensity sometimes makes the essays difficult to interpret so that readers will do well to give them careful and patient attention in order to reconstruct their arguments fairly and accurately.

Recognizing Arguments

Suppose we hear someone say:

John and Mary look alike. They are siblings.

What would we think? Is the speaker simply telling us some things that she believes about John and Mary? Perhaps she knows John and Mary and is merely telling us two things that she knows about them: that they look alike and that they are siblings. That's a plausible interpretation of what was said. But the speaker may be saying something different. She may be telling us that she has inferred that John and Mary are siblings from the fact that they look alike. In other words, she may be saying that the fact that John and Mary look alike constitutes good reason for believing that they are siblings, and that she believes they are siblings for that very reason.

Note that the speaker could have said:

> The reason I believe that John and Mary are siblings is that they look alike.

This would have made it perfectly clear that she was giving an argument and claiming more than that the two statements are true. To be sure, a third possible interpretation of the speaker's statements might be that she is explaining why John and Mary look alike. That is, she might be telling us that the fact that they are siblings explains why they look alike. Note that she could have said:

> Mary and John look alike because they are siblings.

This would have made it clear that she was doing more than merely making two independent claims about John and Mary. She would have been making a third claim, namely, that the truth of one of the claims explains why the other one is true.

We have considered three plausible interpretations of the two sentences. Note that by using words and phrases such as *the reason why I believe* _____ *is* _____, or _____ *because* _____, or _____ *is a reason for believing* _____, the speaker can make it clear that she is making an argument by claiming that one statement provides reason for believing another statement or that one statement explains why another one is true.

In general, arguments cite one or more statements as reason for believing another statement or they cite one or more statements to explain why another statement is true. To consider another example, suppose we read the following:

> It is raining out. The sidewalks are wet.

In interpreting what has been said, we must first determine whether the author is providing an argument. Is he simply telling us two things that he believes? Or is he telling us that there is a connection between the two statements so that one statement serves as reason for believing the other or as an explanation of why the other is true? If the author is not merely making two independent claims, the following possibilities remain:

> The fact that it is raining out explains why the sidewalks are wet.

> The fact that it is raining out provides a reason for believing that the sidewalks are wet.

The fact that the sidewalks are wet provides a reason for believing that it is raining out.

The fact that the sidewalks are wet explains why it is raining out.

We would normally rule out the last interpretation on the grounds that whereas wet sidewalks can provide a reason for believing that it is raining, it is hard to accept wet sidewalks as an explanation of *why* it is raining.

Note that if the author had said:

The sidewalks are wet because it is raining,

it would have been perfectly clear that he was citing the fact that it is raining as an explanation of why the sidewalks are wet. And, if the author had said:

My reason for believing that it is raining is that the sidewalks are wet,

it would have been perfectly clear that he was citing the wet sidewalks as justification for his belief that it is raining. Lastly, if he had said:

My reason for believing that the sidewalks are wet is that it is raining,

it would have been perfectly clear that he was citing his belief that it is raining as justification for believing that the sidewalks are wet.

In general, given any two statements, X and Y, we have the following five possibilities:

1. The author is simply claiming that X is true and that Y is true. In this case, the author is not arguing.

2. The author is claiming that X is true because Y is true.

3. The author is claiming that Y is true because X is true.

4. The author cites X as a reason for believing that Y is true.

5. The author cites Y as a reason for believing that X is true.

In speaking or writing, whenever we connect statements with words and phrases such as *since, because,* or *my reason for believing* _____ is _____, we make it clear that we have joined the statements in an argument. Similarly, in interpreting someone else's statements, when we interpose such terms, we interpret the statements as forming an argument. Thus these locutions are called *argument indicators.*

Sometimes, in the absence of further information in a written passage, we might not be able to tell whether or not the author is arguing. In such cases, we try all the possibilities and then make our best guess. Fortunately, in most cases, and especially where authors are deeply interested in making their thoughts clear to others, we find that authors make abundant use of argument indicators to make it clear when they are using one statement or set of statements as an explanation for another statement or as their reason for believing it. Rather than leaving readers to guess as to whether an argumentative connection among statements is intended, authors are likely to write sentences such as the following:

> *Because* John stopped studying, he failed.
> John stopped studying *because* he failed.
> I *infer from the fact* that John failed that he stopped studying.
> My *reason for believing* that John failed is that he stopped studying.

Readers would do well to make sure they recognize that each of these sentences makes a different claim. In all four, the speaker expresses the belief that John stopped studying as well as the belief that John failed. Beyond that, however, they differ. The first cites the fact that John stopped studying as an explanation of why he failed. The second cites the fact that he failed as an explanation of why he stopped studying. The third cites the fact that he failed as the speaker's reason for believing that he stopped studying. The fourth cites the fact that he stopped studying as the speaker's reason for believing that he failed.

Readers should be aware of argument indicators because authors use them to make it clear that they are providing an argument as well as to make it clear just what argument they are making. Throughout this book readers will be able to practice recognizing argument indicators as part of identifying and laying out arguments.

Basic Argument Structure

The simple examples given so far illustrate the basic form that arguments take: one statement or group of statements is taken to be an explanation of why another statement is true or as a reason for believing that another statement is true. In technical parlance, we call the statement (or group of statements) that provide the author's reason or explanation the *premiss* (or *premisses*) of the argument and the statement for which it is taken to be a reason or an explanation the *conclusion* of the argument. Thus we can represent an argument abstractly as follows:

PREMISS 1

PREMISS 2

PREMISS 3

PREMISS n
_____

CONCLUSION

A premiss is either a reason the author has for believing the conclusion or the author's explanation of why the conclusion is true. Using this language, we can represent the following: "*Since* Mary and John are siblings, they look alike" as:

PREMISS: Mary and John are siblings.

CONCLUSION: They look alike.

Similarly, we can represent the following: "The sidewalks are wet *because* it is raining" as:

PREMISS: It is raining.

CONCLUSION: The sidewalks are wet.

On the other hand, the author could have said: "I infer that it is raining from the fact that the sidewalks are wet." If so, we would structure the argument as follows:

PREMISS: The sidewalks are wet.

CONCLUSION: It is raining.

Sometimes it is useful to represent an argument more graphically. We may think of ourselves as trying to create a visual map of an argument by drawing an arrow from the premiss or premisses to the conclusion. In the first example, when we interpret the statements as an argument, we may represent it as follows:

John and Mary look alike.

They are siblings.

The statement from which the arrow is drawn is the premiss. The statement to which the arrow points is the conclusion.

Sometimes it will be convenient to number the statements contained in the argument:

1. John and Mary look alike.

2. They are siblings.

We can then use the numbers in a simplified graphical representation of the argument:

Sometimes authors present information without constructing an argument. An author may simply be presenting what amounts to a list of facts or, to use a less troublesome term, a list of statements that he or she believes to be true. Consider the following paragraph:

At the end of six weeks all of the internal organs of the fetus will be present, but[1] as yet in a rudimentary stage. The blood vessels leading from the heart will be present, although[2] they too will continue to grow in size with growth of the fetus. By the end of seven weeks, if[3] one tickles the mouth and nose of the developing embryo with a hair, it will flex its neck, while[4] at the end of eight weeks there will be readable electric activity coming from the brain. By now also the fingers and toes will be recognizable. At the end of ten weeks, spontaneous movement is seen. At twelve weeks the brain structure is completely developed.[5]

This passage provides a good example of an author providing a list of facts. Each sentence makes one or two claims about the developing fetus: that at the end of six weeks all its internal organs are present in rudimentary form; that blood vessels will also be present; that, at the end of seven weeks, if one tickles its nose, it will flex its neck; and so on. It seems reasonable to believe that the author is simply presenting some information about the biological development of the fetus.

In this case, it is almost certainly true that the author has reasons for believing these things to be true. For example, the author might be a biologist who has carefully observed developing fetuses over a period of time. Or the author might be reporting the results of others' research into the development of fetuses. Nevertheless, it is evident that in this passage the author is not informing readers of her reasons for believing these things. She is merely reciting some things she believes to be true. There is no suggestion here that one or more of these statements explains another statement or gives the author's reason for believing another statement. Indeed, inserting an argument indicator such as *since* or *because* between any two of the sentences would probably cause readers to misinterpret the passage. Try it:

Since at the end of eight weeks there is detectable brain activity, spontaneous movement is seen at the end of ten weeks.

Or

As a result of the fact that by the end of seven weeks if one tickles the mouth and nose of the developing embryo with a hair, it will flex its neck, there will be readable electric activity coming from the brain at the end of eight weeks.

---

[1] The word *but* serves merely as a conjunction. The sentence contains two claims.

[2] The same is true of the word *although*; it serves merely as a conjunction.

[3] The word *if* introduces the antecedent of a conditional statement. (See p. 17.)

[4] The word *while* serves as a conjunction.

[5] Adapted from Hellegers, Andre E., "Fetal Development," *Theological Studies*, vol. 31, no. 1 (March 1970), pp. 3–9.

Whereas it is possible that the author is making such connections, we are not given any reason in the paragraph to believe that this is so. Furthermore, even rudimentary knowledge of biology would suggest that it is unlikely that she is making such connections. It is more likely that the author is merely putting forward a list of some biologically grounded beliefs about the development of human fetuses.

To say that the paragraph does not contain an argument is not to say that the paragraph is without value. Assuming that the author is in a good position to be sure of the information presented, readers who are not familiar with such facts may be grateful to the author for providing clear information about the biological development of fetuses. Such information is interesting in its own right. Knowing this information also can be of significance for a number of other purposes, including evaluating arguments about the permissibility of abortion.

Consider now the same passage, but with the addition of a new last sentence:

> At the end of six weeks all of the internal organs of the fetus will be present, but as yet in a rudimentary stage. The blood vessels leading from the heart will be present, although they too will continue to grow in size with growth of the fetus. By the end of seven weeks, if one tickles the mouth and nose of the developing embryo with a hair, it will flex its neck, while at the end of eight weeks there will be readable electric activity coming from the brain. By now also the fingers and toes will be recognizable. At the end of ten weeks, spontaneous movement is seen. At twelve weeks the brain structure is completely developed. At this point, it is a person.

What are we to make of this last sentence? Perhaps we should treat it simply as another claim in this long list of claims. But such an interpretation would be troubling, especially when we realize that the term *person* is not a part of the standard language of biology. Whereas we often encounter the term *person* in legal, ethical, sociological, and psychological contexts, we do not find it in biological contexts. Interpreting the author as making a biological claim here would thus certainly shake our confidence in her. Another possibility is to suppose that the author has simply included another one of her beliefs despite the fact that it is different from the others insofar as it goes beyond biology. Perhaps she has included the last sentence as a parenthetical claim. This, too, however, would be a troubling interpretation since the author has not indicated that it is to be taken as a parenthetical remark. Without such indication, we have reason for doubting that interpretation.

The most plausible interpretation of the last sentence is that the author is making an argument. At least for those interested in the abortion issue, it is certainly more interesting to interpret the passage in that way. And, moreover, it makes sense to add one of our argument indicators:

> Since the brain structure is completely developed, the fetus is now a person.

Or

> My reason for believing that the fetus is now a person is that its brain structure is completely developed.

Interpolating an appropriate argument indicator would make explicit our interpretation of this passage as an argument. While we must keep in mind that we are interpreting, in the absence of further information, we have no alternative but to make our best guess.

Having decided to interpret the passage as an argument, we shall next want to determine exactly what the argument is. It seems to be as follows:

> PREMISS: The organism's brain is completely developed.

> CONCLUSION: It is a person.

But this, too, is an interpretation of what we have read, a second stage of interpretation. Not only have we interpreted the passage to be one that contains an argument, but we have also interpreted the passage as containing that particular argument. Here again it is possible for us to be mistaken. The author might also be arguing as follows:

> PREMISS 1: At the end of six weeks all of the internal organs of the fetus will be present, but as yet in a rudimentary stage.

AND

> PREMISS 2: The blood vessels leading from the heart will be present, although they too will continue to grow in size with growth of the fetus.

AND

> PREMISS 3: By the end of seven weeks, if one tickles the mouth and nose of the developing embryo with a hair, it will flex its neck.

AND

> PREMISS 4: At the end of eight weeks there will be readable electric activity coming from the brain.

AND

> PREMISS 5: At the end of eight weeks the fingers and toes also will be recognizable.

AND

> PREMISS 6: At the end of ten weeks, spontaneous movement is seen.

AND

> PREMISS 7: At twelve weeks the brain structure is completely developed.

SO

> CONCLUSION: At twelve weeks the organism is a person.

This interpretation also makes sense. Perhaps the author is arguing that human organisms are persons only when they have completely developed brain structures in addition to the other organic characteristics developed at appropriate intervals. In the absence of further information, it would be difficult for us to tell which argument the author is making. In such cases, we might have to consider both or all of the possibilities.

Argument Indicators

An *argument indicator* is a word or phrase that tells us that an author is arguing. Sometimes, as in some of the examples already discussed, an author omits argument indicators. In such cases we must interpolate them if we think the author is making an argument. Most often, however, authors, especially those who are making a full-faith effort to make their ideas clear, are careful to include them where necessary. It will, therefore, be helpful to readers if they learn to be alert to them.

One of the most common argument indicators is the word *since*. Most often it appears in sentences of the following form:

Since _____, _____.

Here is an example of such a sentence:

Since today is Tuesday, tomorrow is Wednesday.

Note that the sentence below says exactly the same thing, even though the order of the phrases has been reversed:

Tomorrow is Wednesday, since today is Tuesday.

Both sentences express the argument that can be graphically represented as follows:

Today is Tuesday.

Tomorrow is Wednesday.

We find the word *since*, then, in two sentence formats:

Since _____(P)_____, _____(C)_____.

and

_____(C)_____, since _____(P)_____.

The word *since* not only tells us we are dealing with an argument, it also tells us which part of the sentence is the premiss and which part is the conclusion. Note that in both formats, the word *since* precedes the premiss.

The word *because* operates in the same way in these two sentence formats:

Because _____(P)_____, _____(C)_____.

and

———(C)———, because ———(P)———.

Because the words *since* and *because* always precede the premiss, they are sometimes called *premiss indicators*. Other examples of premiss indicators are *it follows from* and *for*, as in these sentence formats:

It follows from ———(P)——— that ———(C)———.
———(C)———, for ———(P)———.

Other words or phrases serve as *conclusion indicators* since they always occur before the conclusion. Here are some examples of sentence formats with the most common conclusion indicators:

——(P)——; therefore ——(C)——.
——(P)——; thus ——(C)——.
——(P)——; so ——(C)——.
——(P)——; hence ——(C)——.
——(P)—— entails ——(C)——.
——(P)—— implies ——(C)——.
From ——(P)—— it follows that ——(C)——.

Neither list given here is a complete one. Readers will do well to try to identify others as they read.

Just one word of caution: Some of these words, like most other words in our language, can have ambiguous meanings. The word *since,* for example, does not always indicate a premiss. Sometimes it indicates a time lapse, as in the sentence, "I have not seen Joe since he was a child." Clearly, this sentence does not contain the following argument:

Joe was a child.

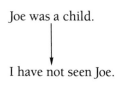

I have not seen Joe.

It is highly unlikely that the author of this sentence is explaining why he has not seen Joe; neither is it likely that the author is giving a reason for not having seen Joe by citing the fact that Joe was a child.

A similar caution must be given with respect to the words *so* and *for.* The word *so* is sometimes used as an intensifier. Consider how it is used in this sentence:

So many people recognize her, she must be famous.

Here the word *so* does not indicate a conclusion. Rather, it operates like the word *very*. The word *for*, on the other hand, is often used as a preposition, as in this example sentence:

He went to bat for me.

Ambiguity aside, the indicators we have discussed so far operate in a fairly straightforward fashion. They are used to indicate an argument, and they identify a particular statement as either a premiss or conclusion. There are also other argument indicators that are often used. Consider again the following sentence:

So many people recognize her, she must be famous.

Even though we have seen that the word *so* does not tell us that this is an argument, the sentence does contain an argument. Here it is the word *must* in the conclusion that indicates the argument. One might be tempted to identify the argument as follows:

So many people recognize her.

She must be famous.

This would be incorrect, however. Rather, the argument is as shown here:

So many people recognize her.

She is famous.

The fact that many people recognize her is evidence that she *is* famous. It is not evidence that she *must be* famous. Sometimes authors introduce the idea of necessity into the conclusion of an argument to signal that they think the premiss or premisses provide a strong reason for believing the conclusion or to signal that the conclusion necessarily follows from the premiss or premisses. They transfer, so to speak, their belief that the argumentative connection is strong to their formulation of the conclusion. Often, then, when words and phrases such as *must, necessarily,* and *has to be* appear in an author's conclusion, we can interpret them as argument indicators.

Arguments, as we have said, cite one or more statements as reason for believing another statement is true or as explanation for why another statement is true. When people argue, therefore, they commit themselves to the truth of the premisses, to the truth of the conclusion, and to the truth of the claim that the premisses constitute reason for believing the conclusion or explain why the conclusion is true. It follows, therefore, that giving an argument is very different from simply claiming that a conditional statement is true. Compare these two statements:

If you have taken the medicine, you'll be better by tomorrow.

Since you have taken the medicine, you'll be better by tomorrow.

The first of these sentences, the if-then sentence,[6] expresses a conditional statement. It is not an argument. The author does not claim that you have taken the medicine, nor does the author claim that you'll be better by tomorrow. The only claim the author does make is that it will not be the case that the antecedent statement (you have taken the medicine) is true while the consequent statement (you'll be better by tomorrow) is false. The second of these sentences does, however, contain an argument. The author of this sentence claims three things: that you have taken the medicine, that you'll be better by tomorrow, and that either the fact that you have taken medicine explains why you'll be better by tomorrow or that fact provides a reason for believing that you'll be better by tomorrow. So, be careful. Conditional statements do not themselves express arguments. They do, however, very often appear as premises of arguments.

Conditional statements occur in many guises. For example, during the course of our readings, we shall frequently come across such statements presented in the following two forms:

> Being conceived by human parents is a *sufficient condition* for being a person.

> Having a concept of a future is a *necessary condition* for having a right to life.

The notions of necessary and sufficient conditions can be readily translated into conditional statements. To claim that X is a sufficient condition for Y is to claim that whenever X is true, Y is also true. In other words, it claims that X will not be true without Y also being true. In short, it is to say:

> If X, then Y.

Thus the first statement above says nothing more than:

> If a being has been conceived by human parents, then it is a person.

To say that X is a necessary condition for Y, on the other hand, is to say that Y will not be true without X being true. In other words, it is to say:

> If Y then X.

---

[6] The standard form of a conditional statement is "If p, then q." Although the words *if* and *then* are separated, they form a single logical connective that joins two simpler statements into a single statement. The word *if* always precedes the antecedent claim. The word *then* precedes the consequent claim. Sometimes, the word *then* is omitted. And sometimes the order is reversed. Consider these three statements:

> If you take this medicine, then you'll be better by tomorrow.

> If you take this medicine, you'll be better by tomorrow.

> You'll be better by tomorrow if you take this medicine.

All three statements make exactly the same claim.

Thus, the second statement above says the same thing as:

> If something has a right to life, then it has a concept of a future.

To say that X is a necessary *and* sufficient condition for Y is to say:

> If X then Y, and if Y then X.

Complex Argument Structures

Arguments often have more than one premiss. In order to exhibit the structure of such arguments, we simply label each premiss separately and then indicate that they are to be taken together by using a plus sign and a bracket. We then draw an arrow from the cluster of premises to the conclusion:

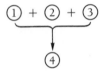

This argument map represents an argument in which three premisses, taken together, are used to explain why a fourth statement is true or to give us reason to believe the fourth statement. Similar argument maps may show either more or fewer premisses joined together to provide a reason or explanation. Consider, for example, the following argument:

> Since John is taller than Mary and Mary is taller than Steve, John is taller than Steve.

This example shows a single argument that has two premisses. We can map this argument as follows:

1. John is taller than Mary.

    +

2. Mary is taller than Steve.

3. John is taller than Steve.

The author is claiming that the first two statements, taken together, constitute reason for concluding that the third statement is true. It is not just because John is taller than Mary that the author concludes that John is taller than Steve, and it is not just because Mary is taller than Steve that the author concludes that John is taller than Steve. It is because the author believes that both the premisses are true. When an argument has more than one premiss, we say that the premisses of the argument are *conjoined*.

Can an argument have more than one conclusion? The strict answer is no. Every argument can have one and only one conclusion. But arguments often nest together to make a complex of arguments. Thus a given piece of writing or speaking may contain several arguments that join together to yield one main conclusion. Consider the following example:

> Since Mary is not yet thirty-five, and since she is not a citizen, she cannot run for president of the United States.

Here, again, we have three statements:

> Mary is not yet thirty-five.

> Mary is not a citizen.

> Mary cannot run for president of the United States.

But how are these three statements related in argument? If we treat the statements as in the previous example, we get the following argument map:

> Mary is not yet thirty-five.
>
>   +
>
> Mary is not a citizen.
>
> |
>
> Mary cannot run for president of the United States.

The two occurrences of the word *since,* however, suggest another structure. Perhaps the author is giving two independent reasons why Mary cannot run for president. Indeed, since each premiss in this example provides an independent basis for the conclusion, it seems most plausible to construe the author as providing two separate arguments, which may be mapped as follows:

> Mary is not yet thirty-five.   Mary is not a citizen.
>
> Mary cannot run for president of the United States.

We say that an argument complex is *convergent* when we interpret it as consisting of two separate arguments that lead to the same conclusion.

Readers might do well to consider why an author might bother to give more than one argument. One answer is because it is often interesting to be aware that one can reach the same conclusion in more than one way. Another answer is that one or more of the arguments may turn out to be unsatisfactory. If so, having multiple arguments leaves open the possibility that one or more of the remaining arguments might provide strong enough reason to believe the conclusion. For example, it might turn out that the author is mistaken in claiming that Mary is not yet thirty-five. If so, that argument would fail to prove that Mary cannot run for president of the United States. Nevertheless, it is possible that the second argument succeeds in establishing its conclusion. Note that in the case of a conjoined argument, one false premiss requires us to discard the entire argument. Should it turn out, for example, that John is not taller than Mary, the argument discussed earlier would fail to prove its conclusion.

It is sometimes difficult to determine whether an author is providing a single argument with conjoined premisses or a convergent argument, leaving it as a matter of interpretation how we construe the passage. As a rule of thumb, subject to limitations that we shall discuss below, we shall interpret passages in whichever way makes the strongest argument. To this extent, then, evaluating arguments is part and parcel of interpreting them. We shall further discuss this interconnection below. For now, consider another example argument:

> Since my horse lost her shoe, I can't ride her, and since I can't ride her, I can't deliver the message.

Once again we have three statements:

> My horse lost her shoe.
>
> I can't ride my horse.
>
> I can't deliver the message.

Here, again, because there are two argument indicators we are most likely dealing with two arguments. The first argument is introduced by the first occurrence of the word *since*:

> My horse lost her shoe.
>
> ↓
>
> I can't ride her.

The second argument, introduced by the second occurrence of the word *since* is as follows:

> I can't ride her.
>
> ↓
>
> I can't deliver the message.

In this example, the second statement occurs in both arguments. It serves as the conclusion of the first argument and the premiss of the second argument. As such, it might seem that the passage would require two maps, one for each of the arguments. Provided, however, that the *very same* statement serves as both the conclusion of one argument and a premiss of the other, there is no reason not to join these arguments into a single map:

> My horse lost her shoe.
>
> ↓
>
> I can't ride her.
>
> ↓
>
> I can't deliver the message.

We call argument complexes in which the same statement occurs as the conclusion of one argument and a premiss of another *sequential arguments*.

Assigning two different roles to one statement in a single argument is not at all problematic. Statements, as we know, are claims. When we make a statement, we claim that something is true. Since we can have reasons for our claim, the claim might be the conclusion of an argument. That is, we can argue *to* a given statement. But statements can also serve as reasons for concluding that something else is true. Thus we can also argue *from* a given statement. In a sequential argument, an author gives reasons for believing a certain statement and then proceeds to draw other conclusions from it. By so doing, the author provides the links in his or her reasoning, from the initial premiss or premisses to the final conclusion.

Note, by the way, that if the preceding example had been originally stated as, "I can't deliver the message because my horse lost her shoe and so I can't ride her," the analysis of it would have been identical to what was presented here. The order in which statements occur in a passage is not necessarily the same as the order in which we shall present them when we reconstruct the argument. In conversation, premisses might be stated either before or after the conclusion.

The following passage has yet a different structure. (For convenience, we have numbered and put brackets around the composite statements within the paragraph.)

> The fact that 1. [John is a professional basketball player][7] implies that 2. [he is probably tall]. It also implies that (3) [he is probably wealthy].

The occurrence of the word *implies* between statements 1 and 2 tells us that statement 1 is a premiss and that statement 2 is a conclusion. Thus the structure of that part of the argument is as follows:

John is a professional basketball player.

He is probably tall.

The second occurrence of the word *implies* tells us that statement 3 is also a conclusion. But from which of the other statements is it derived? The most plausible answer is that statement 3 is also a conclusion drawn from

---

[7]Note that we have ignored the phrase *the fact that* and identified "John is a professional basketball player" as the first statement of the passage. The only difference between someone's claiming that John is a professional basketball player and claiming that it is a fact that John is a professional basketball player is rhetorical. The truth value of the two statements is identical. If it is true that John is a professional basketball player then it is true that it is a fact that John is a professional basketball player, and vice versa. Moreover, if either one is false, so is the other. The phrase "the fact that" is used to emphasize the author's conviction that John is a professional basketball player.

statement 1. Clearly, to construe statement 3 as derived from statement 2 would be to make the argument a weak one. In this case, then, the most plausible interpretation is that two different conclusions are drawn from the same premiss. We should, therefore, map our argument as follows:

We call an argument structure such as this one *divergent*. In arguments with divergent structures, the same premisses (or, as in this case, premiss) are used to establish distinct conclusions.

Complex passages often contain a combination of several different argument structures. Given that arguments may include more than one premiss and may contain several argument structures, there will be many different types of argument maps. Here are just a few examples:

and

and

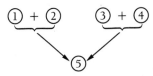

Longer, more complicated passages might have even more complicated maps that combine these sorts of arguments structures. The basic argument map of an essay, for example, might look like this:

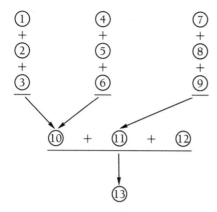

This map represents an argument complex in which two separate arguments of three premisses each—statements 1, 2, and 3 and statements 4, 5, and 6—are provided for statement 10; a single argument of three premisses is given for statement 11; and no argument is given for statement 12. Statements 10, 11, and 12 constitute the premisses of an argument given for statement 13.

We say that every argument consists of a set of statements, one or more of which are the premisses and one of which is the conclusion. An argument can have any number of premisses, but an argument can have one, and only one, conclusion. A complex passage, however, may contain more than one argument. When considering nested arguments, for example, we are likely to discover several conclusions as well as several premisses. Note that whenever the arguments in a passage are connected, we may sometimes speak informally of the "author's argument," even though we recognize that it is actually a complex of several arguments.

Because it is sometimes difficult to determine the arrangement of the particular arguments within an argument complex, we should practice analyzing some nested arguments while we continue to explore the form in which we can most clearly lay them out for our inspection. Consider one of the passages discussed earlier:

> Because a fetus is an organism conceived by human parents, it is a person and so it must not be killed.

The words *because* and *so* tell us immediately that we are dealing with argument, indeed, most likely with two arguments. But which statements are the premisses and which statement is the conclusion? How are they related? The first step in restructuring such a passage is to identify and number the statements within it:

1. A fetus is an organism conceived by human parents.

2. It (a fetus) is a person.

3. It (a fetus) must not be killed.

Note that we treat the argument indicators as external to the statements that comprise the argument. Whereas they give us clues as to how the argument is to be structured, they are not part of the premisses or conclusion themselves. Now we need to think about how the statements are related. The word *because* tells us that statement 1 is a premiss. But more than that, the pattern "Because statement 1, statement 2" tells us that statement 1 must be a premiss and that statement 2 must be a conclusion. Thus this is what we have so far:

PREMISS: A fetus is an organism conceived by human parents.

CONCLUSION: It is a person.

What are we to make of statement 3? The word *so* preceding it informs us that this statement is a conclusion. Thus, because the passage also contains more than one conclusion, it must contain more than one argument. Assuming that the author has presented his or her reasoning completely, statement 3 has to be a conclusion based on either statement 1 or statement 2. This means that the argument can be reconstructed as sequential, as shown on the left, or divergent, as shown on the right:

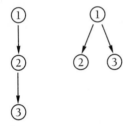

Both of these interpretations make some sense. According to the sequential interpretation, the author is understood to claim that the fact that the organism is conceived by human parents is reason to count it as a person, and that the fact that we have reason to count it as a person is reason to conclude that we must not kill it. Thus in the sequential argument, statement 2 functions as the conclusion of one argument and the premiss of the other. This argument complex can be stated generally as, Since X is true, Y is true, and since Y is true, Z is true.

The divergent interpretation construes the author as drawing two distinct conclusions from the very same premiss. Just as in the first interpretation, the author is understood to argue from the fact that an organism is conceived by human parents to the conclusion that it is a person. The second interpretation differs from the first, however, because here the author is understood to take the same premiss about the organism being conceived by human parents to argue to a different conclusion—that the fetus must not be killed.

In the absence of further information from the author, we will have to make a judgment about how best to interpret the passage. In this case there seems to be more reason to interpret the argument complex as sequential rather than as divergent. According to the divergent interpretation, the author is arguing directly from statement 1 to statement 3. It seems plausible, however, to suppose that the author would not bother to establish statement 2 unless he thought it was a relevant step in the argument from statement 1 to statement 3. According to the sequential interpretation, on the other hand, the author is giving an intermediate step of the argument and thus makes it explicit how he gets from the initial premiss to the main conclusion.

Standard Argument Form

The standard form we shall adopt for presenting arguments can be applied to the argument we have been discussing as follows:

> 1. A fetus is an organism conceived by human parents.   (AP)
>
> 2. [So]^8 A fetus is a person.   (1)
>
> 3. [So] A fetus must not be killed.   (2)

First, each statement which comprises the argument is assigned a number for easy reference. Second, at the far right, each statement is assigned a symbol which indicates the basis on which the author has included the statement in the argument. (AP) stands for "assumed premiss." An assumed premiss occurs when the author simply claims that the statement is true without giving an argument for it. This does not imply that the author could not give reasons for the claim, only that the author has not given a justification for it within the confines of the current presentation of the argument.

    The (1) symbol at the end of line 2 indicates that, at least according to our reconstruction, the author has included statement 2 on the basis of statement 1. Similarly, the (2) symbol at the end of line 3 indicates that we have taken the author to argue for statement 3 on the basis of statement 2. When a conclusion is derived from more than one premiss, we include the numbers of all the statements from which it is derived within the parentheses at the right.

    Suppose we had interpreted this passage as a divergent argument complex. In that case, we would have reconstructed it as follows:

> 1. A fetus is an organism conceived by human parents.   (AP)
>
> 2. It (a fetus) is a person.   (1)
>
> 3. It (a fetus) must not be killed.   (1)

Here the symbol (1) at the end of both lines 2 and 3 indicates that we have taken the author to derive each of statements 2 and 3 from the same premiss.

    In the case of convergent arguments, we assign more than one set of parentheses to the line. The format for this would be as follows:

> 4. _____   (1,2) (3)

---

^{8}We will often include the word *so* in brackets to emphasize that the statement is a conclusion.

This notation indicates that two arguments have been given for statement 4. The premisses of the first argument are statements 1 and 2; the premiss of the second argument is statement 3.

We can continue to examine the standard form for presenting an argument by considering a second example:

> A woman may make any decision with regard to an early fetus because the fetus cannot live apart from the womb and so is merely a part of her body.

Once we have noted the occurrence of argument indicators and satisfied ourselves that the passage is indeed an argument, we can separate the individual statements and number them:

1. A woman may make any decision with regard to an early fetus.

2. The (early) fetus cannot live apart from the womb.

3. It (the early fetus) is merely a part of her body.

What is the most plausible structure here? Actually, this passage presents considerations virtually identical to those outlined for the previous example, except that the order of presentation for the premisses and conclusion differs. In this case, the word *because* appears between statement 1 and statement 2, so we know that statement 1 must be a conclusion and statement 2 a premiss. So far, then, we have the following:

PREMISS: An early fetus cannot live apart from the womb.

CONCLUSION: A woman may make any decision with regard to it.

Now what shall we make of statement 3? The phrase *and so* tells us that statement 3 is also a conclusion. Next we have to decide whether it is derived from statement 1 or statement 2 to determine whether the argument is best understood as sequential or divergent. Here again we have slightly better reason to interpret the argument as sequential because it seems plausible to assume that the author would not bother to establish the claim that the fetus is merely part of the woman's body unless she was going to use that as a reason for concluding that a woman may make any decision with regard to it.

Thus our formal reconstruction of this argument would look like this:

1. The (early) fetus cannot live apart from her womb.   (AP)

2. It (the early fetus) is merely a part of her body.   (1)

3. The woman may make any decision with regard to it (an early fetus).   (2)

Here is a third argument for reconstruction into standard form:

> Since we accept moral constraints on our conduct toward animals, the fact that a fetus is not a person does not mean there are no constraints as to how we treat it.

This example presents a somewhat different problem of interpretation. As usual, however, we begin by taking note of the argument indicators and numbering the statements. We might try to enumerate the statements as follows:

1. We accept moral constraints on our conduct toward animals.

2. A fetus is not a person.

3. There are no constraints as to how we treat a fetus.

This would be a mistake, however, for the author is not claiming that each of these statements is true. Remember that when one argues, one accepts the truth of the premises—even if only tentatively or for the sake of argument—as well as the truth of the conclusion. That means our outline must contain only statements that the author believes are true or is otherwise willing to accept. But while this author accepts statement 1 and can be said to have accepted statement 2 for the sake of argument, he most definitely does not accept statement 3. Rather, what the author is telling us is that because statement 1 is true, statement 2 does not provide a good reason to believe that statement 3 is true, that is, because statement 1 is true, an argument from statement 2 to statement 3 is not a good one. In this case, then, there are only two statements accepted by the author, and the correct diagram of the argument is as follows:

> PREMISS: We accept moral constraints on our conduct toward animals.
>
> CONCLUSION: The argument from the statement, "A fetus is not a person," to the statement, "There are no constraints as to how we treat a fetus," is unsound.

The argument map would be as shown below:

And the argument can be reconstructed formally as follows:

1. We accept moral constraints on our conduct toward animals. (AP)

2. [So] the argument from the statement, "A fetus is not a person," to the statement, "There are no constraints as to how we treat a fetus," is unsound. (1)

In summary of what we have learned so far, arguments are cases of using one or more statements as a reason for believing another statement or for explaining why another statement is true. When we reconstruct a passage in which there is only a single argument, our task is simply to identify the premiss or premisses and the conclusion of that argument. When we reconstruct a passage that contains more than one argument, our tasks are to identify the premiss or premisses and conclusion of each argument and then determine how the multiple arguments connect to each other.

Reconstructing Longer Arguments

Once we understand the basic methods for reconstructing arguments, we can begin to consider arguments in longer passages. Here is the third paragraph of an essay that we shall read later in its entirety. It is from "Abortion and the Concept of a Person," by Jane English.

> At the center of the storm [the abortion controversy] has been the issue of just when it is between ovulation and adulthood that a person appears on the scene. Conservatives draw the line at conception; liberals at birth. In this paper I first examine our concept of a person and conclude that no single criterion can capture the concept of a person and no sharp line can be drawn. Next I argue that if a fetus is a person, abortion is still justifiable in many cases; and if a fetus is not a person, killing it is still wrong in many cases. To a large extent, these two solutions are in agreement. I conclude that our concept of a person cannot and need not bear the weight that the abortion controversy has thrust upon it.

The fact that this paragraph comes early in the author's essay and the fact that it contains the phrase *In this paper, I first examine* give us good reason to think that the author is informing us of what she is going to argue. She is telling us how her argument will proceed.

When we analyze longer passages that contain a complex nest of arguments, our most important task is always to identify the main conclusion. The main conclusion is the single statement that the author is primarily working to establish. Because there are no mechanical ways of identifying the main conclusion, one must read carefully and use all the cues provided by the author. Sometimes, however, authors will spell out the main conclusion early in the essay—and most often we can take the authors at their word. Authors may also reiterate the main conclusion of their argument at the end of the essay. In the paragraph we are working with now, English tells us what her main conclusion will be in the last sentence of the paragraph:

> MAIN CONCLUSION: Our concept of a person cannot and need not bear the weight that the abortion controversy has thrust upon it.

Once we have determined the main conclusion, even if only tentatively, it is always wise to examine it. In this case, we note that the main conclusion contains a conjunction so that the author is going to defend two claims: that the concept of a person cannot bear the weight of the abortion controversy; and that it need not. At this point we might ask ourselves whether either of these claims can be used as a premiss from which to derive the other; that is, whether we have a sequential argument. But it will be immediately apparent that this is unlikely to be the case. To consider a similar argument, I cannot say that the fact that I can't get some gasoline today to start my car means that I don't have to get gasoline to start my car. Neither can I make a good argument by reversing the statements. It is more likely that these are two distinct claims. Thus both in this example and in English's essay, we can expect to find two main arguments.

Looking again at the paragraph from the essay, we should note that the author tells us that she will first examine the concept of a person and conclude that no single criterion can capture our concept of a person and that no sharp line can be drawn. These claims, evidently, will be used to support the first main conclusion. Thus the first part of our argument reconstruction will look like this:

1. No single criterion can capture our concept of a person.   (P)

2. No sharp line (distinguishing person from nonperson) can be drawn.   (P)

3. The concept of a person cannot bear the weight of the abortion controversy.   (1,2)

Before we discuss the use of the label (P), let's consider the author's strategy for establishing her second main conclusion. She tells us that she is going to argue for each of the following claims:

4. If a fetus is a person, abortion is still justifiable in many cases.   (P)

5. If a fetus is not a person, killing it is still wrong in many cases.   (P)

6. To a large extent, these two solutions are in agreement.   (P)

7. Our concept of a person need not bear the weight that the abortion controversy has thrust upon it.   (4–6)

A brief look at the complete essay on pages 159–168 helps us to confirm our tentative structuring of the argument. We can see there that in Section I the author discusses the concept of a person. We can also see that in Section II the author considers "what follows if a fetus is a person," and that in Section III she considers the implications of "supposing a fetus is not after all a person." Because there is no Section IV, we must assume that the author will argue for statement 6 in either the second or third section, or in both. Now that we have laid out the structure of English's essay, what remains is for us to fill in the arguments she provides to support statements 1, 2, 4, 5 and 6.

Let's return to the discussion of the new symbol (P). This is a symbol we shall use primarily in the process of reconstructing an argument to indicate a premiss of an argument whenever an author not only uses that statement as a premiss for a given conclusion but also provides an argument for that premiss. Note that in the final draft of a complete argument outline, we would not need to use this symbol because we would have reconstructed each of the arguments for lines labeled (P), and thus would be able to replace the label with the numbers of the statements from which each one is derived.

Sometimes a complete outline will become so complex and unmanageable that it is useful to divide the presentation of the reconstruction into main and subordinate outlines. Then we can use the symbol (P) in the main outline to indicate that we have reconstructed the argument for that statement in one of the subordinate outlines. Consider what it would mean to add subordinate outlines to the reconstruction of the argument in the English essay.

We have already laid out lines 1–7 as the main argument. Now we can append, say, lines 8–11 and indicate that they constitute the argument(s) for line 1. We would then proceed to outline the argument(s) for line 2, and so on:

Main Argument

[Lines 1–7 as on page 29.]

Argument for Line 1

8. ————————	(AP)
9. ————————	(AP)
10. ————————	(AP)
11. ————————	(AP)

Argument for Line 2

12. ————————	(AP)
13. ————————	(AP)

Similar subordinate outlines would be included for each of the remaining lines labeled (P): lines 4, 5, and 6.

For another example of an extended complex of arguments, we will consider a case in which an author seeks to establish that there is a given point after which abortion is not permissible. Readers will remember that while some people identify that point as the moment of conception, other people accept the possibility of infanticide, and still others identify that point at a whole range of places between the two extremes. Suppose that the author wants his argument to examine and reject several definitions of personhood that have been proposed by others and then provide arguments why his definition is the most acceptable one. (This, in fact, is the structure of the first essay we shall read, "An Almost Absolute Value in History," by John Noonan.) The main outline of such an argument might well look something like this:

1. Criterion w of personhood is unacceptable.	(P)
2. Criterion x of personhood is unacceptable.	(P)
3. Criterion y of personhood is unacceptable.	(P)

4. Criterion z of personhood is unacceptable. (P)

5. (First line of the author's positive argument.) (AP)

6. (Second line of the author's positive argument.) (AP)

n. . . .

Note that the main argument outline includes one line for each criterion examined and rejected, and then proceeds with the reconstruction of the author's positive argument. After completing the main outline, we would append a subordinate outline for each of the lines labeled (P). For example, subordinate outlines with the titles "Argument for Line 1" and "Argument for Line 2" would present the author's arguments for statements 1 and 2, respectively.

The decision whether to include all the subordinate arguments in a single outline or to divide the outline into main and subordinate arguments is a matter of style and manageability of the outline. If for this example we wanted to include the arguments in which the author examines and rejects the criteria cited in lines 1–4 of the main outline, we could simply include the additional arguments in the main outline and replace the symbol (P) as appropriate.

Generating outlines of longer passages is very similar to generating outlines of shorter ones. Our first and primary task is always to look for the main conclusion. Then our second task is to identify the most important premisses, whether assumed or argued for, that the author uses to derive the main conclusion. Finally, we may proceed to reconstruct the arguments for the nonassumed premisses. The amount of detail we include will vary according to the purposes of our work.

Evaluating
Argumentative
Discourse

Evaluating Arguments

We have said that creating an argument outline puts us in a better position to evaluate the argument. To see why this is so, let us suppose that we have generated an argument outline of a particular argument. Abstractly, it might look like the following:

1. _____   (AP)

2. _____   (AP)

3. [So] _____   (1,2)

4. [So] _____   (3)

5. _____   (AP)

6. [So] _____   (4,5)

What information does this outline provide? It tells us exactly which claims comprise the author's argument. Thus it allows us to criticize the argument systematically. Because each line of the outline constitutes an independent claim made by the author each line can be evaluated separately. This particular outline indicates that the author is making the following claims: statement 1 is true; statement 2 is true; the combined truth of statements 1 and 2 provides reason to believe that statement 3 is true; the truth of statement 3 provides good reason to believe that statement 4 is true; statement 5 is true; and, finally, the combined truth of statements 4 and 5 provides reason to believe that statement 6 is true. A map of this argument would look like this:

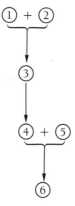

To evaluate the argument, we simply go back over it, line by line, and decide whether we accept each of the author's claims. For a premiss, we must determine whether we believe that the statement is true. For a reasoning step, we must decide whether it is valid. (We shall discuss the notion of validity shortly.) If we reject even a single premiss or a single reasoning step, we will find the argument unsatisfactory. In short, an argument complex is sound, that is cogent, only when all of its premisses are true and all of its reasoning steps are valid.

We should take special note of one thing. When evaluating the truth of any premiss or the validity of any step from a line or lines to another line, it is important to consider each individual claim on its own merits. In other words, when we evaluate a given line of an argument, we must not be influenced by how we evaluated other lines of that argument nor by whether we agree or disagree with the conclusion. Indeed, much of the skill of thinking critically consists of disciplining oneself to focus statement by statement on each individual claim of which an argument is composed.

It is also important to keep in mind that even if we think the main conclusion of the argument complex is mistaken, we need not reject every premiss or every reasoning step within the argument. Rather than simply reject an argument in its entirety, it is important to try to isolate mistaken premisses or invalid reasoning steps. Only by so doing can we make progress in our discussions with those with whom we disagree. By the same token, not every argument given in support of a conclusion with which we agree is necessarily a good one. Sometimes poor arguments are given for conclusions with which we agree.

Consider the following reconstruction of an argument. Note that it has the same form as the argument outline presented earlier.

1. The cerebrum does not develop until the sixth or seventh month. (AP)

2. Being conscious depends upon possessing a cerebrum. (AP)

3. [So] thoughts do not occur until at least the sixth or seventh month.   (1,2)

4. [So] early fetuses do not have a concept of the future.   (3)

5. Only beings that have a concept of the future can have a right to life.   (AP)

6. [So] fetuses prior to six or seven months do not have a right to life.   (4,5)

Let's consider the process of evaluating this argument. We begin with line 1. It's labeled as an assumed premiss, so we must determine whether we think the statement is true. Unless readers are biologists or have otherwise studied fetal development, they are unlikely to know whether or not it is true that the cerebrum does not develop until the sixth or seventh month. One response is to make a judgment based on our confidence in the author with respect to the subject matter at hand. Is the author an expert? Do we have reason to think that the author has researched the topic thoroughly? Is the author emotionally attached to the conclusion and therefore likely, even inadvertently, to misrepresent the case? If we are satisfied with our answers to these questions, we may accept the statement pending further information. Remember that to accept a premiss for the time being is not to commit oneself to it for all time.

Another possibility is to delay judgment pending further research. We may conduct this research on our own, or we may seek out other experts for their evaluation of the premiss. A third response is to reject the premiss and decide that the argument fails. Because a premiss is false, the author has not provided good reason for believing the conclusion. An argument that rests on even one false premiss is obviously unsatisfactory. For example, the argument that it is permissible to abort fetuses younger than five months because fetuses do not feel anything until they are five months old will collapse when it turns out that fetuses feel things earlier than that.

Nevertheless, pinpointing what we think is a false premiss can constitute a significant advance in our inquiry. In situations where we can continue a discussion with the author, we could point to the faulty premiss as a reason for rejecting the argument. Then the author may provide evidence for the premiss or decide to abandon the argument based on it. Thus identifying a premiss that you disagree with is one way to further discussion and inquiry. By focussing the discussion on a specific source of disagreement, people can move on to considering the truth of a particular premiss without getting stuck simply disagreeing about the main conclusion.

Sometimes when we doubt the truth of a premiss it is nevertheless instructive to accept it "for the sake of the argument," just as an author might put forward a premiss primarily for the purpose of considering where it might lead. In other words, authors might assume a given premiss for the sake of argument, even though they have significant doubts about the premiss or even flatly believe that it is false. The author of one of the essays in Part II, "A

Defense of Abortion," Judith Jarvis Thomson, adopts this approach when considering the following premiss:

A fetus is a person.

Although the author explicitly doubts the truth of the premiss, she nevertheless puts it forward as an assumed premiss. She then sets out to determine whether a restrictive abortion policy would follow from it.

Note that our outline format does not distinguish between premisses the author definitely believes and premisses the author has presented for the purpose of determining whether a given conclusion follows from it. In both cases, the label (AP) indicates a statement for which the author provides no further argument. This is because we label the various lines in an argument outline according to the role that each statement plays *within the given argument*. Thus when evaluating an argument, readers who doubt the truth of a particular premiss may find it useful to accept the premiss for the time being, pending further investigation, and decide if the given conclusion follows from it.

Let us, then, accept, if only tentatively, the claim that the cerebrum does not develop until the sixth or seventh month. It helps to know that this claim is widely accepted by experts in fetal development. Statement 2, "Being conscious depends upon possessing a cerebrum," is a somewhat more problematic premiss because it goes beyond biology or physiology in claiming a connection between the occurrence of consciousness and the development of a specific part of the brain. To evaluate this statement, we have to determine whether or not we believe that it is true. If we have doubts about it, we might research it further, accept it tentatively, or reject it. Since as far as this writer knows, the evidence for the claim is strong., let us accept the premiss and proceed.

Statement 3 claims that thoughts do not occur until at least the sixth or seventh month. But unlike statements 1 and 2, statement 3 is not put forward as an assumed premiss. Rather, it is put forward as a conclusion based on the claimed truth of the first two statements. We will discuss the process of evaluating reasoning steps in some detail in the next section of this chapter. For now, let us just note that the question of whether one or more statements provide good reason for believing another statement is different from considering the truth of a premiss. In evaluating the reasoning of an argument, we are not deciding whether the conclusion is true, and we have already decided whether we believe that the premisses are true. Rather, we are deciding whether *if we were to suppose* that the premisses are true, they *would* give us good reason to believe the conclusion. If we decide that they would *and* we have also decided that the premisses *are* true, then we have determined that the argument is sound. Under these circumstances, we have no choice but to believe the conclusion.

That the question of whether given premisses provide good reason for believing a particular conclusion is very different from the question of whether the premisses are true is demonstrated by the fact that we can reject one or more of the premisses and still accept the reasoning that leads to the conclusion. Consider, for example, the following argument:

1. All swans are white birds. (AP)

2. There is a swan in the next room. (AP)

3. There is a white bird in the next room. (1,2)

Even if I know that statement 1 is false (as a matter of fact, there are some black swans) and I believe that statement 2 is false (suppose I think the author is pulling my leg), I nevertheless recognize that *if I were to suppose* that statements 1 and 2 are true, then I would also have to believe that statement 3 is true. Thus, even though I doubt the truth of the premisses, I accept the reasoning that leads from statements 1 and 2 to statement 3. We call such reasoning *valid*.

Similarly, we can accept all the premisses in an argument but reject the reasoning that leads to the conclusion. Consider the following:

1. All professional basketball players are taller than 5' 5".

2. John is taller than 5' 5".

3. [So] John is a professional basketball player.

In this case, even if the premisses are true—which they are—they do not provide good reason for believing the conclusion. The first premiss claims that all professional basketball players are taller than 5' 5". It does not claim that all people who are taller than 5' 5" are professional basketball players. Thus the reasoning that leads from the premisses in statements 1 and 2 to the conclusion in statement 3 is *invalid*.

Let us return to the present case. Assuming it is true that the cerebrum does not develop until the sixth or seventh month and assuming it is also true that being conscious depends upon the organism's having developed a cerebrum, then must it also be true that thoughts do not occur until at least the sixth or seventh month? As it stands, the answer is no. Statement 3 makes a claim about when a human organism first has thoughts, but neither statement 1 nor statement 2 makes any claim about thoughts. If having thoughts had nothing to do with being conscious, then statements 1 and 2 would not support statement 3. If, on the other hand, one can have thoughts only if one is conscious, then the supposed truth of statements 1 and 2 would lead us to conclude that statement 3 must be true.

Having decided that statements 1 and 2 do not, as they stand, provide adequate reason to believe statement 3, we now confront an option. We may reject the argument or we may seek to repair it. In the current case, it seems fair to suppose that the author has simply not bothered to formulate a premiss which, had he done so, would have made the argument valid. Such a premiss might be the following:

2a. One can have thoughts only if one possesses
consciousness. (SP)

An argument from premisses 1, 2, and 2a, to the conclusion, 3, is a valid one. Just as readers may supply missing argument indicators when appropriate, so readers may supply missing premisses (subject to some restrictions which we shall discuss below). Of course, in evaluating the repaired argument, we must evaluate the truth of the supplied premiss just as we evaluate the truth of all stated premisses. Arguments with missing premisses are called *enthymemes*. Indeed, sometimes authors will omit the conclusion of an argument. Such arguments are also called enthymemes. To this point in our evaluation, then we may take the author's argument to be

   1. The cerebrum does not develop until the sixth or seventh month.   (AP)

   2. Being conscious depends upon possessing a cerebrum.   (AP)

  2a. One has thoughts only if one is conscious.   (SP)

   3. [So] an organism doesn't have thoughts until at least the sixth or seventh month.   (1,2)

The (SP) label stands for "suppressed premiss." It indicates a premiss supplied by the reader in the process of reconstructing an author's argument. The fact that we often supply missing premisses while reading or listening to an argument is evidence that we sometimes evaluate an argument at the same time that we are interpreting it. We shall discuss the matter of supplying missing premisses later in this chapter; for now it is enough to recognize that we will sometimes have to add them.

Once we make the suppressed premisses explicit, we have to determine whether they are true. We evaluate suppressed premisses in just the same way that we evaluate stated premisses. Sometimes it will turn out that the only suppressed premisses we can add that will make the argument valid are premisses whose truth we doubt. Consider the following example:

   1. If it is hot, John is uncomfortable.   (AP)

   2. If it is cold, John is uncomfortable.   (AP)

   3. [So] John is always uncomfortable.   (1,2)

As it stands, the argument is invalid. We can repair its validity by adding the premiss:

  2a. It is always either hot or cold.   (SP)

The trouble is that the suppressed premiss is false. Sometimes it is neither hot nor cold. Conscientious readers will seek to repair arguments only by adding premisses that are true[1]. But sometimes no such premiss or premisses can be added, and so the argument must be rejected.

---

[1] Subject to a restriction to be discussed later.

In the current case, it certainly seems very plausible not only to suppose that the author believes that consciousness is a necessary condition for having thoughts but also to accept that claim ourselves. Let us, then, tentatively accept statement 3 based on our tentative acceptance of statements 1, 2, and 2a, as well as our acceptance of the reasoning that leads from these statements to statement 3.

Then we can proceed to statement 4: "So, early fetuses do not have a concept of the future." This statement is taken to follow from statement 3. We must determine whether supposing that statement 3 is true implies that statement 4 is also true. In doing so, we note the introduction of a new idea in statement 4—namely, the idea of having a concept of the future. Here again it is reasonable to suppose that the author has omitted another premiss. Once we add it, our reconstruction of the argument to this point will be as follows:

1. The cerebrum does not develop until the sixth or seventh month. (AP)

2. Being conscious depends upon possessing a cerebrum. (AP)

2a. One can have thoughts only if one is conscious. (SP)

3. [So] thoughts do not occur until at least the sixth or seventh month. (1,2)

3a. Only beings that have thoughts can have a concept of the future. (SP)

4. [So] early embryos do not have a concept of the future. (3,3a)

In the process of reconstructing this argument we have identified two suppressed premisses. We have added them to our reconstruction and labeled them appropriately. In evaluating the argument, we have assessed the truth of the suppressed premisses just as we appraised the truth of the stated premisses. Pending further information, we have decided that the premisses and involved reasoning give good reason for believing statement 4.

Statement 5 is another assumed premiss. It claims that having a concept of the future is a necessary condition for having a right to life. Is this statement true? It is certainly a key claim in the author's argument. It connects the idea of having a right to life with the idea of having a conscious idea of the future. For most readers, such a claim is likely to be, at the very least, startling. We would certainly want to think about the statement before assenting to it or rejecting it, and we would want to consider arguments for it and against it. Since the author has included the statement as an assumed premiss, we are likely to reject the claim, if only tentatively, unless we have previously considered and accepted it. At a minimum, we would likely expect an argument that supports it. In the absence of that, we would probably reject statement 5.

Because the argument from statements 4 and 5 to statement 6 is valid, if statement 5 were true, then it, together with statement 4, would establish the main conclusion of the argument complex, namely, that fetuses prior to six or seven months do not have a right to life.

Now let us suppose that the author has provided an argument for statement 5. The argument would probably consist of examining the characteristics that a being would have to possess to have a right to life. The author would presumably consider the basis on which we assign various rights and try to show that, consistent with our assignations of rights in other contexts, we should accept statement 5 as true. Let us further suppose that, after thorough evaluation of it, some readers come to accept the argument for the truth of statement 5. In combination with their previous approval of statements 1 through 4, they will conclude that the author has provided a cogent, that is, sound, argument for statement 6. Of these readers, some might previously have doubted statement 6 or even have rejected statement 6. The author's argument will have caused them to modify their view of abortion. To others, even to some who had previously believed statement 5, the conclusion of the argument complex might come as a surprise. They might even have previously accepted the truth of statements 1, 2, 2a, 3a, and 5 but never have put them together as in this argument, and so be led to accept the truth of statement 6. Others might never have considered the question whether early fetuses have a right to life and now find themselves forced to accept statement 6.

On the other hand, those who continue to reject statement 6—assuming they wish to continue discussion of the topic—will be forced to identify either a false premiss or an unacceptable reasoning step within the argument complex. Most likely, they will pick statement 5, maybe pointing out, for example, that neonates do not have a concept of a future, yet we think that they have a right to life. Or they might point out that temporarily unconscious persons do not have a concept of a future but we also think that they have a right to life. In so doing, they criticize the argument. They make clear exactly what premisses or what reasoning steps they disagree with, requesting the author to provide further argument on those specific points. It is important to recognize that engaging in a good-faith discussion with an author who has provided an argument for a conclusion with which we disagree requires us to go beyond merely rejecting the conclusion. We have to identify the premisses or the reasoning steps we find unsatisfactory.

It is through this kind of procedure that we can make progress in moral, as well as scientific, discussions. Instead of simply repeating our conclusions and listening to others repeat their conclusions—a process that consists of nothing more than a 'tis/'tisn't quarrel—we may turn our attention to specific premisses or specific steps in the reasoning. With regard to the argument considered here, a thoughtful discussion would undoubtedly lead us to examine the notion of rights more thoroughly to determine on what basis we assign rights in general and the right to life in particular.

One corollary of what we have just discussed should be pointed out immediately: there is an enormous difference between determining that an argument fails to prove its conclusion and determining that its conclusion is false. If we did not distinguish between these two outcomes, we would be able to prove anything by simply giving a bad argument for the negation of what we seek to prove. One could, for example, readily prove that the Red Sox will win next year's World Series by simply arguing that since most apples are red, the Red Sox will not win next year's World Series. The argument would be reconstructed as follows:

1. Most apples are red. (AP)

2. [So] the Red Sox will not win next year's World Series. (1)

Statement 1 is true. But statement 1 clearly does not give us good reason to believe that statement 2 is true. The fact that the argument is invalid does not mean, however, that we should conclude that statement 2 is false and that, therefore, the Red Sox will win next year's World Series. Whereas, the given argument fails to establish that statement 2 is true, we cannot conclude that statement 2 is false. For all we know, another argument might succeed in proving it. We must be content to take its conclusion as unproven.

It is also worth noting that when we agree to accept an assumed premiss as true, we are not claiming that we know for certain that it is true. For example, in accepting as true statements 1 and 2 in the argument about fetuses not having a right to life, we did not suggest we know for certain that they are true. Nevertheless, we chose to believe them. If we later encounter evidence that shows that these statements are not true, the change would require us to alter our evaluation of any argument in which the statements appear as premises.

Valid Reasoning

We say that an argument is *sound* if it succeeds in providing good reasons for believing its conclusion. This will happen only when both of two conditions are met: all its premisses are true and all the reasoning steps are satisfactory. We have already seen that an argument which rests on even one false premiss is unsound. Now we can examine the idea of satisfactory reasoning more carefully. First it will be useful to distinguish between two different kinds of reasoning, *deductive* and *inductive*.

Deductive Reasoning

A reasoning step is deductively valid if, and only if, it is *impossible* for the premiss or premisses to be true and the conclusion to be false. If the combination of true premisses and a false conclusion were possible, then the truth of the premisses could not guarantee the truth of the conclusion, and the argument would fail; the conclusion has not been proved. This strict requirement—that it be impossible for the premisses to be true and the conclusion to be false—is what we mean by the *deductive validity* of an argument. Let's consider again a typical logician's example, similar to the one we discussed in the previous section of this chapter:

1. All swans are white. (AP)

2. The bird in the next room is a swan. (AP)

3. [So] the bird in the next room is white. (1,2)

If the premises are true, the conclusion *has to be* true. If we believe the premises, we are *forced* to believe the conclusion. If we do not believe one or more of the premises, that is a different matter. The point here is that when we *do* believe the premises, if we also insist on denying the conclusion, we are being inconsistent and are making nonsense of our beliefs. By the same token, if we do not believe the conclusion of a valid deductive argument, then we are logically required to reject at least one of the premises. Thus if we enter the next room and discover that there is a black bird in the room, then either it is not true that all swans are white or it is not true that this bird is a swan. To take another example, if we claim that all persons have a right to life and we claim that a particular entity is a person, then we must, if we are to be consistent, agree to the claim that the entity has a right to life. If, however, we deny that this entity has a right to life, then we must deny either that all persons have a right to life or that this entity is a person.

Suppose, however, we were to confront the following argument:

4. All swans are white. (AP)

5. The bird in the next room is not a swan. (AP)

6. [So] the bird in next room is not white. (4,5)

In this case, even if both premises are true, the conclusion *might* turn out to be false. Suppose it turns out that the bird in the next room is an egret. Since egrets are white, statement 6 turns out to be false. Yet it could still be true that all swans are white and that the bird in the next room is not a swan. This argument is, therefore, deductively invalid. Since it is possible for the premisses to be true and the conclusion to be false, its premises do not establish the conclusion.

That the conclusion of an invalid argument might nevertheless turn out to be true—suppose it turns out that the bird in the next room is a crow—makes no difference. Deductively invalid arguments, like arguments with false premises, merely fail to prove their conclusions; that is not the same thing as proving that their conclusions are false. True premises of an invalid argument do not prove the conclusion; true premises of a deductively valid argument *must* yield a true conclusion. Thus if we believe the premises of a deductively valid argument, we have to believe the conclusion.

Note that we can identify the forms of the two arguments if we replace each of the nonlogical terms in the argument with a letter and always replace the same term with the same letter. Thus the form of the first argument is as follows:

1. All X's are Y's.   (AP)

2. Z is an X.   (AP)

3. [So] Z is a Y.   (1,2)

And the form of the second argument is as follows here:

4. All X's are Y's.   (AP)

5. Z is not an X.   (AP)

6. [So] Z is not a Y.   (4,5)

No matter what terms we substitute for X, Y, and Z, as long as we substitute the same term for the same letter throughout a given argument, the first form is always valid and the second form is always invalid. Whenever we encounter an argument of the first form, if we believe the premisses, then logically we must accept the conclusion. With respect to arguments of the second form, however, even if the premisses are true, the conclusion might turn out to be false; that is, even if we believe the premisses, we need not accept the conclusion.

Since the relationship between the premiss or premisses and conclusion of a deductively valid reasoning step is a relationship of necessity—that is, if the premisses are true, then the conclusion *must of necessity* also be true—it follows that the conclusion of a valid argument can never claim anything beyond what is already stated in the premisses. To express it paradoxically, deductive reasoning can serve us no further than enabling us to find out what we already believe or know. In believing that all swans are white and that the bird in the next room is a swan, we already implicitly believe that the bird in the next room is white.

Does it follow that deductive reasoning is useless? The answer is no. For one thing, it is sometimes the case that we haven't recognized the consequences of the beliefs we already possess. Indeed, sometimes by marshalling our beliefs in appropriate order, we discover that they yield surprising consequences. Suppose, for example, that Father Brown writes in his memoirs that his first confessant confessed to having committed murder and that Joe writes in his memoirs that he was Father Brown's first confessant. It follows that unless one of them is mistaken, Joe has confessed to having committed murder. If we believe the statements in both memoirs, then we have to believe that Joe has confessed to committing murder.

Moreover, we use deductive reasoning to explore the logical connections among the concepts we use to express our beliefs. Sometimes we find that we need to adjust those concepts. Suppose, for example, that we have hitherto believed that a swan, by definition, must both be a bird and be white, and suppose, further, that we find a bird that is very much like a swan except that it is black. Should we say that this bird is not a swan, or should we say that some swans are not white? If we say that this bird is not a swan, then we will probably need to introduce a new concept in order to say what the bird is.

We might, for example, say that the bird is a "twan" and define a twan to be a bird that is virtually identical to a swan except that it is not white. If, on the other hand, we decide that it is a swan, then we have to reject the belief that all swans are white and thus surrender the idea of white as being invariant with swans. We would now come to believe that some swans are not white. But that belief, too, has implications. Assuming that the word *swan* is a species-term, for example, our discovery would imply that there is at least one species in which color is not an invariant. And that, too, has implications.

Such reasoning often occurs in moral discussions as well. Suppose we believe that all persons have a right to life and that it is never morally permissible to kill something that has a right to life. Then we are implicitly committed to the claim that it is never permissible to kill a person. Now, suppose we later come to believe that it is sometimes permissible to kill a person, as in the case of self-defense. In other words, we come to accept the claim that it is not always wrong to kill a person. Which of the other two beliefs should we abandon? The process of deciding such a question will cause us to sharpen our understanding of the notion of rights and its connection to our idea of what it is to be a person.

Many people argue that deductive validity provides the only standard of good reasoning and thus is the only standard against which we must measure an argument. These people maintain that we should treat the conclusion of any argument which fails the standard of deductive validity as one that has not been established. Similarly they maintain that the conclusion of any invalid argument has not been proven—even if we are certain of the truth of the premises. The trouble is that many arguments in ordinary discussion fall short of this standard of deductive validity, and yet there are many cases in which we would agree that the argument (assuming the premises are true) does establish (or, at least, provides good reason for believing) its conclusion.

We have already considered one way in which ordinary arguments may fail the test of deductive validity—namely, those in which premises have been omitted. We saw in the argument about fetuses' right to life, for example, that statements 1 and 2 did not establish statement 3 unless we added the additional statement 2a. We also noted that when authors omit premises, principles of good interpretation often require that readers supply the missing premises rather than reject the argument out of hand.

That arguments with suppressed premises sometimes fail to meet the standard of deductive validity is not a challenge to the deductive model of sound reasoning. Indeed, we rely on that very model in order to identify and add the missing premise or premises whenever it is possible to do so.

Inductive Reasoning

There is a second way, however, in which arguments can fall short of the deductive model, which does constitute a serious challenge to the deductive model of sound reasoning. Suppose, instead of using the statement, "All swans are white," as an assumed premise, we ask ourselves what reason we have for believing it. We might answer that we read this fact in Peterson's *Field Guide,* and, suppressing the premiss that everything we read in Peterson's *Field Guide* is true, we have accepted it. But then we might have to question Peterson's basis for concluding that all swans are white. At some point, we will want direct evidence for the truth of the claim that all swans are white. One argument for the conclusion might look like the following:

1.	Sawn a is white.	(AP)
2.	Swan b is white.	(AP)
3.	Swan c is white.	(AP)

.

.

.

50.	Swan n is white.	(AP)
51.	[So] all swans are white.	(1–50)

Assuming that we interpret the word *all* to mean *each and every one,* we will recognize immediately that this argument is deductively invalid, for unless we have examined each and every swan, it always remains possible that at least one of the unexamined swans will turn out not to be white.[2] The truth of statements in lines 1 through 50 does not 100% guarantee the truth of the statement in line 51. The argument is deductively invalid.

It remains the case, however, that this argument does seem to provide us with reason for believing that the statement in line 51 is true, even though its premises do not prove conclusively that its conclusion is true, and even though there is no contradiction in believing that the premises are all true while the conclusion is false. Indeed, statements 1 through 50 would seem to give us even greater reason for believing the following:

52.	The next swan I examine will be white.	(1–50)

This conclusion, however, like the one presented in line 51, cannot be guaranteed by the premises.

One strategy might be to suggest that we can repair these arguments by introducing a suppressed premiss such as this one:

50a. Whenever we examine fifty cases of something and they all possess a given characteristic, then we may validly conclude that all cases (or the next case) of that something will possess that same characteristic. (SP)

---

[2]There is no such problem when the scope of the all-statement is the same as the number of cases examined. That is, if we've examined all fifty marbles in a bag and have verified that each is green, we may validly conclude that all are green. But if we've examined only forty-nine of them, the same conclusion would *not* be deductively valid.

Adding this statement to these arguments would make them deductively valid. But would the argument be sound? Adding a suppressed premiss will enable us to generate a conclusion that must be true only if the premiss we add is true. Remember that we must appraise the truth of every suppressed premiss, just as we appraise the truth of every stated premiss.

There are at least two problems with the claim made in line 50a. The first is that it is highly doubtful whether it is true. Suppose we were to interview fifty people (all of whom happen to be New Yorkers) and discover that they all know who David Dinkins is. May we conclude that all people everywhere know who David Dinkins is?[3] Clearly not. One trouble with this solution is that we must remain in doubt about the truth of the added premiss. As stated, it is simply not true. But even if it were true, the second problem concerns the basis on which we would establish it. Our acceptance of it would presumably rest on the fact that in previous cases, whenever we have identified fifty instances of a regularity, we have correctly inferred to the fifty-first instance. But that argument is itself invalid.

We could, of course, try to modify the statement of the suppressed premiss. For example, we might note that there is a difference between zoologically based information and data concerning well-known people. Then on the basis of this background belief, we might suggest the following revision:

> 50b. Whenever we examine the biological properties of at least fifty animals of the same species and they all have the same characteristic, then we may validly infer that all animals of that species have the same characteristic.

But the trouble remains. Indeed, it is inevitable because the basic argument we can provide for this premiss will itself be based on making an inference from past cases to the next one. It is, therefore, difficult to see how we could have any more confidence in the modified argument than we had in the original argument. This proposed solution, then, while it succeeds in making the argument valid, fails to ensure its soundness. The truth of the added premiss must remain in doubt.

A second proposed solution suffers similar difficulties. The proposal is to modify the conclusions of such arguments to read:

> 51a. *It is likely that* all swans are white. (1–50)

In the case of the second argument, the conclusion would read:

> 52a. *It is likely that* the next swan will be white.

By so modifying the conclusions, we make the arguments deductively valid; their conclusions are weakened to conform to the strength of the evidence for the conclusions. In so doing, we simply raise the question of how weak or strong we should make the conclusions. By introducing the term *it is likely*

---

[3]He's the current mayor of New York.

that into the conclusion, we are claiming only a degree of relative certainty. It turns out that to sustain the validity of such an argument, we must vary the degree of likelihood we attribute to the conclusion. But to do that successfully, we must understand exactly how much evidence the premises provide. Given that we have examined fifty swans and they all turn out to be white, just how likely is it that all swans are white? Given that we have questioned fifty New Yorkers and they all know who David Dinkins is, just how likely is it that all people everywhere know who David Dinkins is?

The two proposed solutions for construing the above arguments as deductive arguments with missing premises share much in common. In the one case, we appraised the strength of the evidence and introduced a premiss indicating that evidence of that strength is sufficient to justify believing the conclusion. In the other case, we appraised the strength of the evidence and then modified the conclusion to reflect the strength of the evidence we have for it. Both solutions call our attention to the deductive invalidity of the argument as originally presented, and so both have the merit of leading us to consider attentively the strength of evidence that the premises actually provide for believing the conclusion. But neither solution provides us with a basis for determining that strength. Both proposed solutions vindicate the deductive model, but the cost is high.

It seems more plausible to suppose that in cases such as the ones above we are dealing with a different sort of reasoning. There can be little doubt that we often draw conclusions that go beyond the available evidence. Suppose we examine fifty marbles from a bag of fifty-one and find that all the marbles are green. Unless we have prior knowledge that they are not all green, we would reasonably conclude that the fifty-first marble will be green. It would be reasonable to give heavy odds (just how heavy?) that the next marble will be green. We would think ourselves justified in drawing this conclusion, even though we recognize it to be a deductively invalid inference. So, too, if we are told, and we believe, that *most* of the marbles in a particular bag are green, other things equal, we would surely bet more on the proposition that the first marble drawn will be green than we would bet on the proposition that it will not be green. And we would bet more on the first proposition even though we recognize that the inference from "Most are green" to "The first one will be green" is not a deductively valid inference.

Arguments with conclusions that go beyond the evidence presented are called *inductive arguments*. Inductive arguments occur frequently and in several guises, one of which is inductive argument by enumeration. Drawing a conclusion about all the members of a group based on evidence about some of its members, as in the conclusion that all swans are white based on the fifty observed swans, is an example of inductive inference by enumeration. The converse of induction by enumeration, reasoning from a generalization to a specific case, as in inferring from "Most are green" to "The first one will be green" is also an example of inductive reasoning. Another frequently used form of inductive argument consists of reasoning from the past to the future, as in the following argument:

1. At sea level, H₂O has always boiled at 212 degrees
   Fahrenheit. (AP)

2. [So] at sea level, H₂O will always (or will tomorrow) boil at 212
   degrees Fahrenheit. (1)

Compare that argument with the following:

1. I've always been healthy.

2. [So] I'll never be sick.

Another form of inductive reasoning is that of reasoning by analogy:

1. Objects of sort X are like objects of sort Y in ways
   A,B,C...N. (AP)

2. [So] objects of sort X are like objects of sort Y in every way
   (or in way O). (AP)

For example:

1. Like adults, fetuses after four months have eyes, ears, and
   detectable brain waves. (AP)

2. Adults have a right to life.

3. [So] fetuses after four months have a right to life. (1–3)

The reasoning we find in developed science goes far beyond these simple types of inductive inferences. For one thing, scientists are often able to perform experiments in which they vary one characteristic and determine whether another characteristic varies with it. Finding such direct variation lends greater strength to and increases confidence in the conclusion. Even imposing the simple discipline of limiting evidence to that obtained only by systematic and precise measurements, as in laboratory experiments or scientific polling, will often strengthen our confidence in the conclusion.

Indirect evidence can also serve to strengthen or weaken our reason for believing the conclusion of an inductive argument. The evidence, for example, that the chromosome count of other species is the same within members of that species lends considerable strength to the inductively arrived at conclusion that the next human being we examine will have forty-six chromosomes, whereas our belief that almost everyone becomes ill periodically significantly weakens our confidence in the inference that we will always be well.

Even more strength is added to predictions and explanations as we come to understand the theoretical connections among phenomena. Theoretical science is characterized by the introduction of theoretical entities, such as waves, quanta, and forces, which enable us to understand the behavior of a wide variety of apparently disparate phenomena by referring to the behavior of these theoretical entities, thus increasing the inductive evidence in support of predictions about the phenomena under consideration. But even in their most rigorous and most inclusive forms, the predictions of and explanatory conclusions of science remain inductive. While the conclusions reached by scientists may sometimes appear to non-scientists to be absolutely certain, in fact they are not. Rather, scientists are usually among the first to acknowledge that each and every conclusion they draw is subject to revision in the event that further information conflicts with their current conclusions. None of our inductively derived beliefs, therefore, should be treated as immune to challenge in the light of further evidence.

It is important to be aware that appraising the strength of a given inductive inference is not a simple matter and that we do not possess a complete canon of rules for drawing inductively justified conclusions. Biologists might want to know whether it is reasonable, given the available evidence, to believe that the genetic structure of all human beings contains forty-six chromosomes. (As a matter of fact, a few do possess forty-eight chromosomes.) Product-quality managers might want to know whether they need to test a given batch of a company's product three, ten, or a hundred times to warrant the company's claim, for example, that its shampoo won't cause tears. Investors who note that the market rose the last three times the price of oil declined might ask now that oil is declining again whether they have good reason to believe the market will go up. The task of developing a comprehensive set of principles for reasonably making such inferences is taken on by statisticians and inductive logicians.

Because beliefs about how the world works also often enter into moral discussions, we will sometimes encounter in those discussions statements whose justification is based on inductive reasoning. On those occasions when inductive arguments appear in the essays included in Parts II and III of this book, our procedure will be to identify them as such by adding an asterisk to the line numbers inside the parenthesis appended to the line. When statements whose ultimate justification is inductive are used as assumed premises, however, we shall continue to label them simply as (AP).

It is also useful to note that in discussions of abortion, because the biological development of fetuses is so well documented, we encounter few disagreements about the facts of the case. (In this respect, the abortion issue is different from many other moral issues. For example, whether capital punishment actually serves as a deterrent is often raised in discussion of that issue.) Thus we shall encounter few inductive arguments with respect to the biological development of fetuses. We shall, however, encounter much disagreement about what these facts imply with respect to our moral responsibilities toward fetuses.

In summary, many ordinary arguments fall short of the deductive standard. Sometimes the reasoning is evidently invalid, and so the argument must be rejected. Sometimes one or more premiss is missing, and so we may try to supply the suppressed premises before evaluating the argument by appraising the truth of both its stated and suppressed premises. Although sound interpretive principles require that we try to supply a true premiss that will make the argument valid, we may conclude that no such premiss exists, and so we have to reject the argument. In the case of inductive reasoning, we must appraise the strength of the evidence carefully in order to evaluate the conclusion. Finally, we will remember that because an unsatisfactory argument can still have a true conclusion, to conclude that a particular argument fails to prove the truth of its conclusion is not the same as proving that its conclusion is false.

The Principles of Charity and Candor

Supplying suppressed premisses as part of interpreting someone else's argument can be an extremely sensitive part of the process. Earlier we said that we may supply a premiss whenever we believe it is necessary to fill a deductive gap in the argument and we believe that the author would accept the premiss as stated. Note that if authors included each and every one of the premisses required to draw their inferences validly, many essays would become exceedingly long. By the same token, if readers, in reconstructing an author's argument, stop to add all the premisses necessary to make each step of a complex argument explicit, they will soon become overwhelmed by premisses. Consequently, while we must be alert to gaps in reasoning since sometimes the suppressed premisses will turn out to be false, the decision whether or not to add a suppressed premiss to an argument outline will depend on our judgment of its significance to the argument and the degree of controversy we believe is connected with it. Consider, for example, a part of the very first argument we discussed in Chapter 1:

> 1. Fetuses are persons.   (AP)
>
> 2. [So] fetuses must not be killed.   (1)

This inference is invalid as it stands. What's missing? How can we make it deductively valid? One thing we might do is add the following suppressed premiss:

> 1a. Persons must never be killed.   (SP)

That would certainly do the trick since if statements 1 and 1a are true, then statement 2 must be true. But remember that in evaluating this argument, we have to determine whether the suppressed premiss is true. While extreme pacifists might accept this premiss as patently true, certainly many other people will not. Most people allow for killing in some situations, such as war, self-defense, capital punishment, or euthanasia. For these people, using this premiss to establish the conclusion will be problematic. At a minimum, they will require justification for the premiss; more likely, they will reject it. It might be the case, however, that this particular premiss is not the one the author was suppressing. Other, less controversial, premisses might also work to make the argument valid. Consider, for example, the two following statements taken together:

> 1b. Innocent persons must never be killed.
>
> 1c. All fetuses are innocent.

The conclusion that fetuses must not be killed follows deductively from statements 1, 1b, and 1c. Whereas the suppressed premises as stated here may also be subject to challenge, they are different from the previous statement and are likely to be accepted by more people.

When deciding how to state a suppressed premiss for which we do not have information from the author, it is important to consider the principles of charity and candor, which we shall refer to as principles of interpretation. The first thing to note about these principles of interpretation is that they are not logical principles; rather, they are more like ethical principles that we can use to guide our interpretive behavior.

When our principal concern is to interpret another person's argument rather than to reach our own conclusion about the issue being discussed, the principle of charity requires that we try, consistent with what we think the author believes, to reconstruct the best argument possible. When we are trying to find our own answers, however, we may decide to consider premises that will make the argument sound, whether we believe the author would accept them or not.

In this respect, the principle of charity requires us to approach another's words in a way quite different from that, say, of a legal counselor, politician, or debater. A lawyer, for example, might properly pounce on every gap in a witness's testimony during cross-examination, if only to make it appear as if the witness is being disingenuous. The lawyer might also try to interpolate troubling premises to make it appear as if the witness is trying to mislead the jury or is giving unreliable testimony. When seeking to arrive at sound answers to difficult ethical issues, however, we need to listen carefully and to reconstruct others' arguments as accurately as we can. In this way, the principle of charity is really a principle of prudence. If we reject an argument just because it has a missing premiss, we may lose an opportunity to give careful consideration to a potentially sound argument. Similarly, if we do not supply premises that suffice to make the argument cogent, we may distort the argument to our own disadvantage.

The principle of candor is the complement of the principle of charity and applies more to giving an argument than to interpreting one. We are all familiar with the principle of candor under the guise of the requirement that we not only tell the truth but that we tell the *whole* truth when testifying in a court of law. By the same token, we expect that authors will provide all the relevant information they have when formulating an argument. Consider, for example, the following argument:

1. At two months, the fetus has toes and fingers. (AP)

2. At two months, the fetus has facial features. (AP)

3. [So] at two months, the fetus looks like a person. (1,2)

Whereas both of the assumed premises stated here are true, the author has not provided all of the relevant information. What the author hasn't said, either because she is ignorant of the additional facts or because she is deliberately omitting them, is that it is also true that at two months fetuses have tails and that their limbs look more like stumps. In these respects, then, fetuses do not look like persons normally do, so argument 3 may not be sound after all. This means that just as the author has not been candid, we as critics fail to be candid if we ignore the other relevant information while evaluating the argument.

The principle of candor becomes particularly important when we are examining inductive arguments, especially arguments from analogy. This is because, in some respects, everything is like everything else and also different from everything else. This means that when we reconstruct and evaluate such arguments, we shall have to pay close attention to whether the author has provided all the relevant information. Also, when we supply the missing premisses for such an argument, we have to be careful not to bias the argument by including information that is either only supportive of or only harmful to the conclusion.

The principles of charity and candor will apply not only to supplying missing premises, but also to cases where it is necessary to reformulate what an author has said. We do this automatically when we encounter typographical errors. It is unlikely, for example, that anyone would hesitate to replace the word *tea* with the word *team* if they read the following sentence in a book:

> Having raised his scholastic average to C, the college's first baseman was allowed to rejoin the tea.

There are, of course, other reasons why we may want to reformulate an author's claim. Sometimes, for example, we may confront ambiguities, often inadvertent on the part of the author, and will want to clear them up. Sometimes we will want to simplify sentences in which an author, in the process of struggling to make an idea clear, has made sentences more complex than they need to be. There is nothing that prevents readers who are developing argument outlines from reformulating what an author has said. Indeed, subject to rigorous application of the principles of charity and candor, it is often advisable to try to do so, since the very process of reformulation often leads to better understanding of the author's arguments.

Part II

Model Argument
Reconstructions

An Almost Absolute Value
in History

John T. Noonan

1   The most fundamental question involved in the long history of thought on abortion is: How do you determine the humanity of a being? To phrase the question in that way is to put in comprehensive humanistic terms what the theologians either dealt with as an explicitly theological question under the heading of "ensoulment" or dealt with implicitly in their treatment of abortion. The Christian position as it originated did not depend on a narrow theological concept. It had no relation to theories of infant baptism.[1] It appealed to no special theory of instantaneous ensoulment. It took the world's view on ensoulment as that view changed from Aristotle to Zacchia. There was, indeed, theological influence affecting the theory of ensoulment finally adopted, and, of course, ensoulment itself was a theological concept, so that the position was always explained in theological terms. But the theological notion of ensoulment could easily be translated into humanistic language by substituting "human" for "rational soul"; the problem of knowing when a man is a man is common to theology and humanism.

2   If one steps outside the specific categories used by theologians, the answer they gave can be analyzed as a refusal to discriminate between human beings on the basis of their varying potentialities. Once conceived, the being was recognized as man because he had man's potential. The criterion for humanity, thus, was simple and all-embracing: if you are conceived by human parents, you are human.

Reprinted by permission of the publishers from *The Morality of Abortion* by John T. Noonan, Cambridge, Massachusetts: Harvard University Press, Copyright © 1970 by the President and Fellows of Harvard College, pp. 51–59.

3   The strength of this position may be tested by a review of some of the other distinctions offered in the contemporary controversy over legalizing abortion. Perhaps the most popular distinction is in terms of viability. Before an age of so many months, the fetus is not viable, that is, it cannot be removed from the mother's womb and live apart from her. To that extent, the life of the fetus is absolutely dependent on the life of the mother. This dependence is made the basis of denying recognition to its humanity.

4   There are difficulties with this distinction. One is that the perfection of artificial incubation may make the fetus viable at any time: it may be removed and artificially sustained. Experiments with animals already show that such a procedure is possible. This hypothetical extreme case relates to an actual difficulty: there is considerable elasticity to the idea of viability. Mere length of life is not an exact measure. The viability of the fetus depends on the extent of its anatomical and functional development. The weight and length of the fetus are better guides to the state of its development than age, but weight and length vary. Moreover, different racial groups have different ages at which their fetuses are viable. Some evidence, for example, suggests that Negro fetuses mature more quickly than white fetuses. If viability is the norm, the standard would vary with race and with many individual circumstances.

5   The most important objection to this approach is that dependence is not ended by viability. The fetus is still absolutely dependent on someone's care in order to continue existence; indeed, a child of one or three or even five years of age is absolutely dependent on another's care for existence; uncared for, the older fetus or the younger child will die as surely as the early fetus detached from the mother. The unsubstantial lessening in dependence at viability does not seem to signify any special acquisition of humanity.

6   A second distinction has been attempted in terms of experience. A being who has had experience, has lived and suffered, who possesses memories, is more human than one who has not. Humanity depends on formation by experience. The fetus is thus "unformed" in the most basic human sense.

7   This distinction is not serviceable for the embryo which is already experiencing and reacting. The embryo is responsive to touch after eight weeks and at least at that point is experiencing. At an earlier stage the zygote is certainly alive and responding to its environment. The distinction may also be challenged by the rare case where aphasia has erased adult memory: has it erased humanity? More fundamentally, this distinction leaves even the older fetus or the younger child to be treated as an unformed inhuman being. Finally, it is not clear why experience as such confers humanity. It could be argued that certain central experiences such as loving or learning are necessary to make a man human. But then human beings who have failed to love or to learn might be excluded from the class called man.

8   A third distinction is made by appeal to the sentiments of adults. If a fetus dies, the grief of the parents is not the grief they would have for a living child. The fetus is an unnamed "it" till birth, and it is not perceived as a personality until at least the fourth month of existence when movements in

the womb manifest a vigorous presence demanding joyful recognition by the parents.

9   Yet feeling is notoriously an unsure guide to the humanity of others. Many groups of humans have had difficulty in feeling that persons of another tongue, color, religion, sex, are as human as they. Apart from reactions to alien groups, we mourn the loss of a ten-year-old boy more than the loss of his one-day-old brother or his 90-year-old grandfather. The difference felt and the grief expressed vary with the potentialities extinguished, or the experience wiped out; they do not seem to point to any substantial difference in the humanity of baby, boy, or grandfather.

10   Distinctions are also made in terms of sensation by the parents. The embryo is felt within the womb only after about the fourth month. The embryo is seen only at birth. What can be neither seen nor felt is different from what is tangible. If the fetus cannot be seen or touched at all, it cannot be perceived as man.

11   Yet experience shows that sight is even more untrustworthy than feeling in determining humanity. By sight, color became an appropriate index for saying who was a man, and the evil of racial discrimination was given foundation. Nor can touch provide the test; a being confined by sickness, "out of touch" with others, does not thereby seem to lose his humanity. To the extent that touch still has appeal as a criterion, it appears to be a survival of the old English idea of "quickening"—a possible mistranslation of the Latin *animatus* used in the canon law. To that extent touch as a criterion seems to be dependent on the Aristotelian notion of ensoulment, and to fall when this notion is discarded.

12   Finally, a distinction is sought in social visibility. The fetus is not socially perceived as human. It cannot communicate with others. Thus, both subjectively and objectively, it is not a member of society. As moral rules are rules for the behavior of members of society to each other, they cannot be made for behavior toward what is not yet a member. Excluded from the society of men, the fetus is excluded from the humanity of men.[2]

13   By force of argument from the consequences, this distinction is to be rejected. It is more subtle than that founded on an appeal to physical sensation, but it is equally dangerous in its implications. If humanity depends on social recognition, individuals or whole groups may be dehumanized by being denied any status in their society. Such a fate is fictionally portrayed in *1984* and has actually been the lot of many men in many societies. In the Roman Empire, for example, condemnation to slavery meant the practical denial of most human rights; in the Chinese Communist world, landlords have been classified as enemies of the people and so treated as non-persons by the state. Humanity does not depend on social recognition, though often the failure of society to recognize the prisoner, the alien, the heterodox as human has led to the destruction of human beings. Anyone conceived by a man and a woman is human. Recognition of this condition by society follows a real event in the objective order, however imperfect and halting the recognition. Any attempt to limit humanity to exclude some groups runs the risk of furnishing authority

and precedent for excluding other groups in the name of the consciousness or perception of the controlling group in the society.

14   A philosopher may reject the appeal to the humanity of the fetus because he views "humanity" as a secular view of the soul and because he doubts the existence of anything real and objective which can be identified as humanity. One answer to such a philosopher is to ask how he reasons about moral questions without supposing that there is a sense in which he and the others of whom he speaks are human. Whatever group is taken as the society which determines who may be killed is thereby taken as human. A second answer is to ask if he does not believe that there is a right and wrong way of deciding moral questions. If there is such a difference, experience may be appealed to: to decide who is human on the basis of the sentiment of a given society has led to consequences which rational men would characterize as monstrous.

15   The rejection of the attempted distinctions based on viability and visibility, experience and feeling, may be buttressed by the following considerations. Moral judgments often rest on distinctions, but if the distinctions are not to appear arbitrary *fiat,* they should relate to some real difference in probabilities. There is a kind of continuity in all life, but the earlier stages of the elements of human life possess tiny probabilities of development. Consider, for example, the spermatozoa in any normal ejaculate: There are about 200,000,000 in any single ejaculate, of which one has a chance of developing into a zygote. Consider the oocytes which may become ova: there are 100,000 to 1,000,000 oocytes in a female infant, of which a maximum of 390 are ovulated. But once spermatozoan and ovum meet and the conceptus is formed, such studies as have been made show that roughly in only 20 percent of the cases will spontaneous abortion occur. In other words, the chances are about 4 out of 5 that this new being will develop. At this stage in the life of the being there is a sharp shift in probabilities, an immense jump in potentialities. To make a distinction between the rights of spermatozoa and the rights of the fertilized ovum is to respond to an enormous shift in possibilities. For about twenty days after conception the egg may split to form twins or combine with another egg to form a chimera, but the probability of either event happening is very small.

16   It may be asked, What does a change in biological probabilities have to do with establishing humanity? The argument from probabilities is not aimed at establishing humanity but at establishing an objective discontinuity which may be taken into account in moral discourse. As life itself is a matter of probabilities, as most moral reasoning is an estimate of probabilities, so it seems in accord with the structure of reality and the nature of moral thought to found a moral judgment on the change in probabilities at conception. The appeal to probabilities is the most commonsensical of arguments; to a greater or smaller degree all of us base our actions on probabilities, and in morals, as in law, prudence and negligence are often measured by the account one has taken of the probabilities. If the chance is 200,000,000 to 1 that the movement in the bushes into which you shoot is a man's I doubt if many persons would

hold you careless in shooting; but if the chances are 4 out of 5 that the movement is a human being's few would acquit you of blame. Would the argument be different if only one out of ten children conceived came to term? Of course this argument would be different. This argument is an appeal to probabilities that actually exist, not to any and all states of affairs which may be imagined.

17 The probabilities as they do exist do not show the humanity of the embryo in the sense of a demonstration in logic any more than the probabilities of the movement in the bush being a man demonstrate beyond all doubt that the being is a man. The appeal is a "buttressing" consideration, showing the plausibility of the standard adopted. The argument focuses on the decisional factor in any moral judgment and assumes that part of the business of a moralist is drawing lines. One evidence of the non-arbitrary character of the line drawn is the difference of probabilities on either side of it. If a spermatozoan is destroyed, one destroys a being which had a chance of far less than 1 in 200 million of developing into a reasoning being, possessed of the genetic code, a heart and other organs, and capable of pain. If a fetus is destroyed, one destroys a being already possessed of the genetic code, organs, and sensitivity to pain, and one which had an 80 percent chance of developing further into a baby outside the womb who, in time, would reason.

18 The positive argument for conception as the decisive moment of humanization is that at conception the new being receives the genetic code. It is this genetic information which determines his characteristics, which is the biological carrier of the possibility of human wisdom, which makes him a self-evolving being. A being with a human genetic code is a man.

19 This review of current controversy over the humanity of the fetus emphasizes what a fundamental question the theologians resolved in asserting the inviolability of the fetus. To regard the fetus as possessed of equal rights with other humans was not, however, to decide every case where abortion might be employed. It did decide the case where the argument was that the fetus should be aborted for its own good. To say a being was human was to say it had a destiny to decide for itself which could not be taken from it by another man's decision. But human beings with equal rights often come in conflict with each other, and some decision must be made as to whose claims are to prevail. Cases of conflict involving the fetus are different only in two respects: the total inability of the fetus to speak for itself and the fact that the right of the fetus regularly at stake is the right to life itself.

20 The approach taken by the theologians to these conflicts was articulated in terms of "direct" and "indirect." Again, to look at what they were doing from outside their categories, they may be said to have been drawing lines or "balancing values." "Direct" and "indirect" are spatial metaphors; "line-drawing" is another. "To weigh" or "to balance" values is a metaphor of a more complicated mathematical sort hinting at the process which goes on in moral judgments. All the metaphors suggest that, in the moral judgments made, comparisons were necessary, that no value completely controlled. The principle of double effect was no doctrine drawn from heaven, but a method of analysis appropriate where two relative values were being compared. In Cath-

olic moral theology, as it developed, life even of the innocent was not taken as an absolute. Judgments on acts affecting life issued from a process of weighing. In the weighing, the fetus was always given a value greater than zero, always a value separate and independent of its parents. This valuation was crucial and fundamental in all Christian thought on the subject and marked it off from any approach which considered that only the parents' interests need be considered.

21   Even with the fetus weighed as human, one interest could be weighed as equal or superior: that of the mother in her own life. The casuists between 1450 and 1895 were willing to weigh this interest as superior. Since 1895, that interest was given decisive weight only in the two special cases of the cancerous uterus and the ectopic pregnancy. In both of these cases the fetus had little chance of survival even if the abortion were not performed. As the balance was once struck in favor of the mother whenever her life was endangered, it could be so struck again. The balance reached between 1895 and 1930 attempted prudentially and pastorally to forestall a multitude of exceptions for interests less than life.

22   The perception of the humanity of the fetus and the weighing of fetal rights against other human rights constituted the work of the moral analysts. But what spirit animated their abstract judgments? For the Christian community it was the injunction of Scripture to love your neighbor as yourself. The fetus as human was a neighbor; his life had parity with one's own. The commandment gave life to what otherwise would have been only rational calculation.

23   The commandment could be put in humanistic as well as theological terms: Do not injure your fellow man without reason. In these terms, once the humanity of the fetus is perceived, abortion is never right except in self-defense. When life must be taken to save life, reason alone cannot say that a mother must prefer a child's life to her own. With this exception, now of great rarity, abortion violates the rational humanist tenet of the equality of human lives.

24   For Christians the commandment to love had received a special imprint in that the exemplar proposed of love was the love of the Lord for his disciples. In the light given by this example, self-sacrifice carried to the point of death seemed in the extreme situations not without meaning. In the less extreme cases, preference for one's own interests to the life of another seemed to express cruelty or selfishness irreconcilable with the demands of love.

Notes

1. According to Glanville Williams (*The Sanctity of Human Life, supra* n. 169, at 193), "The historical reason for the Catholic objection to abortion is the same as for the Christian Church's historical opposition to infanticide: the horror of bringing about the death of an unbaptized child." The statement is made without any citation of evidence. As has been seen, desire to administer baptism could, in the Middle Ages, even be urged as a reason for procuring an abortion. It is highly regrettable that the

American Law Institute was apparently misled by Williams' account and repeated after him the same baseless statement. See American Law Institute, *Model Penal Code: Tentative Draft No. 9* (1959) p. 148, n. 12.

2. . . . Thomas Aquinas gave an analogous reason against baptizing a fetus in the womb: "As long as it exists in the womb of the mother, it cannot be subject to the operation of the ministers of the Church as it is not known to men." (*In sententias Petri Lombardi* 4.6 1.1.2).

Discussion and Outline

of John T. Noonan's
"An Almost Absolute Value in History"

Our procedure will be to read through the essay together, one paragraph at a time, outlining and commenting on arguments as we come across them and, most important, seeking to identify the main argument and its conclusion. Then we will put the parts together to construct a formal argument outline.

Paragraph 1

The main point of this introductory paragraph is stated in the last sentence. Noonan claims that the fundamental problem of knowing when a man is a man—that is, the problem of knowing when a developing organism of the species *Homo sapiens* is to count as a person—is common to theology and humanism. Theologians, he acknowledges, tend to formulate their answer in theological terms, but the answer they give has a secular foundation. He proposes to present that secular basis for he believes that it provides compelling reason to adopt the Church's position, whether or not one accepts the theological basis of Catholicism.

In one respect, of course, the theologically formulated answer is simple: something becomes a person at the very moment that it comes to possess a soul; that is, at the time that ensoulment occurs. Since, however, ensoulment is not an event whose occurrence we can observe, the difficult aspect of this answer is to say when it occurs.[1] It is the Church's answer to this question that Noonan believes has a compelling secular foundation. Thus, his essay will seek to spell out in secular terms the justification for the claim that personhood begins at conception, and, at least tentatively, we may take that to be Noonan's main conclusion.

Paragraph 2

The Church's answer is that personhood begins at conception. It is a simple and all-embracing answer: If you are conceived by human parents, you are a person, and you are a person at the very moment of conception. But on what do the theologians base their answer? Unfortunately, Noonan does not immediately make clear what that basis is, for he does not make clear whether this second paragraph contains a statement of the secular basis for the theologians' answer or merely provides a comment on that answer. The problem in interpreting the paragraph arises with respect to the role of the second clause of the very first sentence of the paragraph: ". . . the answer they gave can be analyzed as a refusal to discriminate between human beings on the basis of their varying potentialities." Is this statement a premiss on which their fundamental answer is based or is it a comment about that answer? If the latter, this part of the argument could be reconstructed as follows:

a1. If you are conceived by human parents, you are human.   (P)

a2. Statement a1 is the theologians' answer.   (AP)

a3. Statement a1 constitutes a refusal to discriminate among
     human beings on the basis of their varying potential.   (AP)

a4. [So] the theologians refuse to discriminate among human
     beings on the basis of their varying potential.   (a1–a3)

This reading takes the paragraph merely to provide a comment on the theologians' answer. The comment as stated in line a3, however, does not provide a justification of the statement in a1 and does not, therefore, tell us the basis of the theologians' answer.

Alternatively, we might read the paragraph as follows:

b1. All things conceived by humans have a human's potential.[2] (AP)

b2. We should not discriminate among things that have
     a human's potential.   (P)

---

[1]Readers should be aware that many people reject the very idea of soul, largely on the basis that no such entity has been observed. At a minimum, the notion of a soul has no place in contemporary psychology and almost none in non-theologically based philosophy.

[2]Note that later in the essay, in paragraph 18, Noonan tells us that what is distinctive about human fetuses is that they have the potential to achieve human wisdom.

b3. [So] we should not discriminate among things conceived by humans. (b1,b2)

b4. Conceptuses[3] are things conceived by humans. (SP)

b5. Adult human beings are both conceived by humans and counted as persons. (SP)

b6. [So] we should count conceptuses as persons. (b3–b5)

According to this interpretation, we understand the paragraph to constitute an argument why conceptuses should be counted as full-fledged persons; that is, we take it to provide a basis for the theologians' support of a conservative abortion policy. There are, however, several things to note about this interpretation. First, in line with the principle of charity, we have reformulated the second premise. Noonan's own formulation—that we should refuse to discriminate among *human beings* on the basis of their varying potentialities—is problematic. In the first place, it is clearly false. Obviously we do discriminate between people on the basis of their varying potential. We would not find it odd, for example, to recommend one program of instruction for one person and a different program for another person based on a judgment of their varying potential. To be sure, the principle of charity requires us to suppose that Noonan is talking about discrimination in assigning different fundamental rights, especially rights dealing with life itself. But second, leaving this difficulty aside, Noonan's formulation clearly begs the question of whether conceptuses are human beings. Even if we agree that we should not discriminate among human beings on the basis of their varying potential, we need not agree that conceptuses are human beings. For these reasons, we have construed Noonan to claim that conceptuses have the *same* potential as adult human beings, namely, as he later says, "the potential for achieving human wisdom."

However, note also that if we adopt this interpretation, then we are forced to reformulate the conclusion of the argument as well. That is, to make the argument valid, we have stated in the conclusion that we *should count* conceptuses as persons. This claim is, of course, different from the claim that conceptuses *are* persons. We have to modify Noonan's conclusion in this way because we have read his argument to contain the premise, "We *should not discriminate* among things that have the same potential." Noonan cannot derive the claim that they are persons from these premises.

Critical evaluation of the argument as we have formulated it here will most likely focus on the premise stated in line b2. Is it true that all things conceived by human parents have the same potential? Consider brain-damaged people. Do they have the potential for human wisdom?

Which is the correct interpretation? The first interpretation is relatively unproblematic, but it does not provide a justification for the theologians'

---

[3]The term *conceptus* denotes organisms at their very earliest stages, including the stage immediately following conception at which they consist of a single cell.

answer. While the second interpretation does provide such a basis, it raises difficulties. Moreover, if the b-interpretation were correct, we would expect Noonan to explicate and perhaps defend its premisses.

Paragraph 3

Unfortunately, Noonan does not proceed directly to explain and defend his answer to the central question of when an organism counts as a person. Rather, he says that he will defend the theologians' answer by reviewing other proposed answers. This suggests that Noonan's defense of his own answer will be a comparative one in which he gives reasons for believing that the theologians' answer is *stronger* than the other answers. He proceeds to present five alternative answers and to offer reasons for rejecting each of them. In evaluating the ensuing discussion, we shall have to consider not only whether Noonan has good reasons for rejecting these alternative answers but also whether he has presented all the important alternatives and presented them in their most compelling formulation.

The first alternative answer Noonan considers is that humanization occurs at viability—that point in the development of the fetus at which it is biologically possible for it to survive apart from the mother's womb.[4] Noonan's formulation of the argument given by those who defend this answer is as follows:

    1. Some people argue: (AP)

        [1. Prior to viability fetuses cannot survive apart from the woman.]   [AP]

        [2. Whatever cannot survive on its own is not human.]   [AP]

        [3. Prior to viability fetuses are not human.]   [1,2]

We have placed brackets around those lines of the argument that constitute Noonan's reconstruction of this and other arguments put forward by other writers. Noonan's claim that others put this argument forward is a premiss of his own argument. Moreover, because he gives no evidence for the claim that others make this argument, we label it AP. But the claims that comprise the argument he is about to criticize are not claims that Noonan accepts. We use the brackets to mark this distinction. Later we may refer to these lines in the argument as lines 1.1, 1.2, and 1.3. It is always important to distinguish between what an author claims and what an author claims others claim.

---

[4]Note that a fetus may be viable but undeliverable because of complications having to do with the woman's health, or even because necessary facilities are not available. Note also, as Noonan will soon point out, that the stage of development at which viability occurs may change as technology develops.

Paragraph 4

Noonan develops his first objection to the claim that personhood begins at viability as follows:

2. Perfection of incubators may make the fetus viable at any time. (AP)

3. The time at which a fetus becomes viable varies with race and individual circumstances. (AP)

4. [So] the viability criterion is elastic. (2)(3)[5]

5. If the criterion for humanity is elastic, then two fetuses conceived at the same time might at a later time not both be persons or might not both be not persons. (SP)

6. But fetuses conceived at the same time must at every time either both be or both not be persons. (SP)

7. [So] an elastic criterion for personhood is not acceptable. (5,6)

8. [So] the viability criterion is not acceptable. (4,7)

Suppose there were some characteristic which appears in all fetuses but which appears in some fetuses earlier than in others, and that, as a result of some future technological development, might appear earlier than it does now in all fetuses. Noonan claims that we would be morally prohibited from using that characteristic as a criterion of personhood. But Noonan does not provide a justification for rejecting elastic criteria. Perhaps he considers it to be obvious, or perhaps he will present his reasons later in the essay. The addition of the suppressed premisses in lines 5 and 6 offers what might be part of Noonan's objection to elastic criteria, but surely does not fill all the gaps in his argument. At a minimum, the fact that some entities come to possess a given characteristic at a later time than others is not an obvious objection to employing the possession of that characteristic as a basis for differential treatment. In other words, it is not obvious why statement 6 would be true, which means we have to consider whether the argument can be made valid without it and what premisses might be used in place of it.

Paragraph 5

Noonan now turns to a second objection to the viability criterion, one which he thinks is more powerful than the previous objection:

9. After viability—indeed, up to age five—the fetus or child is still dependent on someone's care. (AP)

---

[5]Note that this is a convergent argument.

10. [So] there is no substantial lessening of dependence at
    viability. (9)

11. Children are certainly persons well before age five. (SP)

12. [So] viability does not signify any special acquisition of
    personhood. (10,11)

13. [So] the viability criterion is not acceptable. (12)

Note the inference from statement 9 to statement 10. Does statement 9 establish that there is *no substantial* lessening of dependence? If a viable fetus is delivered, it will be dependent on someone's care, but not necessarily on the care of the biological mother. Thus, at viability, there can be a change in the nature of the dependence, from dependence on a specific person to dependence on any of many persons. This fact calls our attention to Noonan's formulation of the statement in line 1.2, which is somewhat broader than defenders of the viability criterion would require. A less general statement—namely, that whatever cannot survive apart from a specific person is not a full-fledged human being—might be used instead. Would this change in the nature of the dependence constitute a substantial lessening of dependence? On what basis are we to decide that question?

Paragraph 6

Here Noonan presents another alternative answer to the main question of when an organism counts as a person. This answer is based on the acquisition of experience, and Noonan formulates it as follows:

14. Some people argue: (AP)

    [1. Humanity, or personhood, depends on formation
    by experience.] [AP]

    [2. Fetuses are unformed by experience.] [AP]

    [3. [So] fetuses are not human.] [1,2]

Paragraph 7

If we assume that the second sentence of this paragraph contains an argument, we can then consider five counterarguments that Noonan develops within this paragraph. The first two counterarguments, which do not directly support his own selection of conception as the point of humanization,[6] are as follows:

---

[6]The second sentence of the seventh paragraph raises a problem of interpretation. The sentence, "The embryo is responsive to touch after eight weeks and at least at that point is experiencing," could be interpreted as merely containing two claims about fetuses, or as presenting the argument that since a fetus is responsive to touch, it is experiencing. The more plausible interpretation is that the sentence does contain this argument.

15. The embryo is responsive to touch after eight weeks.   (AP)

16. [So] at eight weeks it is experiencing and reacting.   (15)

17. The embryo is alive and responding to its environment even earlier than eight weeks.   (AP)

18. [So] if the experience criterion is adopted, embryos even younger than eight weeks are human.   (16)(17)

Note that the inference from statement 15 to statement 16 raises the question, "In what sense is an eight-week fetus experiencing?" Many will draw a much greater gap than Noonan does between the notion of responding to touch and the notion of having experience. Reflex responses, such as the patella reflex, which are not mediated by the cerebrum, are not counted as experiences in most other psychological contexts. The proponents of this criterion surely have something different in mind when they talk of experience. They are more likely to have in mind the acquisition of memories and concepts, the occurrence of which is dependent on the existence of a cerebrum. But the cerebrum does not develop until the sixth or seventh month. That Noonan is aware of this distinction is evidenced by his later remarks.

Moreover, the vagueness of the phrases *even earlier* in line 17 and *even younger* in line 18 raises a problem for Noonan. Even if we were to accept the argument made here, we would remain unclear as to the point at which we may properly say that an early embryo is experiencing. If Noonan claims that conception is the point at which personhood begins, then he is presumably opposed to the use of devices such as the "morning-after pill," which are used much earlier than eight weeks. But the two arguments he has given against using experience to define the point of humanization do not provide reason to reject such pills. Because Noonan does not give us any reason to believe that one-celled zygotes are subjects of experience, his counterarguments so far fail to dispose of experience as the criterion for defining personhood.

Noonan's third counterargument is as follows:

19. Sometimes aphasia erases adult memory.   (AP)

20. Aphasia does not erase personhood.   (AP)

21. [So] formation by experience is an unsatisfactory criterion of personhood.   (19,20)

This argument requires that at least one suppressed premiss be made explicit in order to be valid. And the truth of that premiss is subject to doubt since readers must surely consider the possibility that there is a moral difference in the status of those who have had experiences and lost them either temporarily or permanently and those who have never had them.

The fourth counterargument is as follows:

22. Neonates are also unformed by experience.   (AP)

23. But neonates are persons.   (AP)

24. [So] having experience cannot be a correct criterion of
     personhood.   (22,23)

Note that here Noonan uses the more complex notion of experience. But even
statement 23 may not be patently obvious to all who consider it. As we shall
see in the next essay, by Michael Tooley, there are some who boldly claim that
since neonates lack continuity of experience, they are not persons.

The final argument against the experience criterion, which is presented in the last three sentences of the paragraph, requires considerable sup-
plementation. It seems to be as follows:

25. Proponents of the experience criterion fail to make clear why
     acquisition of experience confers humanity.   (AP)

26. The category of personhood is a moral category.   (SP)

27. In general, a proposed criterion for determining what will be
     included in a given moral category is satisfactory only if the
     criterion identifies a morally relevant basis for determining what
     will be included and it does not arbitrarily exclude entities
     ordinarily included in that category.   (SP)

28. If proponents of the experience criterion identify specific
     experiences, such as loving or learning, then they arbitrarily
     exclude those who either don't love or don't learn.   (AP)

29. Proponents of the experience criterion fail to identify a morally
     relevant distinction or arbitrarily exclude entities ordinarily
     included in the category of persons.   (SP)

30. [So] the experience criterion is
     unsatisfactory.   (25–27,29)(28,29)

Paragraph 8

Noonan proceeds by presenting a third alternative answer to the central question, an answer based on adult sentiments toward fetuses. The argument as he
formulates it is straightforward:

31. Some people argue: (AP)

     [1. If a fetus dies, the grief of the parents is not as great
      as the grief they would have for the death of a
      living child.]   [AP]

     [2. The fetus is an unnamed "it" till birth.]   [AP]

     [3. The fetus is not perceived as a personality until at
      least the fourth month of existence when movements
      in the womb manifest a vigorous presence demanding
      joyful recognition by the parents.]   [AP]

[4. [So] adult sentiments differ toward and are less
engaged with fetuses than with those who have been
born.]   [1][2][3]

[5. [So] fetuses are not persons.]   [4]

Paragraph 9

Noonan's response to this suggestion consists of challenging the suppressed premiss necessary to get from line 31.4 to line 31.5. A plausible formulation of the suppressed premiss is, "If adults' feelings are less engaged toward some things than toward other things, then those other things are not persons." Noonan's response is to claim that having more or less intense feelings toward a given entity is a rather *unsure* guide as to its humanity.

Though reconstructing Noonan's objection to the sentiment criterion for establishing personhood is thus straightforward, it is important to note a shift in the nature of the alternative answers to the central questions that are being addressed by the author. Whereas the first two proposed answers rested on characteristics of fetal organisms, the answer based on this sentiment criterion, as well as the next two proposed answers to be considered, rest on other people's, especially adults', attitudes toward, feelings about, or experiences of fetuses. Noonan claims that all such criteria as the latter are flawed because they are arbitrary and because using them opens up the possibility of justifying morally outrageous conduct. For example, some people's feelings are "less engaged" with the condition of individuals of other races, but would that justify maintaining that individuals of other races are not persons?

Paragraph 10

In this paragraph Noonan presents yet another answer that might be given by others. This answer uses a proposed criterion based on sensations felt by parents:

32. Some people argue: (AP)

[1. The embryo is felt within the womb only after about
the fourth month.]   [AP]

[2. The embryo is seen only at birth.]   [AP]

[3. What can be neither seen nor felt is different from
what is tangible.]   [AP]

[4. If the fetus cannot be seen or touched at all, it cannot
be perceived as man.]   [AP]

[5. [So] the fetus is not a person.]   [1,3,4] [2,3,4]

Paragraph 11

Noonan's rebuttal argument is similar to that directed against the sentiment criterion, except that here the object of attack is a stated premiss, namely the one given in line 32.3. Here Noonan claims that sight and touch (and presumably the other senses) are *untrustworthy* guides to determining humanity. Since the structure of his rebuttal is reasonably evident, we can pass on to the next proposed answer.

Paragraph 12

The last of the five alternative answers to the question of determining personhood to be discussed by Noonan is that of social visibility or social recognition:

33. Some people argue: (AP)

   [1. Fetuses cannot communicate with others.]   [AP]

   [2. [So] they are not socially perceived as human.]   [1]

   [3. [So] fetuses are not members of society.]   [2]

   [4. Moral rules direct the behavior of members of society
   toward one another.]   [AP]

   [5. [So] moral rules cannot be made for behavior toward
   what is not yet a member of society.]   [4]

   [6. [So] fetuses are not persons.]   [3,5]

Paragraph 13

Here Noonan's rebuttal consists of warning against arbitrary determination of who is and who is not a member of society:

34. In the Roman Empire, condemnation to slavery meant the
   practical denial of most human rights.   (AP)

35. In the Chinese Communist world, landlords have been classified
   as enemies of the people and so treated as nonpersons by the
   state.   (AP)

36. [So] if humanity depends on social recognition, individuals or
   whole groups may be dehumanized by being denied any status in
   their society.   (34,35*)

37. If any criterion of humanity yields monstrous consequences,
   then it is unacceptable.   (SP)

38. [So] social visibility is an unacceptable criterion.   (36,37)

Paragraphs 14–18

Having stated and dismissed the arguments in support of the five alternative proposed answers to the central question, Noonan now turns to a defense of his own—that is, the theologians'—answer. Paragraphs 14 through 18 contain that defense. Because the statement of the argument is complex, we shall begin by trying to ferret out the main argument within these paragraphs. We shall adopt the procedure of labeling some of the lines (P), enabling us to postpone reconstructing the arguments given in defense of these premisses. We can then outline the main argument as follows:

MA1. We should seek an objective basis for determining the point of humanization.[7] (P)

MA2. Objective discontinuities—that is, large differences—in probabilities of alternative outcomes provide an objective basis for making well-founded moral *decisions*.[8] (P)

MA3. At conception, a large change occurs in the probability of survival for the conceptus as compared with the probabilities of survival for any given spermatozoan or ovum.[9] (P)

MA4. [So] there is an objective basis for adopting conception as the decisive moment of humanization. (MA2,3)

MA5. The other proposed criteria either have no objective base or are otherwise unsatisfactory. (P)

MA6. [So] we should adopt conception as the decisive moment of humanization. (MA1,4,5)

MA7. At conception, the organism receives the entire human genetic code.[10] (AP)

MA8. Whatever possesses the entire human genetic code is a self-evolving being that has the potential to attain human wisdom. (AP)

MA9. Whatever is a self-evolving being that has the potential to attain human wisdom is a person. (SP)

MA10. [So] whatever has an entire human genetic code is a person. (MA6–9)

Paragraph 14 is apparently intended to provide two arguments for statement MA1. Unfortunately, Noonan's extremely abbreviated presentation

---

[7]Paragraph 14.

[8]Paragraphs 16 and 17.

[9]Paragraph 15.

[10]The remaining statements are in paragraph 18.

of these arguments makes them somewhat unclear. A suggested reconstruction follows:

39. Some people argue (call it A): (AP)

    [1. There is no such thing as a divinely given soul.]   [AP]

    [2. There is nothing real or objective that may be identified as "humanity."]   [AP]

    [3. [So] humanity is an arbitrary category.]   [1,2]

    [4. [So] it is morally permissible not to include fetuses among the class of humans.]   [3]

40. If one reasons about moral questions, then one implicitly recognizes other human beings. (AP)

41. If one identifies other human beings arbitrarily, then one's moral decisions are arbitrary. (AP)

42. Arbitrary decisions cannot be morally justified decisions. (AP)

43. [So] argument A is unsound. (39–42)

44. If there is a right way and a wrong way to decide moral questions, then we may reject criteria that experience shows can generate monstrous consequences. (AP)

45. Experience shows that subjective criteria—that is, criteria based on the attitudes and feelings of those making moral decisions—can yield monstrous consequences. (AP)

46. [So] we should not employ subjective criteria to make moral decisions. (44,45)

MA1. **[So] we should seek an objective basis for determining the point of humanization.** (42)(46)

Whether this reconstruction captures the arguments contained within this paragraph is problematic. Rather than belabor the point, however, we shall simply take paragraph 14 as expressing Noonan's conviction that we are morally obligated, if it is at all possible, to settle the question of when human organisms become persons on the basis of objective criteria. If we accept this claim, then we have good reason to reject the last three of the alternative criteria, because they rest on attitudes and sentiments of members of society toward fetuses rather than on objective grounds.

The argument for statement MA2 proceeds as follows:

47. If the chance is 200 million to 1 that a movement in the bushes into which someone shoots is a person's, few would hold the shooter morally or legally careless in the shooting. (AP)

48. If the chances are 4 to 1 that the movement in the bushes is a person's, few would acquit the shooter of moral or legal blame. (AP)

49. [So] prudence and negligence are often measured by the account one has taken of the probabilities of expected outcomes. (47,48*)

MA2. **[So] objective discontinuities in outcomes can provide the basis for making well-founded moral decisions.** (19–21)

Extremely close criticism of this argument might cause us to question the introduction of the term *objective discontinuity* in the conclusion. It is always a good idea to examine carefully arguments that introduce terms such as this one. They are often introduced only for their persuasive effect. It is not evident, after all, that small shifts in probabilities are any less objective than large shifts or any less serviceable as a basis for making moral decisions, though Noonan rightly points out that large differences in the probabilities of respective outcomes do often serve as the basis for drawing morally relevant lines. Thus, provided we keep clearly in mind that Noonan's contention is that large shifts in probabilities provide good grounds for drawing morally well-founded distinctions, we may treat the term *objective discontinuities* as shorthand for referring to them.

The argument for statement MA3 is evident:

50. The probability of survival of a given spermatozoan is approximately 1 in 200 million. (AP)

51. The probability of survival of a given oocyte is somewhere between 390 in 100,000 and 390 in 1,000,000. (AP)

52. The probability of survival of a given conceptus is approximately 4 in 5. (AP)

MA3. **[So] at conception, a large change occurs in the probability of survival for the conceptus as compared with the probabilities of survival for any given spermatozoan or ovum.** (50–52)

According to our reconstruction, Noonan proceeds by drawing two inferences. The first is the unproblematic inference from statements MA2 and MA3 to MA4: The conception criterion is objectively based. The second is the more problematic inference from statements MA4 and MA5—that the other alternative criteria are either not objectively based or are otherwise unsatisfactory—to statement MA6: That we should adopt conception as the decisive point of humanization.

Whereas we may overlook the introduction of the term *objective discontinuities,* we may not overlook some of the difficulties that accompany this latter inference. Note that Noonan does not consider whether the occurrence of such discontinuities is the *only* basis for making well-founded moral distinctions, nor does he consider whether such discontinuities *always* constitute a basis for drawing morally justified lines. May we draw a line whenever there is a large shift in probabilities? It is probable that Noonan believes that while the occurrence of objective discontinuities provides a necessary condition for drawing morally proper lines, other factors are also relevant. His comment that this discontinuity is a "buttressing consideration" suggests such an interpretation. But if so, he must explain to his readers just what are these other factors, and his defense of these other factors must be independent of the occurrence of accompanying objective discontinuities whenever competing answers are also accompanied by such discontinuities.

Consider the situation when someone's brain is severely injured and there is a large shift in the probability that the person will ever have another thought, let alone ever again possess human wisdom. Can we draw a morally well-founded line here and maintain that he or she may be killed? From Noonan's discussion of the proposed experience criterion, we would expect that Noonan would answer "no." Yet such a distinction would be drawn on the basis of an objective discontinuity in probabilities of outcomes. Again, there is a large shift in the probability of an individual's having experience before and after it develops a brain, and a large shift in the probability of the individual having thoughts before and after the development of a cerebrum. Why, then, are these not objectively based criteria? Finally, isn't there a significant shift in the probability of a woman's survival when she becomes pregnant? There certainly is in some places in the contemporary world, and there certainly was at the time the theologians formulated their answer.

Noonan's failure to examine the above-stated questions is a serious flaw in his essay. Moreover, Noonan would have helped his readers considerably had he let them know before examining the five alternative answers that his argument would turn on the relative objectivity of the competing criteria. If he had told readers this at the beginning, he might well have put them in a better position to understand and evaluate, if only in a preliminary fashion, his objections to the various criteria. Moreover, he might have made it easier for readers to interpret the introductory paragraphs, especially the second paragraph. For we are now led to suspect that the statement that puzzled us at the very beginning of the essay—the claim that theologians refuse to discriminate among human beings on the basis of their potential—is a miscast way of claiming that theologians are resolute in seeking objective grounds for determining the point of humanization.

The question of how to interpret the connection between the "buttressing consideration" and what he calls the "positive argument for conception as the decisive moment of humanization" arises again in considering the last three claims of the argument:

> MA8. Whatever possesses the entire human genetic code is a self-evolving being that has the potential to attain human wisdom. (AP)

> MA9. Whatever is a self-evolving being that has the potential to attain human wisdom is a person. (SP)

MA10. [So] whatever has an entire human genetic code is
a person. (MA8,9)

For one thing, statement MA8, as it stands, is not true. Every cell of
the human being, including pathogenic cells such as cancer cells, contains an
entire human genetic code. But more importantly, what is the relationship
between the so-called buttressing claim that an objective shift in probabilities
of survival occurs at conception and this main argument? Is it the fact that the
conceptus has received the entire genetic code or the fact that the probabilities
of its survival have radically shifted that constitutes the objective moral basis
for identifying conception as the point of humanization? Granted, they are the
same point. But which constitutes the reason? Why is having the possibility
of human wisdom the chosen point rather than the point at which one comes
to have at least some human wisdom? If, to answer this question, Noonan
points to the buttressing consideration, then he has placed greater weight on
the buttress than it can sustain. If, to answer the question why the shift in
probabilities at conception is the appropriate shift in probabilities to consider
in answering the main question, then Noonan must provide a defense of that
argument.

This is Noonan's positive argument for his answer to the main
question. In the following discussion, during which Noonan draws some
of the implications of his main conclusion, we shall refer to that main conclusion as:

53. Conception is the point of humanization.

Paragraph 19

Having argued for statement 53, conception as the point of humanization,
Noonan proceeds in the remainder of his essay to draw the implications that
this holds for the question of abortion. He begins by making a number of
assertions:

54. If something is human, then it has a destiny to make its own
decisions, which may not be taken away by another man's
decision. (AP)

55. If something has a destiny to make its own decisions, which may
not be taken away by another man's decision, then it may not be
aborted for its own good. (AP)

56. Fetuses may not be aborted for their own good. (53–55)[11]

57. If fetuses are persons, then fetuses have equal rights with all
other persons. (AP)

58. The rights of fetuses may conflict with others' rights. (AP)

---

[11]Note that this is a suppressed conclusion.

    59. Fetuses cannot speak for themselves.   (AP)

    60. In cases of conflict, the stake for the fetus is the right to life
        itself.   (AP)

Paragraph 20

This paragraph draws a further inference from the previous one:

    61. The life even of the innocent is not absolute.   (AP)

    62. In weighing the life of the fetus against another person's life, the
        fetus is always to be given a value greater than zero and always a
        value separate from its parents.   (53,58,61)

Paragraph 21

Only the last sentence of this paragraph contains an argument. It seeks to
explain why a restrictive abortion policy was adopted between 1895 and 1930.
Otherwise, it contains merely a brief historical account of the Church's policy
changes.

    63. A multitude of questionable exceptions arose when the Church's
        policy permitted abortions only in the case of a cancerous uterus
        or ectopic pregnancy.   (AP)

    64. [So] the Church returned to its position of absolute prohibition
        of abortion.   (63)

Paragraphs 22–24

    65. One should love one's neighbor as oneself.   (AP)

    66. [So] abortion is never right except in self-defense.   (53,57)

    67. [So] reason alone cannot say that a mother must prefer a child's
        life to her own.   (53,65)

    68. Jesus was an exemplar of and urged self-sacrifice.   (AP)

    69. [So] it is morally exemplary to sacrifice one's own life to the
        interests of the fetus.   (53,67,68)

Model Outline

Having carefully read through each paragraph of this essay and delineated the
arguments contained within them, our task now is to put the pieces together
and consider the whole. The primary question addressed by the essay is

evident: It is to determine when in the process of its development an organism of the species *Homo sapiens* becomes a person. Although at least half the essay is devoted to rejecting five proposed answers to that central question, Noonan has told us that his main objective in this essay is to provide the secular basis for the theologians' claim that conception is the point of humanization. His grounds for thinking that this answer is superior to the others are that at conception the organism receives the entire human genetic code, which carries with it the potential for human wisdom, and that at that very moment there occurs what he calls an objective discontinuity in the probability of the survival of the organism. This shift in the probability of the organism's survival, he claims, constitutes an objective basis for identifying conception as the crucial point. It is evident that our tentative identification of his main argument, which was given previously as MA1 through MA10, was accurate.

Main Argument

1. We should seek an objective basis for determining the point of humanization. (P)

2. Objective discontinuities—that is, large differences—in probabilities of alternative outcomes can provide the basis for making well-founded moral distinctions. (P)

3. At conception, a large change occurs in the probability of survival for the conceptus as compared with the probabilities of survival for any given spermatozoan or ovum. (P)

4. [So] there is an objective basis for adopting conception as the decisive moment of humanization. (2,3)

5. The other proposed criteria either have no objective base or are otherwise unsatisfactory. (P)

6. [So] we should adopt conception as the decisive moment of humanization. (1,4,5)

7. At conception, the organism receives the entire human genetic code. (AP)

8. Whatever possesses the entire human genetic code is a self-evolving being that has the potential to attain human wisdom. (AP)

9. Whatever is a self-evolving being that has the potential to attain human wisdom is a person. (SP)

10. [So] whatever has an entire human genetic code is a person. (6–9)

Argument for line 1

11. If one arbitrarily determines who is a human being, then all one's decisions about moral questions are arbitrary. (38)

12. Arbitrary decisions cannot be morally justified decisions. (AP)

13. If there is a right way and a wrong way to decide moral questions, then we may reject criteria that experience shows can generate monstrous consequences. (AP)

14. Experience shows that subjective criteria—that is, criteria based on the attitudes and feelings of those making moral decisions—can yield monstrous consequences. (AP)

 1. [So] we should adopt only an objective basis for determining the point of humanization. (11,12)(13,14)

Argument for line 2

15. The probability of survival of a given spermatozoan is approximately 1 in 200 million. (AP)

16. The probability of survival of a given oocyte is somewhere between 390 in 100,000 and 390 in 1,000,000. (AP)

17. The probability of survival of a conceptus is approximately 4 in 5. (AP)

18. Extremely large shifts in probabilities of outcomes constitute objective discontinuities in nature. (AP)

 2. [So] at conception, an objective discontinuity occurs in the probability of survival for the conceptus as compared with the probabilities of survival for any given spermatozoan or ovum. (15–18)

Argument for line 3

19. If the chance is 200 million to 1 that a movement in the bushes into which someone shoots is a person's, few would hold the shooter morally or legally careless in the shooting. (AP)

20. If the chances are 4 to 5 that the movement in the bushes is a person's, few would acquit the shooter of moral or legal blame. (AP)

21. [So] prudence and negligence are often measured by the account a person has taken of the probabilities of expected outcomes. (13,14*)

 3. [So] objective discontinuities in outcomes can provide the basis for making well-founded moral decisions. (19–21)

Argument for line 5[12]

22. Factors such as individual circumstances, race, and technological development might make different fetuses viable at different times. (AP)

23. [So] the viability criterion is elastic. (22)

24. If the criterion for humanity is elastic, then two fetuses conceived at the same time might at a later time not both be persons or might not both be not persons. (SP)

25. But fetuses conceived at the same time must at every time either both be or not be persons. (SP)

26. [So] an elastic criterion for humanity is not acceptable. (23–25)

27. After viability, indeed, up to age 5, the fetus or child is still dependent on someone's care. (AP)

28. [So] there is no substantial lessening of dependence at viability. (27)

29. [So] viability does not signify any special acquisition of humanity. (28)

30. [So] the viability criterion is not acceptable. (23,26)(29)

31. The embryo is responsive to touch after eight weeks. (AP)

32. [So] at eight weeks it is experiencing and reacting. (31)

33. The embryo is alive and responding to its environment at an even earlier stage. (AP)

34. [So] if the experience criterion is adopted, embryos even younger than eight weeks are not to be aborted. (32)(33)

35. Sometimes aphasia erases adult memory. (AP)

36. Aphasia does not erase personhood. (AP)

37. Neonates are also unformed by experience. (AP)

38. But neonates are persons. (AP)

39. Proponents of the experience criterion fail to make clear why acquisition of experience confers humanity. (AP)

40. The category of personhood is a moral category. (SP)

---

[12]We shall include only the main grounds for objecting to the proposed alternative criteria. See the discussion above for full treatments of the arguments against these criteria.

41. In general, a proposed criterion for determining what will be
    . included in a given moral category is satisfactory only if the
    criterion identifies a morally relevant basis for determining what
    will be included and it does not arbitrarily exclude entities
    ordinarily included in that category. (SP)

42. If proponents of the experience criterion identify specific
    experiences, such as loving or learning, then they arbitrarily
    exclude those who either don't love or don't learn. (AP)

43. Proponents of the experience criterion fail to identify a morally
    relevant distinction or arbitrarily exclude entities ordinarily
    included in the category of persons. (SP)

44. [So] the experience criterion of personhood
    is unsatisfactory. (39–41,43)(42,43)

45. It is not the case that if we have less intense feelings toward some
    individuals than toward others, it follows that they are not
    persons. (AP)

46. [So] the adult-sentiment criterion of personhood is
    unsatisfactory. (45)

47. Sensations are untrustworthy guides for determining what
    something is. (AP)

48. [So] the criterion that rests on parental sensations is an
    untrustworthy guide to humanity. (47)

49. In the Roman Empire, condemnation to slavery meant the
    practical denial of most human rights. (AP)

50. In the Chinese Communist world, landlords have been classified
    as enemies of the people and so treated as nonpersons by the
    state. (AP)

51. [So] if humanity depends on social recognition, individuals or
    whole groups may be dehumanized by being denied any status in
    their society. (49,50*)

52. If any criterion of humanity can yield monstrous consequences,
    then it is unacceptable. (SP)

53. [So] social visibility is an unacceptable criterion of
    personhood. (51,52)

54. The above-discussed criteria are the primary alternatives to
    conception. (AP)

5. [So] the primary alternatives to conception are either not
   objectively based or otherwise unsatisfactory.
   (30,44,46,48,53,54)

Implications[13]

55. If fetuses are persons, then fetuses have equal rights with all other persons. (AP)

56. [So] fetuses have equal rights with all other persons. (10,55)

57. If an individual has equal rights with all other persons then the individual may be killed only in self-defense. (AP)

58. [So] fetuses may only be killed in self-defense. (56,57)

59. If fetuses are persons, then reason alone cannot say that a woman must prefer a child's life to her own. (SP)

60. [So] reason alone cannot say that a mother must prefer a child's life to her own. (10,59)

61. Jesus was an exemplar of and urged self-sacrifice. (AP)

62. [So] it is morally exemplary to sacrifice one's own life to the interests of the fetus. (60,61)

---

[13] I have treated what follows as implications drawn from the main conclusion rather than integral parts of the main argument.

In Defense of Abortion
and Infanticide

Michael Tooley

¹   This essay deals with the question of the morality of abortion and
infanticide. The fundamental objection traditionally advanced against these
practices rests on the contention that human fetuses and infants have a right
to life. It is this claim that will be the focus of attention here. The basic issue
to be discussed, then, is what properties a thing must have in order to have a
right to life. My approach will be to set out and defend a basic moral principle
specifying a condition an organism must satisfy if it is to have a right to life.
It will be seen that this condition is not satisfied by human fetuses and infants,
and thus that they do not have a right to life. So unless there are other objections to abortion and infanticide which are sound, one is forced to conclude
that these practices are morally acceptable ones.[1] In contrast, it may turn out
that our treatment of adult members of some other species is morally indefensible. For it is quite possible that some nonhuman animals do possess properties that endow them with a right to life.

I. Abortion and Infanticide

² What reason is there for raising the question of the morality of infanticide?
One reason is that it seems very difficult to formulate a completely satisfactory
pro-abortion position without coming to grips with the infanticide issue. For
the problem that the liberal on abortion encounters here is that of specifying a

cutoff point which is not arbitrary: at what stage in the development of a human being does it cease to be morally permissible to destroy it, and why?

3   It is important to be clear about the difficulty here. The problem is not, as some have thought, that since there is a continuous line of development from a zygote to a newborn baby, one cannot hold that it is seriously wrong to destroy a newborn baby without also holding that it is seriously wrong to destroy a zygote, or any other intermediate stage in the development of a human being. The problem is rather that if one says that it is wrong to destroy a newborn baby but not a zygote or some intermediate stage, one should be prepared to point to a morally relevant difference between a newborn baby and the earlier stage in the development of a human being.

4   Precisely the same difficulty can, of course, be raised for a person who holds that infanticide is morally permissible, since one can ask what morally relevant difference there is between an adult human being and a newborn baby. What makes it permissible to destroy a baby, but wrong to kill an adult? So the challenge remains. But I shall argue that in the latter case there is an extremely plausible answer.

5   Reflecting on the morality of infanticide forces one to face up to this challenge. In the case of abortion a number of events—quickening or viability, for instance—might be taken as cutoff points, and it is easy to overlook the fact that none of these events involves any morally significant change in the developing human. In contrast, if one is going to defend infanticide, one has to get very clear about what it is that gives something a right to life.

6   One of the interesting ways that the abortion issue differs from most other moral issues is that the plausible issues on abortion appear to be the extreme cases. For if a human fetus has a right to life, one is inclined to say that, in general, one would be justified in killing it only to save the life of the mother, and perhaps not even in that case. Such is the extreme anti-abortion position. On the other hand, if the fetus does not have a right to life, why should it be seriously wrong to destroy it? Why would one need to point to special circumstances—such as the presence of genetic disease, or a threat to the woman's health—in order to justify such action? The upshot is that there does not appear to be any room for a moderate position on abortion such as one finds, for example, in the Model Penal Code recommendations.[2]

7   Aside from the light it may shed on the abortion question, the issue of infanticide is both interesting and important in its own right. The theoretical interest has been mentioned above: it forces one to face up to the question of what it is that gives something a right to life. The practical importance need not be labored. Most people would prefer to raise children who do not suffer from gross deformities or from severe physical, emotional or intellectual handicaps. If it could be shown that there is no moral objection to infanticide, the happiness of society could be significantly and justifiably increased.

8   The suggestion that infanticide may be morally permissible is not an idea that many people are able to consider dispassionately. Even philosophers tend to react in a way which seems primarily visceral—offering no arguments, and dismissing infanticide out of hand.

9   Some philosophers have argued, however, that such a reaction is not inappropriate, on the ground that, first, moral principles must, in the final analysis, be justified by reference to our moral feelings, or intuitions, and secondly, infanticide is one practice that is judged wrong by virtually everyone's moral intuition. I believe, however, that this line of thought is unsound, and I have argued elsewhere that even if [one] grants, at least for the sake of argument, that moral intuitions are the final court of appeal regarding the acceptability of moral principles, the question of the morality of infanticide is not one that can be settled by an appeal to our intuitions concerning it.[3] If infanticide is to be rejected, an argument is needed, and I believe that the considerations advanced in this essay show that it is unlikely that such an argument is forthcoming.

II: What Sort of Being Can Possess a Right to Life?

10 The issues of the morality of abortion and of infanticide seem to turn primarily on the answers to the following four questions:

1. What properties, other than potentialities, give something a right to life?

2. Do the corresponding potentialities also endow something with a right to life?

3. If not, do they at least make it seriously wrong to destroy it?

4. At what point in its development does a member of the biologically defined species *Homo sapiens* first possess those nonpotential properties that give something a right to life?

The argument to be developed in the present section bears upon the answers to the first two questions.

11   How can one determine what properties endow a being with a right to life? An approach that I believe is very promising starts out from the observation that there appear to be two radically different sorts of reasons why an entity may lack a certain right. Compare, for example, the following two claims:

1. A child does not have a right to smoke.

2. A newspaper does not have a right to be torn up.

The first claim raises a substantive moral issue. People might well disagree about it, and support their conflicting views by appealing to different moral theories. The second claim, in contrast, seems an unlikely candidate for moral dispute. It is natural to say that newspapers just are not the sort of thing that can have any rights at all, including a right not to be torn up. So there is no need to appeal to a substantive moral theory to resolve the question whether a newspaper has a right not to be torn up.

12   One way of characterizing this difference . . . is to say that the second claim, unlike the first, is true in virtue of a certain *conceptual* connection, and that is why no moral theory is needed in order to see that it is true. The explanation, then, of why it is that a newspaper does not have a right not to be torn up is that there is some property P such that, first, newspapers lack property P, and secondly, it is a conceptual truth that only things with property P can be possessors of rights.

13   What might property P be? A plausible answer is, I believe, set out and defended by Joel Feinberg in his paper, "The Rights of Animals and Unborn Generations."[4] It takes the form of what Feinberg refers to as the *interest principle:* ". . . the sorts of beings who *can* have rights are precisely those who have (or can have) interests."[5] And then, since "interests must be compounded somehow out of conations,"[6] it follows that things devoid of desires, such as newspapers, can have neither interests nor rights. Here, then, is one account of the difference in status between judgments such as (1) and (2) above.

14   Let us now consider the right to life. The interest principle tells us that an entity cannot have any rights at all, and *a fortiori,* cannot have a right to life, unless it is capable of having interests. This in itself may be a conclusion of considerable importance. Consider, for example, a fertilized human egg cell. Someday it will come to have desires and interests. As a zygote, however, it does not have desires, nor even the *capacity* for having desires. What about interests? This depends on the account one offers of the relation between desires and interests. It seems to me that a zygote cannot properly be spoken of as a subject of interests. My reason is roughly this. What is in a thing's interest is a function of its present and future desires, both those it will have and those it could have. In the case of an entity that is not presently capable of any desires, its interest must be based entirely upon the satisfaction of its future desires. Then, since the satisfaction of its future desires presupposes the continued existence of the entity in question, anything which has an interest which is based upon the satisfaction of future desires must also have an interest in its own continued existence. Therefore something which is not presently capable of having any desires at all—like a zygote—cannot have any interests at all unless it has an interest in its own continued existence. I shall argue shortly, however, that a zygote cannot have such an interest. From this it will follow that it cannot have any interests at all, and this conclusion, together with the interest principle, entails that not all members of the species *Homo sapiens* have a right to life.

15   The interest principle involves, then, a thesis concerning a necessary condition which something must have if it is to have a right to life, and it is a thesis which has important moral implications. It implies, for example, that abortions, if performed sufficiently early, do not involve any violation of a right to life. But on the other hand, the interest principle provides no help with the question of the moral status of human organisms once they have developed to the point where they do have desires, and thus are capable of having interests.

The interest principle states that they *can* have rights. It does not state whether they *do* have rights—including, in particular, a right not to be destroyed.

16   It is possible, however, that the interest principle does not exhaust the conceptual connections between rights and interests. It formulates only a very general connection: a thing cannot have any rights at all unless it is capable of having at least some interest. May there not be more specific connections, between particular rights and particular sorts of interests? The following line of thought lends plausibility to this suggestion. Consider animals such as cats. Some philosophers are inclined to hold that animals such as cats do not have any rights at all. But let us assume, for the purpose of the present discussion, that cats do have some rights, such as a right not to be tortured, and consider the following claim:

3. A cat does not have a right to a university education.

How is this statement to be regarded? In particular, is it comparable in status to the claim that children do not have a right to smoke, or, instead, to the claim that newspapers do not have a right not to be torn up? To the latter, surely. Just as a newspaper is not the sort of thing that can have any rights at all, including a right not to be destroyed, so one is inclined to say that a cat, though it may have some rights, such as a right not to be tortured, is not the sort of thing that possibly can have a right to a university education.

17   This intuitive judgment about the status of claims such as (3) is reinforced, moreover, if one turns to the question of the grounds of the interest principle. Consider, for example, the account offered by Feinberg, which he summarizes as follows:

> Now we can abstract from our discussion of animal rights a crucial principle for tentative use in the resolution of the other riddles about the applicability of the concept of a right, namely, that the sorts of beings who *can* have rights are precisely those who have (or can have) interests. I have come to this tentative conclusion for two reasons: (1) because a right holder must be capable of being represented and it is impossible to represent a being that can have no interests, and (2) because a right holder must be capable of being a beneficiary in his own person, and a being without interests is a being that is incapable of being harmed or benefited, having no good or 'sake' of its own. Thus a being without interests has no 'behalf' to act in, and no 'sake' to act for.[7]

If this justification of the interest principle is sound, it can also be employed to support principles connecting particular rights with specific sorts of interests. Just as one cannot represent a being that has no interests at all, so one cannot, in demanding a university education for a cat, be representing the cat unless one is thereby representing some interest that the cat has, and that would be served by its receiving a university education. Similarly, one cannot be acting for the sake of a cat in arguing that it should receive a university education unless the cat has some interest that will thereby be furthered. The conclusion, therefore, is that if Feinberg's defense of the interest principle is sound, other more specific principles must also be correct. These more specific principles can be summed up, albeit somewhat vaguely, by the following, *particular-interests principle:*

> It is a conceptual truth that an entity cannot have a particular right, R, unless it is at least capable of having some interest, I, which is furthered by its having right R.

18   Given this particular-interests principle, certain familiar facts, whose importance have not often been appreciated, become comprehensible. Compare an act of killing a normal adult human being with an act of torturing one for five minutes. Though both acts are seriously wrong, they are not equally so. Here, as in most cases, to violate an individual's right to life is more seriously wrong than to violate his right not to have pain inflicted on him. Consider, however, the corresponding actions in the case of a newborn kitten. Most people feel that it is seriously wrong to torture a kitten for five minutes, but not to kill it painlessly. How is this difference in the moral ordering of the two types of acts, between the human case and the kitten case, to be explained? One answer is that while normal adult human beings have both a right to life and a right not to be tortured, a kitten has only the latter. But why should this be so? The particular-interests principle suggests a possible explanation. Though kittens have some interests, including, in particular, an interest in not being tortured, which derives from their capacity to feel pain, they do not have an interest in their own continued existence, and hence do not have a right not to be destroyed. The answer contains, of course, a large promissory element. One needs a defense of the view that kittens have no interest in continued existence. But the point here is simply that an important question about the rationale underlying the moral ordering of certain sorts of acts, and the particular-interests principle points to a possible answer.

19   This fact lends further plausibility, I believe, to the particular-interests principle. What one would ultimately like to do, of course, is to set out an analysis of the concept of a right, show that the analysis is indeed satisfactory, and then show that the particular-interests principle is entailed by the analysis. Unfortunately, it will not be possible to pursue such an approach here, since formulating an acceptable analysis of the concept of a right is a far from trivial matter. What I should like to do, however, is to touch briefly upon the problem of providing such an analysis, and then to indicate the account that seems to me most satisfactory—an account which does entail the particular-interests principle.

20   It would be widely agreed, I believe, both that rights impose obligations, and that the obligations they impose upon others are conditional upon certain factors. The difficulty arises when one attempts to specify what the obligations are conditional upon. There seem to be two main views in this area. According to the one, rights impose obligations that are conditional upon the interests of the possessor of the right. To say that Sandra has a right to

something is thus to say, roughly, that if it is in Sandra's interest to have that thing, then others are under an obligation not to deprive her of it. According to the second view, rights impose obligations that are conditional upon the right's not having been waived. To say that Sandra has a right to something is to say, roughly, that if Sandra has not given others permission to take the thing, then they are under an obligation not to deprive her of it.

21   Both views encounter serious difficulties. On the one hand, in the case of minors, and nonhuman animals, it would seem that the obligations that rights impose must be taken as conditional upon the interests of those individuals, rather than upon whether they have given one permission to do certain things. On the other, in the case of individuals who are capable of making informed and rational decisions, if that person has not given one permission to take something that belongs to him, it would seem that one is, in general, still under an obligation not to deprive him of it, even if having that thing is no longer in his interest.

22   As a result, it seems that a more complex account is needed of the factors upon which the obligations imposed by rights are conditional. The account which I now prefer, and which I have defended elsewhere,[8] is this:

> A has a right to X

means the same as

> A is such that it can be in A's interest to have X, and either (1) A is not capable of making an informed and rational choice whether to . grant others permission to deprive him of X, in which case, if it is in A's interest not to be deprived of X, then, by that fact alone, others are under a *prima facie* obligation not to deprive A of X, or (2) A is capable of making an informed and rational choice whether to grant others permission to deprive him of X, in which case others are under a *prima facie* obligation not to deprive A of X if and only if A has not granted them permission to do so.

And if this account, or something rather similar is correct, then so is the particular-interests principle.

23   What I now want to do is to apply the particular-interests principle to the case of the right to life. First, however, one needs to notice that the expression, "right to life," is not entirely happy, since it suggests that the right in question concerns the continued existence of a biological organism. That this is incorrect can be brought out by considering possible ways of violating an individual's right to life. Suppose, for example, that future technological developments make it possible to change completely the neural networks in a brain, and that the brain of some normal adult human being is thus completely reprogrammed, so that the organism in question winds up with memories (or rather, apparent memories), beliefs, attitudes, and personality traits totally different from those associated with it before it was subjected to reprogramming. (The pope is reprogrammed, say, on the model of Bertrand Russell.) In such a case, however beneficial the change might be, one would surely want to say

that someone had been destroyed, that an adult human being's right to life had been violated, even though no biological organism had been killed. This shows that the expression, "right to life," is misleading, since what one is concerned about is not just the continued existence of a biological organism.

24   How, then, might the right in question be more accurately described? A natural suggestion is that the expression "right to life" refers to the right of a subject of experiences and other mental states to continue to exist. It might be contended, however, that this interpretation begs the question against certain possible views. For someone might hold—and surely some people in fact do—that while continuing subjects of experiences and other mental states certainly have a right to life, so do some other organisms that are only potentially such continuing subjects, such as human fetuses. A right to life, on this view, is either the right of a subject of experiences to continue to exist, or the right of something that is only potentially a continuing subject of experiences to become such an entity.

25   This view is, I believe, to be rejected, for at least two reasons. In the first place, this view appears to be clearly incompatible with the interest principle, as well as with the particular-interests principle. Secondly, this position entails that the destruction of potential persons is, in general, *prima facie* seriously wrong, and I shall argue, in the next section,[9] that the latter view is incorrect.

26   Let us consider, then, the right of a subject of experiences and other mental states to continue to exist. The particular-interests principle implies that something cannot possibly have such a right unless its continued existence can be in its interest. We need to ask, then, what must be the case if the continued existence of something is to be in its interest.

27   It will help us to focus our thinking, I believe, if we consider a crucial case, stressed by Derek Parfit. Imagine a human baby that has developed to the point of being sentient, and of having simple desires, but that is not yet capable of having any desire for continued existence. Suppose, further, that the baby will enjoy a happy life, and will be glad that it was not destroyed. Can we or can we not say that it is in the baby's interest not to be destroyed?

28   To approach this case, let us consider a closely related one, namely, that of a human embryo that has not developed sufficiently far to have any desires, or even any states of consciousness at all, but that will develop into an individual who will enjoy a happy life, and who will be glad that his mother did not have an abortion. Can we or can we not say that it is in the embryo's interest not to be destroyed?

29   Why might someone be tempted to say that it is in the embryo's interest that it not be destroyed? One line of thought which, I believe, tempts some people, is this. Let Mary be an individual who enjoys a happy life. Then, though some philosophers have expressed serious doubts about this, it might very well be said that it was certainly in Mary's interest that a certain embryo was not destroyed several years earlier. And this claim, together with the tendency to use expressions such as "Mary before she was born" to refer to the

embryo in question, may lead one to think that it was in the embryo's interest not to be destroyed. But this way of thinking involves a conceptual confusion. A subject of interests, in the relevant sense of "interest," must necessarily be a subject of conscious states, including experience and desires. This means that in identifying Mary with the embryo, and attributing to it her interest in its earlier nondestruction, one is treating the embryo as if it were itself a subject of consciousness. But by hypothesis the embryo being considered has not developed to the point where there is any subject of consciousness associated with it. It cannot, therefore, have any interests at all, and *a fortiori*, it cannot have any interest in its own continued existence.

30   Let us now return to the first case—that of a human baby that is sentient, and which has simple desires, but which is not yet capable of having more complex desires, such as a desire for its own continued existence. Given that it will develop into an individual who will lead a happy life, and who will be glad that the baby was not destroyed, does one want to say that the baby's not being destroyed is in the baby's own interest?

31   Again, the following line of thought may seem initially tempting. If Mary is the resulting individual, then it was in Mary's interest that the baby not have been destroyed. But the baby just *is* Mary when she was young. So it must have been in the baby's interest that it not have been destroyed.

32   Indeed, this argument is considerably more tempting in the present case than in the former, since here there is something that is a subject of consciousness, and which it is natural to identify with Mary. I suggest, however, that when one reflects upon the case, it becomes clear that such an identification is justified only if further things are the case. Thus, on the one hand, suppose that Mary is able to remember quite clearly some of the experiences that the baby enjoyed. Given that sort of causal and psychological connection, it would seem perfectly reasonable to hold that Mary and the baby are one and the same subject of consciousness, and thus, that if it is in Mary's interest that the baby not have been destroyed, then this must also have been in the baby's interest. On the other hand, suppose that not only does Mary, at a much later time, not remember any of the baby's experiences, but the experiences in question are not psychologically linked, either via memory or in any other way, to mental states enjoyed by the human organism at *any* later time. Here it seems to me clearly incorrect to say that Mary and the baby are one and the same subject of consciousness, and therefore it cannot be correct to transfer, from Mary to the baby, Mary's interest in the baby's not having been destroyed.

33   Let us now return to the question of what must be the case if the continued existence of something is to be in [its] own interest. The picture that emerges from the two cases just discussed is this. In the first place, nothing at all can be in an entity's interest unless it has desires at some time or other. But more than this is required if the continued existence of the entity is to be in its own interest. One possibility, which will generally be sufficient, is that the individual have, at the time in question, a desire for its own continued

be in its own interest even when such a desire is not present. What is needed, existence. Yet it also seems clear that an individual's continued existence can apparently, is that the continued existence of the individual will make possible the satisfaction of some desires existing at other times. But not just any desires existing at other times will do. Indeed, as is illustrated by the deprogramming/reprogramming example, it is not even sufficient that they be desires associated with the same physical organism. It is crucial that they be desires that belong to one and the same subject of consciousness.

34   The critical question, then, concerns the conditions under which desires existing at different times can be correctly attributed to a single, continuing subject of consciousness. The question raises a number of difficult issues which cannot be considered here. Part of the rationale underlying the view I wish to advance will be clear, however, if one considers the role played by memory in the psychological unity of the individual over time. When I remember a past experience, what I know is not merely that there was a certain experience which someone or other had, but that there was an experience that belonged to the *same* individual as the present memory beliefs, and it seems clear that this feature of one's memories is, in general, a crucial part of what it is that makes one a continuing subject of experiences, rather than merely a series of psychologically isolated, momentary subjects of consciousness. This suggests something like the following principle:

> Desires existing at different times can belong to a single, continuing subject of consciousness only if that subject of consciousness possesses, at some time, the concept of a continuing self or mental substance.[10]

35   Given this principle, together with the particular-rights principle, one can set out the following argument in support of a claim concerning a necessary condition which an entity must satisfy if it is to have a right to life:

1. The concept of a right is such that an individual cannot have a right at time t to continued existence unless the individual is such that it can be in its interest at time t that it continue to exist.

2. The continued existence of a given subject of consciousness cannot be in that individual's interest at time t unless *either* that individual has a desire, at time t, to continue to exist as a subject of consciousness, *or* that individual can have desires at other times.

3. An individual cannot have a desire to exist as a subject of consciousness unless it possesses the concept of a continuing self or mental substance.

4. An individual existing at one time cannot have desires at other times unless there is at least one time at which it possesses the concept of a continuing self or mental substance.

Therefore:

> 5. An individual cannot have a right to continued existence unless there is at least one time at which it possesses the concept of a continuing self or mental substance.

36   This conclusion is obviously significant. But precisely what implications does it have with respect to the morality of abortion and infanticide? The answer will depend on what relationship there is between, on the one hand, the behavioral and neurophysiological development of a human being, and, on the other, the development of that individual's mind. Some people believe that there is no relationship at all. They believe that a human mind, with all its mature capacities, is present in a human from conception onward, and so is there before the brain has begun to develop, and before the individual has begun to exhibit behavior expressive of higher mental functioning. Most philosophers, however, reject this view. They believe, on the one hand, that there is, in general, a rather close relation between an individual's behavioral capacities and its mental functioning, and, on the other, that there is a very intimate relationship between the mind and the brain. As regards the latter, some philosophers hold that the mind is in fact identical with the brain. Others maintain that the mind is distinct from the brain, but causally dependent upon it. In either case, the result is a view according to which the development of the mind and the brain are closely tied to one another.

37   If one does adopt the view that there is a close relation between the behavioral and neurophysiological development of the human being, and the development of its mind, then the above conclusion has a very important, and possibly decisive implication with respect to the morality of abortion and infanticide. For when human development, both behavioral and neurophysiological, is closely examined, it is seen to be most unlikely that human fetuses, or even newborn babies, possess any concept of a continuing self.[11] And in the light of the above conclusion, this means that such individuals do not possess a right to life.

38   But is it reasonable to hold that there is a close relationship between human behavioral and neurophysiological development, and the development of the human mind? Approached from a scientific perspective, I believe that there is excellent reason for doing so. Consider, for example, what is known about how, at later stages, human mental capacities proceed in step with brain development, or what is known about how damage to different parts of the human brain can affect, in different ways, an individual's intellectual capacities.

39   Why, then, do some people reject the view that there is a close relationship between the development of the human mind, and the behavioral and neurophysiological development of human beings? There are, I think, two main reasons. First, some philosophers believe that the scientific evidence is irrelevant, because they believe that it is possible to establish, by means of purely metaphysical argument, that a human mind, with its mature capacities,

is present in a human being from conception onward. I have argued elsewhere that the argument in question is unsound.[12]

40   Secondly, and more commonly, some people appeal to the idea that it is a divinely related truth that human beings have minds from conception onward. There are a number of points to be made about such an appeal. In the first place, the belief that a mind, or soul, is infused into a human body at conception by God is not an essential belief within many of the world religions. Secondly, even within religious traditions, such as Roman Catholicism, where that belief is a very common one, it is by no means universally accepted. Thus, for example, the well-known Catholic philosopher, Joseph Donceel, has argued very strongly for the claim that the correct position of the question of ensoulment is that the soul enters the body only when the human brain has undergone a sufficient process of development.[13] Thirdly, there is the question of whether it is reasonable to accept the religious outlook which is being appealed to in support of the contention that humans have minds which are capable of higher intellectual activities from conception onward. This question raises very large issues in philosophy of religion which cannot be pursued here. But it should at least be said that many contemporary philosophers who have reflected on religious beliefs have come to the view that there is not sufficient reason for believing in the existence of God, let alone for accepting the much more detailed religious claims which are part of a religion such as Christianity. Finally, suppose that one nevertheless decides to accept the contention that it is a divinely revealed truth that humans have, from conception onward, minds that are capable of higher mental activities, and that one appeals to this purported revelation in order to support the claim that all humans have a right to life. One needs to notice that if one then goes on to argue, not merely that abortion is morally wrong, but that there should be a law against it, one will encounter a very serious objection. For it is surely true that it is inappropriate, at least in a pluralistic society, to appeal to specific religious beliefs of a non-moral sort—such as the belief that God infuses souls into human bodies at conception—in support of legislation that will be binding on everyone, including those who either accept different religious beliefs, or none at all.

IV: *Summary and Conclusions*[14]

41 In this paper I have advanced three main philosophical contentions:

1. An entity cannot have a right to life unless it is capable of having an interest in its own continued existence.

2. An entity is not capable of having an interest in its own continued existence unless it possesses, at some time, the concept of a continuing self, or subject of experiences and other mental states.

3. The fact that an entity will, if not destroyed, come to have properties that would give it a right to life does not in itself make it seriously wrong to destroy it.

42   If these philosophical contentions are correct, the crucial question is a factual one: At what point does a developing human being acquire the concept of a continuing self, and at what point is it capable of having an interest in its own continued existence? I have not examined these issues in detail here, but I have suggested that careful scientific studies of human development, both behavioral and neurophysiological, strongly support the view that even newborn humans do not have the capacities in question. If this is right, then it would seem that infanticide during a time interval shortly after birth must be viewed as morally acceptable.

43   But where is the line to be drawn? What is the precise cutoff point? If one maintained, as some philosophers do, that an individual can possess a concept only if it is capable of expressing that concept linguistically, then it would be a relatively simple matter to determine whether a given organism possessed the concept of a continuing subject of experiences and other mental states. It is far from clear, however, that this claim about the necessary connection between the possession of concepts and the having of linguistic capabilities is correct. I would argue, for example, that one wants to ascribe mental states of a conceptual sort—such as beliefs and desires—to animals that are incapable of learning a language, and that an individual cannot have beliefs and desires unless it possesses the concepts involved in those beliefs and desires. And if that view is right—if an organism can acquire concepts without thereby acquiring a way of expressing those concepts linguistically—then the question of whether an individual possesses the concept of a continuing self may be one that requires quite subtle experimental techniques to answer.

44   If this view of the matter is roughly correct, there are two worries that one is left with at the level of practical moral decisions, one of which may turn out to be deeply disturbing. The lesser worry is the question just raised: Where is the line to be drawn in the case of infanticide? This is not really a troubling question since there is no serious need to know the exact point at which a human infant acquires a right to life. For in the vast majority of cases in which infanticide is desirable due to serious defects from which the baby suffers, its desirability will be apparent at birth or within a very short time thereafter. Since it seems clear that an infant at this point in its development is not capable of possessing the concept of a continuing subject of experiences and other mental states, and so is incapable of having an interest in its own continued existence, infanticide will be morally permissible in the vast majority of cases in which it is, for one reason or another, desirable. The practical moral problem can thus be satisfactorily handled by choosing some short period of time, such as a week after birth, as the interval during which infanticide will be permitted.

45   The troubling issue which arises out of the above reflections concerns whether adult animals belonging to species other than *Homo sapiens* may not also possess a right to life. For once one allows that an individual can possess concepts, and have beliefs and desires, without being able to express those concepts, or those beliefs and desires, linguistically, then it becomes very much an open question whether animals belonging to other species do not possess

properties that give them a right to life. Indeed, I am strongly inclined to think that adult members of at least some nonhuman species do have a right to life. My reason is that, first, I believe that some nonhuman animals are capable of envisaging a future for themselves, and of having desires about future states of themselves. Secondly, that anything which exercises these capacities has an interest in its own continued existence. And thirdly, that having an interest in one's own continued existence is not merely a necessary, but also a sufficient condition for having a right to life.

46   The suggestion that at least some nonhuman animals have a right to life is not unfamiliar, but it is one that most of us are accustomed to dismissing very casually. The line of thought advanced here suggests that this attitude may very well turn out to be tragically mistaken. Once one reflects upon the question of the *basic* moral principles involved in the ascription of a right to life to organisms, one may find oneself driven to the conclusion that our every-day treatment of members of other species is morally indefensible, and that we are in fact murdering innocent persons.

Notes

1. My forthcoming book, *Abortion and Infanticide,* contains a detailed study of other important objections.

2. Section 230.3 of the American Law Institute's *Model Penal Code* (Philadelphia, 1962).

3. *Abortion and Infanticide,* Chapter 10.

4. In *Philosophy and Environmental Crisis,* edited by William T. Blackstone (Athens, Georgia, 1974), pp. 43–68.

5. Op. Cit., p. 51.

6. Ibid., pp. 49–50.

7. Ibid., p. 51.

8. Op. Cit., section 5.2.

9. This section has been omitted—Ed.

10. For a fuller discussion, and defense of this principle, see op. cit., section 5.3.

11. For a detailed survey of the scientific evidence concerning human development, see op. cit., section 11.5.

12. Op. cit., section 11.42.

13. For a brief discussion, see Joseph F. Donceel, "A Liberal Catholic's View," in *Abortion in a Changing World,* Volume I, edited by R. E. Hall, New York, 1970. A more detailed philosophical discussion can be found in Donceel's "Immediate Animation and Delayed Hominization," *Theological Studies,* Volume 31, 1970, pp. 76–105.

14. Section III: "Is It Morally Wrong to Destroy Potential Persons" has been omitted.—Ed.

Discussion and Outline

of Michael Tooley's
"In Defense of Abortion and Infanticide"

As we did with Noonan's article, we will produce our model outline in two stages. First, we will proceed paragraph by paragraph (or, where more profitable, section by section) identifying and reconstructing arguments as we come across them. Then we will put them together into a model outline. As always, we keep our eyes out for the main conclusion, and then, once we have identified it, we will continue to keep one eye on it as we read the rest of the essay.

Paragraph 1

In the introductory paragraph Tooley tells us that he will examine—and reject—not only the claim that fetuses have a right to life but also the claim that newborn infants have such a right. His strategy will be to identify a property (or set of properties) P which a thing must have in order to have a right to life and then to argue, first, that since zygotes, fetuses, and neonates do not possess P, they do not have a right to life, and, second, that since some adult members of other species might very well possess P, they might well have such a right. We may expect, then, that much of Tooley's article will be devoted to specifying this property P as clearly as he can and to justifying his claim that in order to possess a right to life, an individual must possess this property.

Thus the structure of the main argument of this essay is as follows:

    a. To possess a right to life, an entity must possess property P (to be specified).   (P)

b. Zygotes, fetuses, and neonates do not possess P.　　　　(P)

c. [So] zygotes, fetuses, and neonates do not possess a right
to life.　　　　(a,b)

d. Some adult members of other species might have such a
property.　　　　(AP)

e. [So] some adult members of other species might have a right
to life.　　　　(a,d)

Note that we have labeled the above lines as lines a–e. This is because our complete reconstruction of Tooley's main argument will incorporate his specification of the property P. Nevertheless, it is evident right from the start that Tooley's main conclusion is stated in line c.[1]

Note also that Tooley's first premiss claims that possessing P is a *necessary*—as opposed to *sufficient*—condition for something to have a right to life. Tooley is claiming that everything that has a right to life possesses P, the property which he is going to identify. He has not claimed that everything that possesses this property possesses a right to life, which is what he would have claimed if he had said that possessing P is a sufficient condition for having a right to life.[2]

Attending to this distinction between necessary and sufficient conditions helps us understand why Tooley limits his second conclusion in statement e, to the claim that members of other species *might* possess a right to life. In claiming that P is a necessary condition for someone's having a right to life we do not rule out the possibility that there are other necessary conditions for having that right in addition to P, and since there might be other necessary conditions, Tooley cannot validly conclude that whatever possesses P possesses a right to life. He can only validly conclude that if adult members of other species do have this characteristic, they meet this condition of having a right to life. That is, they *might* have a right to life. But there is a second reason for Tooley to qualify his conclusion in statement e. Tooley does not claim in statement d that adult members of other species possess P. He claims only that, given the current evidence, we cannot plausibly rule out that they have such characteristics. So, he can claim only that they *might* possess P. For two reasons, then, he can only validly conclude that adult members of other species might have a right to life. His conclusion as stated in line e, then, is doubly qualified.

Let's turn again to the central argument in lines a–c. As usual, we first attend to its conclusion. It is that zygotes, fetuses, and neonates do not have a

---

[1] It might be suggested that Tooley's argument contains two main conclusions: statements c and e. While we would have no serious objection to such an interpretation, nevertheless, in view of the title of the essay and in view of the fact that the bulk of Tooley's argument is devoted to statement c, it seems more reasonable to construe the essay as having a single main conclusion. In any case, we shall focus our attention primarily on the argument for statement c.

[2] See the discussion of necessary and sufficient conditions in Chapter 1.

right to life. Note that Tooley tells us in the very next sentence that he is not here defending the claim that abortion and infanticide are morally permissible. To get to that further conclusion, he says, he would also have to show that there are no other sound bases for rejecting infanticide. A complete defense of infanticide, then, must include the following:

    f. Unless there are other (sound) objections to abortion and
       infanticide, these practices are morally acceptable.   (c)

    g. There are no other sound objections to abortion and
       infanticide.[3]   (P)

    h. [So] infanticide is morally permissible.   (c,f,g)

But these other claims are not to be the focus of this article, and he refers us to his book for his examination of these other putative objections. Here he will argue to the conclusion that fetuses do not have a right to life.

It is perhaps worth pausing here to consider what, if anything, is the difference between the two conclusions in statements c and h. Consider the following example: Suppose a stranger asks you for a match. You have plenty of matches and plenty of time to give one to the stranger. Now ask yourself, "Should I give the stranger a match?" Then, ask, "Does the stranger have a right to receive a match from me?" If you give different answers to these questions—most likely, that one ought to give the stranger a match but that the stranger does not have a right to it—then you imply that answers to questions about rights are not always identical to answers to questions of what one, or others, ought to do. Generally, on this conception, if one establishes that someone has a right to be treated in a given way, then it follows that others ought to treat that person in that way. But it does not follow from the fact that the individual does not have that right that it is not the case that the individual ought not to be treated in that way. The possession of rights is only one consideration relevant to determining how others ought to treat an individual, and it is for this reason that Tooley suggests that the premiss in statement g is needed in order to make a full defense of infanticide.

It is well to be aware, however, that there are many who, despite the distinctions drawn above, tend to use the notion of possessing a right to something as nothing more than shorthand for saying that it is morally obligatory for others to treat an individual in that way. So, for example, there are many who when they say that fetuses have a right to life are simply expressing their belief that it is morally impermissible to perform abortions. That is, they conclude that fetuses have a right to life on the ground that they think that it is impermissible to kill fetuses. To adopt this latter view is to subsume all issues of the existence of rights under the question of moral permissibility.

Whatever the more satisfactory approach, readers should be warned that despite the frequency and intensity with which people make claims that

---

[3]We shall soon confront authors who argue that Tooley is mistaken in claiming what he does in statement g. They maintain that although it is true that fetuses and neonates do not have a right to life, it is nevertheless morally impermissible to kill them.

we have rights of certain sorts, it is notoriously difficult to say just what we are claiming or doing when we attribute them. Moreover, this is as much a problem for conservatives as it is for liberals, like Tooley, who argue their position in terms of rights. Conservatives often (at least seem to) base their restrictive abortion policy on the claim that fetuses have a right to life. However, when one pushes them to make clear the basis on which they attribute this right to fetuses, one discovers that they are simply using the term "right" to express the strength of their conviction that it is morally impermissible to engage in abortion.

Paragraphs 2–9

In Section I Tooley explains why he raises the controversial issue of infanticide. In common with John Noonan, he accepts the following line of argument:

1. From conception to adulthood there is a continuous line of development of the organism. (AP)

2. [So] if there is some point in that development prior to which it is not seriously wrong to destroy the organism and after which it is seriously wrong, then there must be a specifiable, nonarbitrary, morally relevant difference between the stages adjacent to that point. (1)

Moreover, also in common with Noonan, he claims the following:

3. None of the proposed prebirth cutoff points involves any morally significant change in the developing human. (P)[4]

Unlike Noonan, however, Tooley maintains what follows here:

4. There is an extremely plausible basis for drawing a line during infancy. (P)

Tooley notes that many will reject his arguments out of hand either because they cannot confront the question of infanticide dispassionately or because they take it as evident that infanticide is morally impermissible and conclude that since any argument with a false conclusion must be unsound, Tooley's argument must be unsound. As to the latter, there is, as we pointed out in Part I of this book, a considerable difference between rejecting the conclusion of someone's argument and pinpointing the source of disagreement, which involves identifying the premises or reasoning steps which one thinks have led the author astray. Tooley thus challenges readers who disagree with him to go beyond mere out-of-hand rejection of his conclusion. As to those who cannot consider the question dispassionately, he can only urge them to do so. Although our unanalyzed moral beliefs are not to be lightly discarded, we are justified in adopting a moral belief only after we have subjected our initial

---

[4]We may omit his brief argument for this claim.

beliefs to examination. Moreover, he suggests, much human misery might well be prevented by permitting infanticide of seriously defective infants.

Paragraphs 10–13

Tooley begins his positive argument by asking why newspapers don't have a right not to be torn up. His answer is that newspapers don't have desires, that having desires is a necessary condition of having interests, and that having interests is a necessary condition of having rights:

5. Newspapers don't have desires. (AP)

6. Only things that have desires can have interests—that is, can be better or worse off, benefited or harmed. (AP)

7. [So] newspapers don't have interests. (5,6)

8. Only things that can have interests have rights. (AP)

9. [So] newspapers don't have rights. (7,8)

Although Tooley provides some cursory discussion of the statements in lines 6 and 8, which he bases on Feinberg's analysis of rights (see paragraphs 17–22), we will label them as assumed premises. He calls the claim expressed in line 8 the "interests-principle." The underlying idea is that a minimum condition of attributing rights to something is that it has—or is capable of having—interests that can be furthered or frustrated. Moreover, as Tooley claims in line 6, a minimum condition of having interests is that one have—or be capable of having—desires. Without desires, or preferences, one cannot be better or worse off.[5]

It is evident that Tooley does not identify having interests with having desires. The latter are claimed only to be a necessary condition of the former. What is in one's interest might be a function of desires that one will or could come to have, as for instance, we might say that a child's interest is served by insisting that he or she go to school even though the child desires not to go to school, for we think that the child will, or at least could, come to have desires whose satisfaction will be furthered by having gone to school. Interests are thus predicated on desires that one will or could have. But if something has no desires, and, moreover, never can have any desires, then, according to Tooley, it makes no conceptual sense to say that the thing has interests and so no conceptual sense to say that it has rights.

---

[5]Note that Tooley recognizes a distinction between having interests and having desires, though he tells us only that the latter are somehow compounded out of the former. There is, however, good reason for drawing the distinction. We sometimes want to say that individuals' interests are most furthered by denying them an object they desire. Thus, Tooley does not maintain that an entity's desires are the same as its interests; he maintains only that if an entity doesn't (and can't) have any desires at all, then it cannot have any interests, and it follows, then, that it cannot have any rights.

Note also that the same argument applies to anything that never has desires. Since trees, for example, do not have—and never will have—desires, they can have no interests and thus no rights, including, of course, a right to life. Accordingly, one can never do a tree a serious wrong by cutting it down. It does not follow, however, that it is never wrong to fell a tree. Others may have interests in sustaining trees (or in sustaining a given tree), and consequently one might be violating another's rights by felling a tree, just as one may do a human being a wrong by tearing up his newspaper. Moreover, as we saw above, there might be other reasons not to fell a tree, reasons that do not have to do with its having rights.

Now, of course, zygotes also don't have desires. May we conclude that zygotes don't have rights? Well, no, some people will say, since, unlike newspapers and trees, in the normal course of things, some—most—zygotes will come to be individuals who have desires. Perhaps we can base a claim that zygotes have interests, and therefore that zygotes meet this condition of having rights, on the claim that, unlike newspapers, it is now true of them that they will have desires—that is, that they now have "future desires." In short, we may insist that the statement of the interest-principle in line 8 be amended in such a way as to make explicit the idea that possessing rights does not rest solely upon possessing current desires. Thus, we have the following:

10. Only individuals who currently have desires or who will have desires in the future—which is to say they now have future desires—can have interests. (6)

And to this statement we may add the following argument:

11. Zygotes don't have current desires. (AP)

12. [So] if zygotes have rights, they will come to have desires, which is also to say they now have future desires. (10,11)

Paragraph 14

Tooley proceeds by telling us that he is going to deny that zygotes have interests that are based on having future desires. In this paragraph, he previews that argument:

13. Satisfaction of future desires presupposes the continued existence of the entity in question. (AP)

14. [So] anything that has an interest which is based upon the satisfaction of future desires must also have an interest in its own continued existence. (13)[6]

15. [So] if zygotes have interests at all, they must have an interest in their own continued existence. (12,14)

---

[6]Note the use of a suppressed premise here: If A has an interest in X, and Y is a necessary condition of X, then A has an interest in Y.

16. But zygotes do not have an interest in their own continued existence. (P)

17. [So] zygotes do not have any interests at all. (15,16)

18. [So] zygotes do not have any rights. (8,17)

We assign the label (P) to the critical premiss in line 16 since Tooley wishes to postpone his defense of it until later.

Paragraphs 15–18

Before turning to his defense of the statement in line 16, Tooley chooses to consider fetuses, which present a somewhat different problem. Fetuses, he points out, do have current desires. Does it follow that they have a right to life? Tooley's answer is no. To defend his answer, he introduces what he calls the *particular-interests principle*, which he thinks follows from the same considerations as does the interests-principle itself: An entity can have a particular right, R, only if it is capable of having a particular interest, I, which would be furthered by its having that right. In other words, the rights a given individual has depend in part upon which interests, and thus which desires, it has or could have. If something can't ever have a desire for a particular thing, then it can never have a right to it. It is conceptually absurd, he claims, to attribute to cats a right to a university education, even though cats do have some desires. It is conceptually absurd because having that right will not contribute to the satisfaction of any desire cats actually have or could come to have, and so having that right could not further any interest that they could have. On the other hand, cats do have—or at least meet the minimum condition for having—the right not to be tortured, since their having that right does further an interest they have—namely, an interest derived from their aversion to, or desire to avoid, pain. The argument may be reconstructed as follows:

19. Only things that can have a particular interest, I, which can be furthered by their having a particular right, R, can have that right. (AP)[7]

20. [So] only things that have current or future desires can have an interest which can be furthered by its possessing a given right. (11,19)

21. Cats have an aversion to, or desire to avoid, pain. (AP)

22. [So] cats can have an interest in not feeling pain. (20,21)

23. Possessing a right not to be tortured can further the interests of anything that has an aversion to pain. (AP)

24. [So] cats satisfy this condition for having—that is, they might have—a right not to be tortured. (22,23)

---

[7]As with the interests principle, we label the particular-interests principle as an assumed premiss since Tooley's discussion is at best cursory. See the discussion of paragraphs 17–22.

But what about the right to life? Tooley continues as follows:

> 25. But cats do not have an interest in their own continued
>   existence.   (P)
>
> 26. [So] cats do not have a right not to be destroyed.[8]   (20,24)

As with zygotes, so with cats. The critical premiss consists of denying that the entity in question has an interest in its own continued existence. Indeed, the argument is the same for fetuses and neonates. They, too, so Tooley claims, do not have an interest in their own continued existence. Since zygotes, as we have seen, do not have current desires and, if Tooley is right, no interest in their own continued existence, they have no rights at all. Cats, fetuses, and neonates do have some current desires. So they do have some rights, or rather, they satisfy this necessary condition for having some rights—those which further the interests derived from the desires they do and can now have. But these entities do not have an interest in their own continued existence, or so Tooley proposes to show. So, while they have some rights, they do not have a right to continued existence.

Paragraphs 19–22

Here Tooley provides a brief analysis of the notion of having a particular right to something. Since, according to this account, having an interest in something is a necessary condition of having a right to it he claims that if his account of having a right is correct, then so is the particular-interests principle.

Paragraphs 23–29

Here Tooley considers the application of the particular-interests principle to the right of zygotes, fetuses, and neonates to continue to exist. His first step is to note that the notion of a right to life is misleading since it suggests that the right in question concerns the continued existence of biological organisms. It doesn't—or at least it doesn't concern *only* that. It is to entities that possess consciousness—that is, entities that are subjects of experience or other mental states—that we attribute the right to continue to exist. The argument is outlined as follows:

> 27. If future technological developments make it possible to change
>   completely the neural networks in a brain, and the brain of some
>   normal adult human being is reprogrammed so that it winds up
>   with memories (or, rather, apparent memories), beliefs, attitudes,

---

[8]It is worth noting here that many people who believe that fetuses have a right to life and who believe that kittens have a right not to be tortured, do not believe that kittens have a right to life, and even fewer of those believe that zygotes of cats have a right to life.

and personality traits totally different from those associated with it before it was reprogrammed, then that person has been destroyed, even though that human organism continues to exist. (AP)

28. To perform, without consent, such an operation on an individual would be to violate that person's right to life. (AP)

29. [So] the right to life is not just a matter of the continued existence of a biological organism. (27,28)

30. The expression "right to life" refers to the right of a subject of experiences and other mental states to continue to exist. (29)

A question arises here whether Tooley thinks that the right to life can be attributed only to entities that possess continuing consciousness. If so, we must note that the statement in line 27 does not establish this claim. We must suppose that, in addition to the statements in lines 27 and 28, Tooley also holds the following claim:

31. If, by virtue of future technological developments, we were to retain an individual's consciousness but destroy his body, say, by transferring that consciousness to another body, we would conclude that the individual has not ceased to exist—and thus would conclude that although we might have violated some rights of that individual, we would not have violated his right to life. (SP)

Tooley's purpose in trying to establish that the right to life is to be attributed only to conscious entities is to enable him to consider the argument in terms of continuity of development. Even if there is a continuous development of the physical organism from conception to birth, it would not follow that there is continuous development of the consciousness belonging to, or associated with, that entity. And, indeed, Tooley denies that such continuity exists. It is his claim that continuity of consciousness begins some time after birth.

To establish this claim, Tooley asks readers to imagine a fetus that has developed to the point of being sentient and having simple desires, but which is not yet capable of having any desire for continued existence, and which, moreover, will enjoy a happy life and be glad that it was not destroyed. He asks whether it is in that fetus's interest not to be destroyed. His reply is that even though we often say things like, "Mary before she was born," when referring later to a particular fetus, it is conceptually confusing to identify Mary with the fetus unless there is some psychological link between the conscious states of Mary and the fetus. Thus Tooley makes the following claim:

32. A necessary condition for two states of consciousness (two experiences or other mental states) that occur at different times to belong to the same individual—that is, one and the same subject of consciousness—is that the two states of consciousness

be psychologically linked to one another via memory or in some
other way.   (AP)[9]

This claim is critical in Tooley's argument. It is not just that a right to
life can be sensibly attributed only to entities that possess consciousness, they
must be entities that possess continuing consciousness, entities whose mental
states are linked with each other. Imagine a being which is such that it has
mental states, but each state is entirely unconnected with the next, so that the
entity never anticipates future states and never possesses memories of past
conscious states. Now Tooley claims that such an individual, from the point of
view, so to speak, of its consciousness, is not one individual, but rather, it is a
different individual at each moment. Its future states of consciousness do not
belong to the same individual as the current states. Moreover, the argument
continues as follows:

33. The continued existence of a given subject of consciousness
    cannot be in that individual's interest at time t unless either that
    individual has a desire, at time t, to continue to exist as a subject
    of consciousness or *that very same* individual can have desires at
    other times.   (AP)

34. The fact that when one remembers a past experience what one
    knows is not merely that there was a certain experience that
    someone or other had, but that there was an experience that
    belonged to the *same* individual as the present memory beliefs is
    a crucial part of what it is that makes one a continuing subject of
    experiences, rather than merely a series of psychologically
    isolated, momentary subjects of consciousness.   (AP)

35. [So] two states of consciousness existing at different times can
    belong to a single, continuing subject of consciousness only if
    that subject of consciousness possesses, at some time, the
    concept of a continuing self or mental substance.   (34)

36. [So] desires existing at different times can belong to a single,
    continuing subject of consciousness only if that subject of
    consciousness possesses, at some time, the concept of a
    continuing self or mental substance.   (35)

Paragraphs 30–35

In this part of the essay Tooley brings the strands of his argument together:

37. The concept of a right is such that an individual cannot have
    a right at time t to continue to exist unless the individual is

---

[9]We label this statement as an assumed premiss because Tooley does not actually provide an
argument for it. The cases he examines merely "suggest" to him that this premiss is true.

such that it can be in its interest at time t that it continue
to exist. (20)

38. The continued existence of a given subject of consciousness
cannot be in that individual's interest at time t unless *either* that
individual has a desire, at time t, to continue to exist as a subject
of consciousness, *or* that individual can have desires at other
times. (AP)

39. An individual cannot have a desire to exist as a subject of
consciousness unless it possesses the concept of a continuing self
or mental substance. (AP)

40. An individual existing at one time cannot have desires at other
times unless there is at least one time at which it possesses the
concept of a continuing self or mental substance. (36)

41. [So] an individual cannot have a right to continued existence
unless there is at least one time at which it possesses the concept
of a continuing self or mental substance. (39,40)

It turns out, then, that the claim Tooley makes in line 32 is critical. To
have a right to life, it is not only necessary that an individual have conscious
states, it is also necessary that future conscious states be linked to current
conscious states in such a way that we may attribute them to the same
consciousness.

Paragraphs 36–40

These paragraphs contain a brief discussion of Tooley's reasons for believing
that even neonates do not have a concept of a continuing self; that is, they
contain a brief argument in defense of the following statement:

42. Neither fetuses nor newborn babies possess a concept of a
continuing self or mental substance. (P)

Tooley's grounds for believing this claim rest on the claim that there is a close
relation between the development of the brain and the development of consciousness. While this is not universally accepted, it is certainly widely accepted among psychologists and neurophysiologists. Those who reject it, he
claims, rest their arguments on religious or other *a priori* grounds. It is not
necessary for us to rehearse these discussions. Tooley directs us to his book
Abortion and Infanticide for a detailed survey of the scientific evidence.

Of course, together with the statement in line 41, the statement in line
42 enables Tooley to derive his main conclusion:

43. Zygotes, fetuses, and neonates do not possess a right to
continued existence. (41,42)

This is Tooley's answer to the challenge to identify a morally relevant
point in the continuous development of an organism before which destroying

the organism is not seriously wrong and after which it is seriously wrong. The point is that at which the organism comes to have a concept of a continuing self, an awareness of a future. Until that time, there exists at most a concatenation of conscious states associated with the same body, and thus, until that time, it does not possess interests based on its future, for even though the same physical organism might in the future have desires, those desires will not belong to the same subject of consciousness as do its current desires. Finally, since it turns out that the crucial change in the organism occurs sometime after birth, it follows that to kill a neonate is not to violate that entity's right to life.

Paragraphs 41–46

Here Tooley makes some additional comments. The first concerns the practical consequences of his position. He acknowledges that we cannot know precisely when a human organism comes to have a concept of itself as a continuing subject of consciousness. He is satisfied, however, that it occurs well after the first few weeks of infancy, and since practical decisions can be made most often within the first week of infancy, he believes we can adopt that time period as the cutoff point for infanticide.

He also raises the question whether adult members of other species possess such a concept, and he expresses his belief that some adult members of other species are capable of envisaging a future for themselves; so he concludes that we may well be acting immorally in killing them.

Model Outline

Having completed our initial analysis while reading the essay part by part, we may now proceed to constructing a formal outline of the whole argument. With respect to this essay, either of two approaches seems appropriate. The first approach would be to return to the outline we constructed of Tooley's strategy, as stated at the very beginning of his essay and fill in the characteristic that Tooley has identified as necessary for having a right to life. According to this approach, our final outline would be constructed as follows:

Main Argument

A1. An individual can have a right to continued existence only if there is at least one time at which it possesses the concept of a continuing self or mental substance. (P)

A2. Zygotes, fetuses, and neonates do not now and never have possessed a concept of a continuing self or mental substance. (P)

A3. [So] zygotes, fetuses, and neonates do not possess a right to life. (1,2)

A4. Some adult members of other species might have such a
concept. (P)

A5. [So] some adult members of other species might have a right
to life. (1,4)

Argument for line A1[10]

A6. Having interests is a necessary condition for having rights.(AP)

A7. Having a particular interest, I, which can be furthered by
having a particular right, R, is a necessary condition for
having R. (AP)

A8. Having desires is a necessary condition for having
interests. (AP)

A9. [So] only things that have current or future desires can have
interests. (8)

A10. An individual cannot have a right at time t to continue to exist
unless it can be in its interest at time t that it continue to
exist. (7)

A11. At time t, continued existence can be in the interest of a given
subject of consciousness only if either that individual has a
desire, at time t, to continue to exist as a subject of
consciousness, *or* that individual can have desires at other
times. (AP)

A12. An individual cannot have a desire to continue to exist as a
subject of consciousness unless it possesses the concept of a
continuing self or mental substance. (AP)

A13. Experiences or other mental states existing at different times
can belong to a single, continuing subject of consciousness
only if that subject of consciousness possesses, at some time,
the concept of a continuing self or mental substance. (AP)[11]

A14. An individual existing at one time cannot have desires at other
times unless there is at least one time at which it possesses the
concept of a continuing self or mental substance. (13)

A1. **[So] an individual can have a right to continued existence only
if there is at least one time at which it possesses the concept
of a continuing self or mental substance.** (12,14)

---

[10]This is nothing more than Tooley's own summary, slightly reformulated.

[11]We label this statement as an assumed premiss because Tooley tells us that his lengthy
discussions of both the programming/reprogramming example and of the Mary/baby example
merely "suggest" to him the claim made in this line.

Arguments for lines A2 and A4

The arguments for lines A2 and A4 are not developed in the essay. We are referred to Tooley's book for a summary of the available neurophysiological and psychological evidence. That evidence, he says, supports the claims (1) that zygotes are not subjects of consciousness at all (and thus can have neither current nor future desires) and (2) that while fetuses and neonates are subjects of experience, and thus can have current desires and thus also the rights which could further those desires, they do not possess a concept of a continuing self or mental substance and thus can neither have a desire to continue to exist nor future desires. Therefore they do not have a right to continued existence.

If, on the other hand, we use a second approach and try to construct an outline that incorporates a more thorough sense of the flow of Tooley's argument, our final outline would be more like the following:

Main Argument

B1. Only things that have desires have interests. (AP)

B2. Only things that have current desires or that will come in the future to have desires that can be satisfied (that now have future desires) can have interests. (1)

B3. Newspapers don't ever have desires. (AP)

B4. [So] newspapers don't have interests. (2,3)

B5. Only things that have interests have rights. (AP)[12]

B6. [So] newspapers don't have rights. (4,5)

B7. Zygotes don't have current desires. (AP)

B8. [So] if zygotes have interests, they have future desires. (2,7)

B9. Continuing to exist is a necessary condition of satisfying future desires. (AP)

B10. If X is a necessary condition of Y, then having an interest in X is a necessary condition of having an interest in Y. (SP)

B11. [So] having an interest in one's continued existence is a necessary condition of having interests based on future desires. (9,10)

B12. [So] if zygotes have interests, they must have an interest in their own continued existence. (8,11)

---

[12]We label lines B5 and B16 as assumed premises even though Tooley does provide some cursory discussion of them. These lines state the interests principle and the particular-interests principle.

B13. But zygotes do not have an interest in their own continued existence. (P)

B14. [So] zygotes do not have any interests at all. (12,13)

B15. [So] zygotes cannot have any rights. (5,14)

B16. Only things that can have a particular interest, I, which can be furthered by their having a particular right, R, can have that right. (AP)

B17. [So] only things that have current or future desires can have an interest which can be furthered by a given right. (2,16)

B18. Cats, fetuses, and neonates feel pain. (AP)

B19. [So] cats, fetuses, and neonates can have an interest in not feeling pain. (17–18)

B20. Possessing a right not to be tortured can further the interests of anything that has a desire not to feel pain. (AP)

B21. [So] cats, fetuses, and neonates satisfy this condition for having a right not to be tortured. (19,20)

B22. But cats, fetuses, and neonates do not have an interest in their own continued existence. (P)

B23. [So] cats, fetuses, and neonates do not have a right not to be destroyed. (17,22)

Argument for lines B13 and B22

B24. A necessary condition for having an interest in one's continued existence is that one have a concept of a continuing self or other mental substance. (P)

B25. Zygotes, cats, fetuses, and neonates do not possess a concept of a continuing self or other mental substance. (P)

B13. [So] zygotes do not have an interest in their own continued existence. (24,25)

B22. [So] cats, fetuses, and neonates do not have an interest in their own continued existence. (24,25)

Argument for line B24

B26. A necessary condition for having an interest in one's continued existence is either that one have a desire now to continue to exist or that one can have future desires. (AP)

B27. A necessary condition for having a desire now to continue to exist is that one have a concept of a continuing self or other mental substance. (AP)

B28. A necessary condition of one's having future desires is that the future states of consciousness and the present state of consciousness belong to the very same individual. (AP)

B29. A necessary condition for a future state of consciousness to belong to the very same individual as a current state of consciousness is that at some time the two states of consciousness be psychologically linked to each other via memory or in some other way. (AP)

B30. A necessary condition of linking a present and a future state of consciousness is that the individual possess at some time the concept of a continuing self or other mental substance. (AP)

B31. [So] a necessary condition for an individual to have future desires is the individual possess at some time the concept of a continuing self or mental substance. (28–30)

B24. [So] a necessary condition for having an interest in one's continued existence is that one have a concept of a continuing self or other mental substance. (26,27,30)

Argument for line B25

Same as for lines A2 and A4.

A Defense of Abortion[1]

Judith Jarvis Thomson

Most opposition to abortion relies on the premise that the fetus is a human being, a person, from the moment of conception. The premise is argued for, but as I think, not well. Take, for example, the most common argument. We are asked to notice that the development of a human being from conception through birth into childhood is continuous; then it is said that to draw a line, to choose a point in this development and say "before this point the thing is not a person, after this point it is a person" is to make an arbitrary choice, a choice for which in the nature of things no good reason can be given. It is concluded that the fetus is, or anyway that we had better say it is, a person from the moment of conception. But this conclusion does not follow. Similar things might be said about the development of an acorn into an oak tree, and it does not follow that acorns are oak trees, or that we had better say they are. Arguments of this form are sometimes called "slippery slope arguments"—the phrase is perhaps self-explanatory—and it is dismaying that opponents of abortion rely on them so heavily and uncritically.

I am inclined to agree, however, that the prospects for "drawing a line" in the development of a fetus look dim. I am inclined to think also that we shall probably have to agree that the fetus has already become a human person well before birth. Indeed, it comes as a surprise when one first learns how early in life it begins to acquire human characteristics. By the tenth week, for example, it already has a face, arms, legs, fingers and toes; it has internal organs, and brain activity is detectable.[2] On the other hand, I think that the

From *Philosophy and Public Affairs,* Vol. 1, no. 1 (Princeton University Press) 1971, pp. 47–66. Copyright © 1971 by Princeton University Press. Reprinted by permission of the publisher.

premise is false, that the fetus is not a person from the moment of conception. A newly fertilized ovum, a newly implanted clump of cells, is no more a person than an acorn is an oak tree. But I shall not discuss any of this. For it seems to me to be of great interest to ask what happens if, for the sake of argument, we allow the premise. How, precisely, are we supposed to get from there to the conclusion that abortion is morally impermissible? Opponents of abortion commonly spend most of their time establishing that the fetus is a person, and hardly any time explaining the step from there to the impermissibility of abortion. Perhaps they think the step too simple and obvious to require much comment. Or perhaps instead they are simply being economical in argument. Many of those who defend abortion rely on the premise that the fetus is not a person, but only a bit of tissue that will become a person at birth; and why pay out more arguments than you have to? Whatever the explanation, I suggest that the step they take is neither easy nor obvious, that it calls for closer examination than it is commonly given, and that when we do give it this closer examination we shall feel inclined to reject it.

3   I propose, then, that we grant that the fetus is a person from the moment of conception. How does the argument go from here? Something like this, I take it. Every person has a right to life. So the fetus has a right to life. No doubt the mother has a right to decide what shall happen in and to her body; everyone would grant that. But surely a person's right to life is stronger and more stringent than the mother's right to decide what happens in and to her body, and so outweighs it. So the fetus may not be killed; an abortion may not be performed.

4   It sounds plausible. But now let me ask you to imagine this. You wake up in the morning and find yourself back to back in bed with an unconscious violinist. A famous unconscious violinist. He has been found to have a fatal kidney ailment, and the Society of Music Lovers has canvassed all the available medical records and found that you alone have the right blood type to help. They have therefore kidnapped you, and last night the violinist's circulatory system was plugged into yours, so that your kidneys can be used to extract poisons from his blood as well as your own. The director of the hospital now tells you, "Look, we're sorry the Society of Music Lovers did this to you—we would never have permitted it if we had known. But still, they did it, and the violinist now is plugged into you. To unplug you would be to kill him. But never mind, it's only for nine months. By then he will have recovered from his ailment, and can safely be unplugged from you." Is it morally incumbent on you to accede to this situation? No doubt it would be very nice of you if you did, a great kindness. But do you have to accede to it? What if it were not nine months, but nine years? Or longer still? What if the director of the hospital says, "Tough luck. I agree, but you've now got to stay in bed, with the violinist plugged into you, for the rest of your life. Because remember this. All persons have a right to life, and violinists are persons. Granted you have a right to decide what happens in and to your body, but a person's right to life outweighs your right to decide what happens in and to your body. So you cannot ever be unplugged from him." I imagine you would regard this as outrageous, which

suggests that something really is wrong with that plausible-sounding argument I mentioned a moment ago.

5   In this case, of course, you were kidnapped; you didn't volunteer for the operation that plugged the violinist into your kidneys. Can those who oppose abortion on the ground I mentioned make an exception for a pregnancy due to rape? Certainly. They can say that persons have a right to life only if they didn't come into existence because of rape; or they can say that all persons have a right to life, but that some have less of a right to life than others, in particular, that those who came into existence because of rape have less. But these statements have a rather unpleasant sound. Surely the question of whether you have a right to life at all, or how much of it you have, shouldn't turn on the question of whether or not you are the product of a rape. And in fact the people who oppose abortion on the ground I mentioned do not make this distinction, and hence do not make an exception in case of rape.

6   Nor do they make an exception for a case in which the mother has to spend the nine months of her pregnancy in bed. They would agree that would be a great pity, and hard on the mother; but all the same, all persons have a right to life, the fetus is a person, and so on. I suspect, in fact, that they would not make an exception for a case in which, miraculously enough, the pregnancy went on for nine years, or even the rest of the mother's life.

7   Some won't even make an exception for a case in which continuation of the pregnancy is likely to shorten the mother's life: they regard abortion as impermissible even to save the mother's life. Such cases are nowadays very rare, and many opponents of abortion do not accept this extreme view. All the same, it is a good place to begin: a number of points of interest come out in respect to it.

8   1. Let us call the view that abortion is impermissible even to save the mother's life "the extreme view." I want to suggest first that it does not issue from the argument I mentioned earlier without the addition of some fairly powerful premises. Suppose a woman has become pregnant, and now learns that she has a cardiac condition such that she will die if she carries the baby to term. What may be done for her? The fetus, being a person, has a right to life, but as the mother is a person too, so has she a right to life. Presumably they have an equal right to life. How is it supposed to come out that an abortion may not be performed? If mother and child have an equal right to life, shouldn't we perhaps flip a coin? Or should we add to the mother's right to life her right to decide what happens in and to her body, which everybody seems to be ready to grant—the sum of her rights now outweighing the fetus' right to life?

9   The most familiar argument here is the following. We are told that performing the abortion would be directly killing[3] the child, whereas doing nothing would not be killing the mother, but only letting her die. Moreover, in killing the child, one would be killing an innocent person, for the child has committed no crime, and is not aiming at his mother's death. And then there are a variety of ways in which this might be continued. (1) But as directly

killing an innocent person is always and absolutely impermissible, an abortion may not be performed. Or, (2) as directly killing an innocent person is murder, and murder is always and absolutely impermissible, an abortion may not be performed.[4] Or, (3) as one's duty to refrain from directly killing an innocent person is more stringent than one's duty to keep a person from dying, an abortion may not be performed. Or, (4) if one's only options are directly killing an innocent person or letting a person die, one must prefer letting the person die, and thus an abortion may not be performed.[5]

10   Some people seem to have thought that these are not further premises which must be added if the conclusion is to be reached, but that they follow from the very fact that an innocent person has a right to life.[6] But this seems to me to be a mistake, and perhaps the simplest way to show this is to bring out that while we must certainly grant that innocent persons have a right to life, the theses in (1) through (4) are all false. Take (2), for example. If directly killing an innocent person is murder, and thus is impermissible, then the mother's directly killing the innocent person inside her is murder, and thus is impermissible. But it cannot seriously be thought to be murder if the mother performs an abortion on herself to save her life. It cannot seriously be said that she must refrain, that she must sit passively by and wait for her death. Let us look again at the case of you and the violinist. There you are, in bed with the violinist, and the director of the hospital says to you, "It's all most distressing, and I deeply sympathize, but you see this is putting an additional strain on your kidneys, and you'll be dead within the month. But you have to stay where you are all the same. Because unplugging you would be directly killing an innocent violinist, and that's murder, and that's impermissible." If anything in the world is true, it is that you do not commit murder, you do not do what is impermissible, if you reach around to your back and unplug yourself from that violinist to save your life.

11   The main focus of attention in writings on abortion has been on what a third party may or may not do in answer to a request from a woman for an abortion. This is in a way understandable. Things being as they are, there isn't much a woman can safely do to abort herself. So the question asked is what a third party may do, and what the mother may do, if it is mentioned at all, is deduced, almost as an afterthought, from what it is concluded that third parties may do. But it seems to me that to treat the matter in this way is to refuse to grant to the mother that very status of person which is so firmly insisted on for the fetus. For we cannot simply read off what a person may do from what a third party may do. Suppose you find yourself trapped in a tiny house with a growing child. I mean a very tiny house, and a rapidly growing child—you are already up against the wall of the house and in a few minutes you'll be crushed to death. The child on the other hand won't be crushed to death; if nothing is done to stop him from growing he'll be hurt, but in the end he'll simply burst open the house and walk out a free man. Now I could well understand it if a bystander were to say, "There's nothing we can do for you. We cannot choose between your life and his, we cannot be the ones to decide who is to live, we cannot intervene." But it cannot be concluded that you too

can do nothing, that you cannot attack it to save your life. However innocent the child may be, you do not have to wait passively while it crushes you to death. Perhaps a pregnant woman is vaguely felt to have the status of house, to which we don't allow the right of self-defense. But if the woman houses the child, it should be remembered that she is a person who houses it.

12   I should perhaps stop to say explicitly that I am not claiming that people have a right to do anything whatever to save their lives. I think, rather, that there are drastic limits to the right of self-defense. If someone threatens you with death unless you torture someone else to death, I think you have not the right, even to save your life, to do so. But the case under consideration here is very different. In our case there are only two people involved, one whose life is threatened, and one who threatens it. Both are innocent: the one who is threatened is not threatened because of any fault, the one who threatens does not threaten because of any fault. For this reason we may feel that we bystanders cannot intervene. But the person threatened can.

13   In sum, a woman surely can defend her life against the threat to it posed by the unborn child, even if doing so involves its death. And this shows not merely that the theses in (1) through (4) are false: it shows also that the extreme view of abortion is false, and so we need not canvass any other possible ways of arriving at it from the argument I mentioned at the outset.

14   2. The extreme view could of course be weakened to say that while abortion is permissible to save the mother's life, it may not be performed by a third party, but only by the mother herself. But this cannot be right either. For what we have to keep in mind is that the mother and the unborn child are not like two tenants in a small house which has, by an unfortunate mistake, been rented to both: the mother owns the house. The fact that she does adds to the offensiveness of deducing that the mother can do nothing from the supposition that third parties can do nothing. But it does more than this: it casts a bright light on the supposition that third parties can do nothing. Certainly it lets us see that a third party who says "I cannot choose between you" is fooling himself if he thinks this is impartiality. If Jones has found and fastened on a certain coat, which he needs to keep him from freezing, but which Smith also needs to keep him from freezing, then it is not impartiality that says "I cannot choose between you" when Smith owns the coat. Women have said again and again "This body is my body!" and they have reason to feel angry, reason to feel that it has been like shouting into the wind. Smith, after all, is hardly likely to bless us if we say to him, "Of course it's your coat, anybody would grant that it is. But no one may choose between you and Jones who is to have it."

15   We should really ask what it is that says "no one may choose" in the face of the fact that the body that houses the child is the mother's body. It may be simply a failure to appreciate this fact. But it may be something more interesting, namely the sense that one has a right to refuse to lay hands on people, even where it would be just and fair to do so, even where justice seems to require that somebody do so. Thus justice might call for somebody to get Smith's coat back from Jones, and yet you have a right to refuse to be the one

to lay hands on Jones, a right to refuse to do physical violence to him. This, I think, must be granted. But then what should be said is not "no one may choose," but only "*I* cannot choose," and indeed not even this, but "I will not *act*," leaving it open that somebody else can or should, and in particular that anyone in a position of authority, with the job of securing people's rights, both can and should. So this is no difficulty. I have not been arguing that any given third party must accede to the mother's request that he perform an abortion to save her life, but only that he may.

16   I suppose that in some views of human life the mother's body is only on loan to her, the loan not being one which gives her any prior claim to it. One who held this view might well think it impartiality to say "I cannot choose." But I shall simply ignore this possibility. My own view is that if a human being has any just, prior claim to anything at all, he has a just, prior claim to his own body. And perhaps this needn't be argued for here anyway, since, as I mentioned, the arguments against abortion we are looking at do grant that the woman has a right to decide what happens in and to her body.

17   But although they do grant it, I have tried to show that they do not take seriously what is done in granting it. I suggest the same thing will reappear even more clearly when we turn away from cases in which the mother's life is at stake, and attend, as I propose we now do, to the vastly more common cases in which a woman wants an abortion for some less weighty reason than preserving her own life.

18   3. Where the mother's life is not at stake, the argument I mentioned at the outset seems to have a much stronger pull. "Everyone has a right to life, so the unborn person has a right to life." And isn't the child's right to life weightier than anything other than the mother's own right to life, which she might put forward as ground for an abortion?

19   This argument treats the right to life as if it were unproblematic. It is not, and this seems to me to be precisely the source of the mistake.

20   For we should now, at long last, ask what it comes to, to have a right to life. In some views having a right to life includes having a right to be given at least the bare minimum one needs for continued life. But suppose that what in fact is the bare minimum a man needs for continued life is something he has no right at all to be given? If I am sick unto death, and the only thing that will save my life is the touch of Henry Fonda's cool hand on my fevered brow, then all the same, I have no right to be given the touch of Henry Fonda's cool hand on my fevered brow. It would be frightfully nice of him to fly in from the West Coast to provide it. It would be less nice, though no doubt well meant, if my friends flew out to the West Coast and carried Henry Fonda back with them. But I have no right at all against anybody that he should do this for me. Or again, to return to the story I told earlier, the fact that for continued life that violinist needs the continued use of your kidneys does not establish that he has a right to be given the continued use of your kidneys. He certainly has no right against you that you should give him continued use of your kidneys. For nobody has any right to use your kidneys unless you give him such a right;

and nobody has the right against you that you shall give him this right—if you do allow him to go on using your kidneys, this is a kindness on your part, and not something he can claim from you as his due. Nor has he any right against anybody else that they should give him continued use of your kidneys. Certainly he had no right against the Society of Music Lovers that they should plug him into you in the first place. And if you now start to unplug yourself, having learned that you will otherwise have to spend nine years in bed with him, there is nobody in the world who must try to prevent you, in order to see to it that he is given something he has a right to be given.

21   Some people are rather stricter about the right to life. In their view, it does not include the right to be given anything, but amounts to, and only to, the right not to be killed by anybody. But here a related difficulty arises. If everybody is to refrain from killing that violinist, then everybody must refrain from doing a great many different sorts of things. Everybody must refrain from slitting his throat, everybody must refrain from shooting him—and everybody must refrain from unplugging you from him. But does he have a right against everybody that they shall refrain from unplugging you from him? To refrain from doing this is to allow him to continue to use your kidneys. It could be argued that he has a right against us that we should allow him to continue to use your kidneys. That is, while he had no right against us that we should give him the use of your kidneys, it might be argued that he anyway has a right against us that we shall not now intervene and deprive him of the use of your kidneys. I shall come back to third-party interventions later. But certainly the violinist has no right against you that you shall allow him to continue to use your kidneys. As I said, if you do allow him to use them, it is a kindness on your part, and not something you owe him.

22   The difficulty I point to here is not peculiar to the right to life. It reappears in connection with all the other natural rights; and it is something which an adequate account of rights must deal with. For present purposes it is enough just to draw attention to it. But I would stress that I am not arguing that people do not have a right to life—quite to the contrary, it seems to me that the primary control we must place on the acceptability of an account of rights is that it should turn out in that account to be a truth that all persons have a right to life. I am arguing only that having a right to life does not guarantee having either the right to be given the use of or a right to be allowed continued use of another person's body—even if one *needs* it for life itself. So the right to life will not serve the opponents of abortion in the very simple and clear way in which they seem to have thought it would.

23   4. There is another way to bring out the difficulty. In the most ordinary sort of case, to deprive someone of what he has a right to is to treat him unjustly. Suppose a boy and his small brother are jointly given a box of chocolates for Christmas. If the older boy takes the box and refuses to give his brother any of the chocolates, he is unjust to him, for the brother has been given a right to half of them. But suppose that, having learned that otherwise it means nine years in bed with that violinist, you unplug yourself from him.

You surely are not being unjust to him, for you gave him no right to use your kidneys, and no one else can have given him any such right. But we have to notice that in unplugging yourself, you are killing him; and violinists, like everybody else, have a right to life, and thus in the view we were considering just now, the right not to be killed. So here you do what he supposedly has a right you shall not do, but you do not act unjustly to him in doing it.

24   The emendation which may be made at this point is this: the right to life consists not in the right not to be killed, but rather in the right not to be killed unjustly. This runs a risk of circularity, but never mind: it would enable us to square the fact that the violinist has a right to life with the fact that you do not act unjustly toward him in unplugging yourself, thereby killing him. For if you do not kill him unjustly, you do not violate his right to life, and so it is no wonder you do him no injustice.

25   But if this emendation is accepted, the gap in the argument against abortion stares us plainly in the face: it is by no means enough to show that the fetus is a person, and to remind us that all persons have a right to life—we need to be shown also that killing the fetus violates its right to life, i.e., that abortion is unjust killing. And is it?

26   I suppose we may take it as a datum that in a case of pregnancy due to rape the mother has not given the unborn person a right to the use of her body for food and shelter. Indeed, in what pregnancy could it be supposed that the mother has given the unborn person such a right? It is not as if there were unborn persons drifting about the world, to whom a woman who wants a child says "I invite you in."

27   But it might be argued that there are other ways one can have acquired a right to the use of another person's body than by having been invited to use it by that person. Suppose a woman voluntarily indulges in intercourse, knowing of the chance it will issue in pregnancy, and then she does become pregnant; is she not in part responsible for the presence, in fact the very existence, of the unborn person inside her? No doubt she did not invite it in. But doesn't her partial responsibility for its being there itself give it a right to the use of her body?[7] If so, then her aborting it would be more like the boy's taking away the chocolates, and less like your unplugging yourself from the violinist— doing so would be depriving it of what it does have a right to, and thus would be doing it an injustice.

28   And then, too, it might be asked whether or not she can kill it even to save her own life: If she voluntarily called it into existence, how can she now kill it, even in self-defense?

29   The first thing to be said about this is that it is something new. Opponents of abortion have been so concerned to make out the independence of the fetus, in order to establish that it has a right to life, just as its mother does, that they have tended to overlook the possible support they might gain from making out that the fetus is dependent on the mother, in order to establish that she has a special kind of responsibility for it, a responsibility that gives it rights against her which are not possessed by any independent person—such as an ailing violinist who is a stranger to her.

30   On the other hand, this argument would give the unborn person a right to its mother's body only if her pregnancy resulted from a voluntary act, undertaken in full knowledge of the chance a pregnancy might result from it. It would leave out entirely the unborn person whose existence is due to rape. Pending the availability of some further argument, then, we would be left with the conclusion that unborn persons whose existence is due to rape have no right to the use of their mothers' bodies, and thus that aborting them is not depriving them of anything they have a right to and hence is not unjust killing.

31   And we should also notice that it is not at all plain that this argument really does go even as far as it purports to. For there are cases and cases, and the details make a difference. If the room is stuffy, and I therefore open a window to air it and a burglar climbs in, it would be absurd to say, "Ah, now he can stay, she's given him a right to the use of her house—for she is partially responsible for his presence there, having voluntarily done what enabled him to get in, in full knowledge that there are such things as burglars, and that burglars burgle." It would be still more absurd to say this if I had had bars installed outside my windows precisely to prevent burglars from getting in, and a burglar got in only because of a defect in the bars. It remains equally absurd if we imagine it is not a burglar who climbs in, but an innocent person who blunders or falls in. Again, suppose it were like this: people-seeds drift about in the air like pollen, and if you open your windows, one may drift in and take root in your carpets or upholstery. You don't want children, so you fix up your windows with fine mesh screens, the very best you can buy. As can happen, however, and on very, very rare occasions does happen, one of the screens is defective; and a seed drifts in and takes root. Does the person-plant who now develops have a right to the use of your house? Surely not—despite the fact that you voluntarily opened your windows, you knowingly kept carpets and upholstered furniture, and you knew that screens were sometimes defective. Someone may argue that you are responsible for its rooting, that it does have a right to your house, because after all you could have lived out your life with bare floors and furniture, or with sealed windows and doors. But this won't do—for by the same token anyone can avoid a pregnancy due to rape by having a hysterectomy, or anyway by never leaving home without a (reliable!) army.

32   It seems to me that the argument we are looking at can establish at most that there are some cases in which the unborn person has a right to the use of its mother's body, and therefore some cases in which abortion is unjust killing. There is room for much discussion and argument as to precisely which, if any. But I think we should sidestep this issue and leave it open, for at any rate the argument certainly does not establish that all abortion is unjust killing.

33   5. There is room for yet another argument here, however. We surely must all grant that there may be cases in which it would be morally indecent to detach a person from your body at the cost of his life. Suppose you learn that what the violinist needs is not nine years of your life, but only one hour:

all you need do to save his life is to spend one hour in that bed with him. Suppose also that letting him use your kidneys for that one hour would not affect your health in the slightest. Admittedly you were kidnapped. Admittedly you did not give anyone permission to plug him into you. Nevertheless it seems to me plain you ought to allow him to use your kidneys for that hour—it would be indecent to refuse.

34   Again, suppose pregnancy lasted only an hour, and constituted no threat to life or health. And suppose that a woman becomes pregnant as a result of rape. Admittedly she did not voluntarily do anything to bring about the existence of a child. Admittedly she did nothing at all which would give the unborn person a right to the use of her body. All the same it might well be said, as in the newly emended violinist story, that she ought to allow it to remain for that hour—that it would be indecent of her to refuse.

35   Now some people are inclined to use the term "right" in such a way that it follows from the fact that you ought to allow a person to use your body for the hour he needs, that he has a right to use your body for the hour he needs, even though he has not been given that right by any person or act. They may say that it follows also that if you refuse, you act unjustly toward him. This use of the term is perhaps so common that it cannot be called wrong: nevertheless it seems to me to be an unfortunate loosening of what we would do better to keep a tight rein on. Suppose that box of chocolates I mentioned earlier has not been given to both boys jointly, but was given only to the older boy. There he sits, stolidly eating his way through the box, his small brother watching enviously. Here we are likely to say "You ought not to be so mean. You ought to give your brother some of those chocolates." My own view is that it just does not follow from the truth of this that the brother has any right to any of the chocolates. If the boy refuses to give his brother any, he is greedy, stingy, callous—but not unjust. I suppose that the people I have in mind will say it does follow that the brother has a right to some of the chocolates, and thus that the boy does act unjustly if he refuses to give his brother any. But the effect of saying this is to obscure what we should keep distinct, namely the difference between the boy's refusal in this case and the boy's refusal in the earlier case, in which the box was given to both boys jointly, and in which the small brother thus had what was from any point of view clear title to half.

36   A further objection to so using the term "right" that from the fact that A ought to do a thing for B, it follows that B has a right against A that A do it for him, is that it is going to make the question of whether or not a man has a right to a thing turn on how easy it is to provide him with it; and this seems not merely unfortunate, but morally unacceptable. Take the case of Henry Fonda again. I said earlier that I had no right to the touch of his cool hand on my fevered brow, even though I needed it to save my life. I said it would be frightfully nice of him to fly in from the West Coast to provide me with it, but that I had no right against him that he should do so. But suppose he isn't on the West Coast. Suppose he has only to walk across the room, place a hand briefly on my brow—and lo, my life is saved. Then surely he ought to do it, it

would be indecent to refuse. Is it to be said, "Ah, well, it follows that in this case she has a right to the touch of his hand on her brow, and so it would be an injustice in him to refuse"? So that I have a right to it when it is easy for him to provide it, though no right when it's hard? It's rather a shocking idea that anyone's rights should fade away and disappear as it gets harder and harder to accord them to him.

37   So my own view is that even though you ought to let the violinist use your kidneys for the one hour he needs, we should not conclude that he has a right to do so—we should say that if you refuse, you are, like the boy who owns all the chocolates and will give none away, self-centered and callous, indecent in fact, but not unjust. And similarly, that even supposing a case in which a woman pregnant due to rape ought to allow the unborn person to use her body for the hour he needs, we should not conclude that he has a right to do so; we should conclude that she is self-centered, callous, indecent, but not unjust, if she refuses. The complaints are no less grave; they are just different. However, there is no need to insist on this point. If anyone does wish to deduce "he has a right" from "you ought," then all the same he must surely grant that there are cases in which it is not morally required of you that you allow that violinist to use your kidneys, and in which he does not have a right to use them, and in which you do not do him an injustice if you refuse. And so also for mother and unborn child. Except in such cases as the unborn person has a right to demand it—and we were leaving open the possibility that there may be such cases—nobody is morally required to make large sacrifices, of health, of all other interests and concerns, of all other duties and commitments, for nine years, or even for nine months, in order to keep another person alive.

38   6. We have in fact to distinguish between two kinds of Samaritan: the Good Samaritan and what we might call the Minimally Decent Samaritan. The story of the Good Samaritan, you will remember, goes like this:

> A certain man went down from Jerusalem to Jericho, and fell among thieves which stripped him of his raiment, and wounded him, and departed, leaving him half dead.
>
> And by chance there came down a certain priest that way; and when he saw him, he passed by on the other side.
>
> And likewise a Levite, when he was at the place, came and looked on him, and passed by on the other side.
>
> But a certain Samaritan, as he journeyed, came where he was, and when he saw him he had compassion on him.
>
> And went to him, and bound up his wounds, pouring in oil and wine, and set him on his own beast, and brought him to an inn, and took care of him.
>
> And on the morrow, when he departed, he took out two pence, and gave them to the host, and said unto him, "Take care of him, and whatsoever thou spendest more when I come again, I will repay thee."

The Good Samaritan went out of his way, at some cost to himself, to help one in need of it. We are not told what the options were, that is, whether or not the priest and the Levite could have helped by doing less than the Good Samaritan did, but assuming they could have, then the fact they did nothing at all shows they were not even Minimally Decent Samaritans, not because they were not Samaritans, but because they were not even minimally decent.

39   These things are a matter of degree, of course, but there is a difference, and it comes out perhaps most clearly in the story of Kitty Genovese, who, as you will remember, was murdered while thirty-eight people watched or listened, and did nothing at all to help her. A Good Samaritan would have rushed out to give direct assistance against the murderer. Or perhaps we had better allow that it would have been a Splendid Samaritan who did this, on the ground that it would have involved risk of death for himself. But the thirty-eight not only did not do this, they did not even trouble to pick up a phone to call the police. Minimally Decent Samaritanism would call for doing at least that, and their not having done it was monstrous.

40   After telling the story of the Good Samaritan, Jesus said, "Go, and do thou likewise." Perhaps he meant that we are morally required to act as the Good Samaritan did. Perhaps he was urging people to do more than is morally required of them. At all events it seems plain that it was not morally required of any of the thirty-eight that he rush out to give direct assistance at the risk of his own life, and that it is not morally required of anyone that he give long stretches of his life—nine years or nine months—to sustaining the life of a person who has no special right (we were leaving open the possibility of this) to demand it.

41   Indeed, with one rather striking class of exceptions, no one in any country in the world is legally required to do anywhere near as much as this for anyone else. The class of exceptions is obvious. My main concern here is not the state of the law in respect to abortion, but it is worth drawing attention to the fact that in no state in this country is any man compelled by law to be even a Minimally Decent Samaritan to any person; there is no law under which charges could be brought against the thirty-eight who stood by while Kitty Genovese died. By contrast, in most states in this country women are compelled by law to be not merely Minimally Decent Samaritans, but Good Samaritans to unborn persons inside them. This doesn't by itself settle anything one way or the other, because it may well be argued that there should be laws in this country—as there are in many European countries—compelling at least Minimally Decent Samaritanism.[8] But it does show that there is a gross injustice in the existing state of the law. And it shows also that the groups currently working against liberalization of abortion laws, in fact working toward having it declared unconstitutional for a state to permit abortion, had better start working for the adoption of Good Samaritan laws generally, or earn the charge that they are acting in bad faith.

42   I should think, myself, that Minimally Decent Samaritan laws would be one thing, Good Samaritan laws quite another, and in fact highly improper. But we are not here concerned with the law. What we should ask is not

whether anybody should be compelled by law to be a Good Samaritan, but whether we must accede to a situation in which somebody is being compelled—by nature, perhaps—to be a Good Samaritan. We have, in other words, to look now at third-party interventions. I have been arguing that no person is morally required to make large sacrifices to sustain the life of another who has no right to demand them, and this even where the sacrifices do not include life itself: we are not morally required to be Good Samaritans or anyway Very Good Samaritans to one another. But what if a man cannot extricate himself from such a situation? What if he appeals to us to extricate him? It seems to me plain that there are cases in which we can, cases in which a Good Samaritan would extricate him. There you are, you were kidnapped, and nine years in bed with that violinist lie ahead of you. You have your own life to lead. You are sorry, but you simply cannot see giving up so much of your life to the sustaining of his. You cannot extricate yourself, and ask us to do so. I should have thought that—in light of his having no right to the use of your body—it was obvious that we do not have to accede to your being forced to give up so much. We can do what you ask. There is no injustice to the violinist in our doing so.

43   7. Following the lead of the opponents of abortion, I have throughout been speaking of the fetus merely as a person, and what I have been asking is whether or not the argument we began with, which proceeds only from the fetus' being a person, really does establish its conclusion. I have argued that it does not.

44   But of course there are arguments and arguments, and it may be said that I have simply fastened on the wrong one. It may be said that what is important is not merely the fact that the fetus is a person, but that it is a person for whom the woman has a special kind of responsibility issuing from the fact that she is its mother. And it might be argued that all my analogies are therefore irrelevant—for you do not have that special kind of responsibility for that violinist, Henry Fonda does not have that special kind of responsibility for me. And our attention might be drawn to the fact that men and women both are compelled by law to provide support for their children.

45   I have in effect dealt (briefly) with this argument in section 4 above; but a (still briefer) recapitulation now may be in order. Surely we do not have any such "special responsibility" for a person unless we have assumed it, explicitly or implicitly. If a set of parents do not try to prevent pregnancy, do not obtain an abortion, and then at the time of birth of the child do not put it out for adoption, but rather take it home with them, then they have assumed responsibility for it, they have given it rights, and they cannot now withdraw support from it at the cost of its life because they now find it difficult to go on providing for it. But if they have taken all reasonable precautions against having a child, they do not simply by virtue of their biological relationship to the child who comes into existence have a special responsibility for it. They may wish to assume responsibility for it, or they may not wish to. And I am suggesting that if assuming responsibility for it would require large sacrifices, then

they may refuse. A Good Samaritan would not refuse—or anyway, a Splendid Samaritan, if the sacrifices that had to be made were enormous. But then so would a Good Samaritan assume responsibility for that violinist; so would Henry Fonda, if he is a Good Samaritan, fly in from the West Coast and assume responsibility for me.

46   8. My argument will be found unsatisfactory on two counts by many of those who want to regard abortion as morally permissible. First, while I do argue that abortion is not impermissible, I do not argue that it is always permissible. There may well be cases in which carrying the child to term requires only Minimally Decent Samaritanism of the mother, and this is a standard we must not fall below. I am inclined to think it a merit of my account precisely that it does not give a general yes or a general no. It allows for and supports our sense that, for example, a sick and desperately frightened fourteen-year-old schoolgirl, pregnant due to rape, may of course choose abortion, and that any law which rules this out is an insane law. And it also allows for and supports our sense that in other cases resort to abortion is even positively indecent. It would be indecent in the woman to request an abortion, and indecent in a doctor to perform it, if she is in her seventh month, and wants the abortion just to avoid the nuisance of postponing a trip abroad. The very fact that the arguments I have been drawing attention to treat all cases of abortion, or even all cases of abortion in which the mother's life is not at stake, as morally on a par ought to have made them suspect at the outset.

47   Secondly, while I am arguing for the permissibility of abortion in some cases, I am not arguing for the right to secure the death of the unborn child. It is easy to confuse these two things in that up to a certain point in the life of the fetus it is not able to survive outside the mother's body; hence removing it from her body guarantees its death. But they are importantly different. I have argued that you are not morally required to spend nine months in bed, sustaining the life of that violinist; but to say this is by no means to say that if, when you unplug yourself, there is a miracle and he survives, you then have a right to turn round and slit his throat. You may detach yourself even if this costs him his life; you have no right to be guaranteed his death, by some other means, if unplugging yourself does not kill him. There are some people who will feel dissatisfied by this feature of my argument. A woman may be utterly devastated by the thought of a child, a bit of herself, put out for adoption and never seen or heard of again. She may therefore want not merely that the child be detached from her, but more, that it die. Some opponents of abortion are inclined to regard this as beneath contempt—thereby showing insensitivity to what is surely a powerful source of despair. All the same, I agree that the desire for the child's death is not one which anybody may gratify, should it turn out to be possible to detach the child alive.

48   At this place, however, it should be remembered that we have only been pretending throughout that the fetus is a human being from the moment

of conception. A very early abortion is surely not the killing of a person, and so is not dealt with by anything I have said here.

Notes

1. I am very much indebted to James Thomson for discussion, criticism, and many helpful suggestions.

2. Daniel Callahan, *Abortion: Law, Choice, and Morality* (New York, 1970), p. 373. This book gives a fascinating survey of the available information on abortion. The Jewish tradition is surveyed in David M. Feldman, *Birth Control in Jewish Law* (New York, 1968) Part 5; the Catholic tradition in John T. Noonan, Jr. "An Almost Absolute Value in History," in *The Morality of Abortion*, ed. John T. Noonan, Jr., Cambridge, Mass., 1970).

3. The term "direct" in the arguments I refer to is a technical one. Roughly, what is meant by "direct killing" is either killing as an end in itself, or killing as a means of some end, for example, the end of saving someone else's life. See footnote 6 for an example of its use.

4. Cf. *Encyclical Letter of Pope Pius XI on Christian Marriage*, St. Paul Editions (Boston, n.d.) p. 32: "however much we may pity the mother whose health and even life is gravely imperiled in the performance of the duty allotted to her by nature, nevertheless what could ever be a sufficient reason for excusing in any way the direct murder of the innocent? This is precisely what we are dealing with here." Noonan (*The Morality of Abortion*, p. 43) reads this as follows: "What cause can ever avail to excuse in any way the direct killing of the innocent? For it is a question of that."

5. The thesis in (4) is in an interesting way weaker than those in (1), (2), and (3): they rule out abortion even in cases in which both mother and child will die if the abortion is not performed. By contrast, one who held the view expressed in (4) could consistently say that one needn't prefer letting two persons die to killing one.

6. Cf. the following passage from Pius XII, *Address to the Italian Catholic Society of Midwives:* "The baby in the maternal breast has the right to life immediately from God.—Hence there is no man, no human authority, no science, no medical, eugenic, social, economic or moral 'indication' which can establish or grant a valid juridical ground for a direct deliberate disposition of an innocent human life, that is a disposition which looks to its destruction either as an end or as a means to another end perhaps in itself not illicit.—The baby, still not born, is a man in the same degree and for the same reason as the mother" (quoted in Noonan, *The Morality of Abortion*, p. 45).

7. The need for a discussion of this argument was brought home to me by members of the Society for Ethical and Legal Philosophy, to whom this paper was originally presented.

8. For a discussion of the difficulties involved, and a survey of the European experience with such laws, see *The Good Samaritan and the Law*, ed. James M. Ratcliffe (New York, 1966).

Discussion and Outline

of Judith Jarvis Thomson's
"A Defense of Abortion"

Paragraphs 1 and 2

Like many philosophers, Thomson begins her essay by informing readers of what she is not going to discuss. She is not going to discuss whether human organisms are persons from the moment of conception. To be sure, she tells us that she thinks they are not persons, at least they are not persons early in their development. Moreover, she tells us that the most frequently offered argument for the claim that they are persons—the argument based on the moral arbitrariness of selecting a cutoff point during the organism's development—is unsound. (An acorn, after all, is not an oak tree even though there is no precisely determined point at which the one becomes the other.) On the other hand, she says that proabortionists shall probably have to acknowledge that fetuses become persons much earlier in their development than many of them think. But she is not going to discuss any of these matters; indeed, she despairs of settling the question of when a conceptus becomes a person. Rather, she is going to examine what *follows from* the claim that personhood begins at conception. For purposes of this essay, anyway, she is going to assume that this claim is true. Thus, the first line of our argument outline must be:

> 1. Human organisms are persons from the moment of
>   conception. (AP)

Thomson's essay, then, is one of those in which the author accepts a premiss for the sake of argument—that is, for the sake of examining what follows from it. Readers who disagree with the premiss will not accept conclusions that depend on it, even if they are otherwise soundly drawn. Those who do believe the premiss will have no quarrel with Thomson at this point. They are well advised nevertheless to consider her essay, for Thomson tells us that she will question whether arguments from that claim to the conclusion that abortion is never (or almost never) morally permissible are indeed soundly drawn.

Paragraph 3

Her first step must be to reconstruct the basic argument which antiabortionists use to get from the premiss that fetuses are persons to the conclusion that abortion is always (or almost always) impermissible. In reconstructing others' arguments, of course, she must be guided by the principles of charity and candor. The argument, she says, goes as follows:

   2. Some people argue (call it A):   (AP)

> [1. A human organism is a person from the moment of conception.]   [AP]

> [2. Every person has a right to life.]   [AP]

> [3. [So] the fetus has a right to life.]   [1,2]

> [4. A woman has a right to decide what happens in and to her body.]   [AP]

> [5. A person's right to life is stronger and more stringent than a woman's right to decide what happens in and to her body.]   [AP]

> [6. [So] the fetus's right to life outweighs the woman's right to decide what happens in and to her body.]   [3–5]

> [7. [So] the fetus may not be aborted (except to save the woman's life).]   [6]

It is worthwhile to compare Noonan's formulation of the conservatives' conclusion: "In the weighing [of the rights of the fetus against the rights of the woman], the fetus was always given a value greater than zero, always a value separate and independent of its parents."[1] Using Noonan's terms, we can say that Thomson undertakes to weigh the conflicting rights. Do they always balance on the side of the fetus?

Paragraph 4

Thomson begins her examination by asking the reader to imagine a scenario in which a person, call him K, awakens to discover himself attached to another

---

[1]See paragraph 20 in Noonan's article as reprinted here.

person—a famous violinist, V—such that if K is detached within the next nine months, V will die. (We need not rehearse all the details of the scenario.) Thomson claims that it is permissible to detach oneself from V, even if V will die, and she maintains that if the analogy holds, it follows that the basic argument is unsound. Formally:

3. Assume the scenario. [K is the kidnapped person; V is the violinist.] (AP)

4. V has a right to life. (AP)

5. K has a right to decide what happens in and to his body. (AP)

6. V's right is stronger and more stringent than K's right. (AP)

7. Lines 3 to 6 are relevantly similar to the premisses of argument A. (AP)

8. [So] if A is sound, K may not detach himself. (3–7)

9. But K may detach himself. (AP)

10. Any argument whose conclusion is false is unsound. (AP)

11. [So] A is unsound. (8–10)

Thomson notes, of course, that K is not obligated to detach himself and that it would be "frightfully nice" of him to remain attached, but nevertheless, she claims, K is not obligated to remain attached to V.

Paragraphs 5 and 6

The imagined case is very much like that of a pregnancy brought about by rape, for in such a case the fetus has been forcibly attached to the woman. Note that the violinist has not acted to bring about his attachment, anymore than the fetus has acted to bring about its attachment. If one agrees with Thomson that it is permissible for K to detach himself from V, then one has *prima facie* reason to agree that the woman may detach herself from the fetus. And this is so despite the fact that the fetus has a right to life. If it is permissible to detach oneself from the violinist, who unquestionably has a right to life, then it is permissible to detach oneself from the fetus.

Now many people who adopt a conservative position on abortion nevertheless permit abortion when the fetus is conceived as a result of forcible rape. Thomson is quick to call their attention to the difficulties involved in making such an exception, for those who do make such an exception must either claim that unlike other fetuses, such fetuses do not have a right to life (or have less of a right to life than do the other fetuses)—a difficult position to sustain—or they must find some other grounds on which to justify aborting such fetuses. In either case, they must acknowledge that the basic conservative argument is unsatisfactory. On the other hand, those who do not make exceptions in such cases are nevertheless challenged by

Thomson's argument to examine themselves carefully. Do they believe that they are morally obligated to remain connected to the violinist? To answer that question in the affirmative is to adopt an extreme commitment to the survival of others.

Paragraphs 7–17

Most pregnancies, of course, are not caused by rape. In most, the woman is a more active participant than is the kidnapped person who is forcibly attached to the violinist. Thomson, however, reserves discussion of these cases. She turns first to those extreme conservatives who will not make an exception even when the woman's life is at stake. Since the basic argument speaks only of the greater strength of the right to life when compared with the right to decide what happens in and to one's body, it does not account for why the life of the fetus should weigh more heavily than the life of the woman. Thomson considers several efforts to supplement the basic conservative argument. (We consider one.)

12. Some people say: (AP)

    [1. Performing an abortion is directly killing a
    person.] [AP]

    [2. Not performing an abortion when one knows that the
    mother will die is letting someone die.] [AP]

    [3. The duty not to kill a person is stronger than the duty
    not to let someone die.] [AP]

    [4. So, one may not perform an abortion *even* to save the
    mother's life.] [1–3]

But this argument, too, is unsound. For though it might apply to third parties—say, to a doctor asked to perform an abortion—it certainly does not apply to the threatened woman herself. Killing another in self-defense when one's life is threatened is ordinarily thought permissible, even if a threatener is not a voluntary agent.[2] And so Thomson's argument continues as follows:

13. X finds herself trapped in a very tiny house with a rapidly
    growing child such that if nothing is done to stop the child's
    growth X will soon be crushed to death, while the child will
    survive unharmed. (AP)

14. A third party may not choose between the lives of X and the
    child. (AP)

---

[2]While it is usually true that those who threaten another's life are not innocent, it is not necessarily so. In an article by Jane English we shall read later on pages 159–168, the author hypothesizes individuals who are hypnotized to kill others. She claims that if one is attacked by such an innocent threat, one may kill that individual.

15. [So] a third party may not kill the child.   (13,14)

16. X may kill the child.   (AP)

17. [So] in a case where one party threatens a second party's life, we may not infer what the second party may do from what the third party may do.   (15,16)

18. [So] it does not follow from the claim that a doctor may not choose between the mother's life and the fetus's life that a woman may not choose to save her own life.   (17)

19. [So] at most, the extreme conservatives' argument can show that a third party may not perform an abortion.   (12,18)

Later, Thomson will further discuss the question of third-party involvement. For now she is content to show that the basic argument together with the supplementary argument provide insufficient grounds for objecting to abortion in cases where the mother's life is threatened.

Paragraphs 18–22

How does the conservatives' argument fare when dealing with cases in which the woman's life is not at stake? On the surface, it certainly seems to have greater force, for the right to life seems clearly stronger than other rights with which the fetus's right to life might conflict. But just what is implied by having a right to life? Does it imply having the right to be given whatever is necessary to sustain that life? Suppose that to sustain X's life it is necessary for X to have what she otherwise has no right to obtain.

20. It is not necessarily the case that if the only thing that will save X's life is the touch of Y's hand on X's brow that X has a right to have that touch.   (AP)

21. [So] having a right to life does not imply having either the right to be given the use of or a right to continued use of another person's body—even if needed for life itself.   (21)

Paragraphs 23–25

The above point is critical. Indeed, it is the pivotal claim in Thomson's argument. Unless one grants to another the right to the use of one's body, no one has that right, even if it is necessary in order to sustain one's life. To have a right to something consists only in having the right not to be deprived of it *unjustly*. To detach oneself from the violinist is not to treat him unjustly, for he has just claim to use your body only if you have granted him that right.

So, too, for a fetus. Even if we assume that it has a right to life, the woman does it no injustice if she detaches herself from it, for the fetus has no right to the use of the woman's body—unless, that is, the woman has somehow given the fetus the right to use her body. Indeed, even if we believe that the woman ought to carry the baby—for example, if the pregnancy were to last only an hour and no complications were expected—it still would not be the case that the fetus has a right against the woman that she carry it. In short, having the right to life does not imply having the right to receive any and everything necessary to sustain that life. Rather, having the right to life is having the right not to be deprived of life *unjustly*. The assumed premiss in line 1 leads to the following:

> 22. [So] it is impermissible to kill a fetus only if one kills it
>   unjustly. (1)

Paragraphs 26–32

Under what circumstances, then, does a woman treat a fetus unjustly if she refuses to provide her body to sustain the fetus's life? Thomson's answer is that unless the woman has given the fetus a right to use her body, she never deprives it unjustly. It follows that, for Thomson, the question of the permissibility of abortion resolves into the question of determining the circumstances under which a woman has given the fetus a right to use her body. It is clear that in cases of rape, consent has not been given. On the other hand, one might well claim that if a woman freely engages in intercourse in full knowledge that she is likely to conceive, then she has, at least implicitly, consented to the fetus's use of her body. The fetus, of course, would not otherwise exist.

> 23. Unless a woman has given a fetus the right to use her body, the
>   fetus has no right to use her body even if it is necessary to
>   sustain the fetus's life. (21)
>
> 24. In the case of rape, the woman has not given the fetus the right
>   to use her body. (AP)
>
> 25. The fetus has been given a right to use its mother's body if her
>   pregnancy results from a voluntary act, undertaken in full
>   knowledge that pregnancy will probably result. (AP)

Between these two extremes, there is room for argument. The details make a difference, and Thomson proceeds to explore the details:

> 26. If X opens a window to air a room and a burglar climbs in, X has
>   not consented to the burglar's use of her house even though she
>   is partially responsible for his presence, having voluntarily done
>   what enabled him to get in, in full knowledge that there are
>   burglars and that burglars burgle. (AP)
>
> 27. If X has bars installed outside her windows to prevent burglars,
>   and a burglar gets in because of a defect in the bars, X has not
>   consented to the burglar's use of her house. (AP)
>
> 28. Suppose people-seeds drift about like pollen and if X opens her
>   windows, a seed may take root in her carpets. X doesn't want

children, so she installs fine mesh screens. But it happens that one of the screens is defective and a seed drifts in and takes root. The person-plant who now develops does not have a right to the use of X's house. (AP)

29. [So] actual circumstances make a difference to whether the fetus has a right to the use of the woman's body. (26–28)

30. [So] the basic argument does not establish that all abortion is unjust killing. (29)

Paragraphs 33–37

Assume for the moment that we are now talking about a pregnancy in which we are agreed that the woman has not consented to the fetus's use of her body. Does it follow that it is morally permissible for her to abort? Thomson's answer is no. Sometimes, she thinks, the woman ought to continue the pregnancy. Suppose, she says, that Henry Fonda need only cross the room to place his hand on a dying person's head, so that we would think him heartless if he refused to do it. Does it follow that the dying person has a right to Fonda's touch? The answer, Thomson claims, is no, even though we might well believe that Henry Fonda should do it.

Some people maintain that if X ought to treat Y in a given way, then it follows that Y has a right to be treated in that way. Thomson, however, denies this. It is better, she thinks, to keep considerations related to rights distinct from considerations related to "oughts." While it is true that if Y has a right to be treated in a certain way by X then X ought to treat Y in that way, the converse is not true. It does not follow from the claim that Y ought to treat X in a given way, that X has a right to be treated in that way. Similarly, it does not follow from the fact that X does not violate Y's rights by treating Y in a given way that X ought so to treat Y.

31. If, of two siblings, X and Y, X is given a box of chocolates and X eats them all and refuses to share with Y, then X is greedy but not unjust to Y. (AP)

32. If two siblings, X and Y, are given a box of chocolates and X eats them all and refuses to share with Y, then X is both greedy and unjust. (AP)

33. One ought not be greedy. (AP)

34. Again, if Henry Fonda need only cross the room to put his hand on X's brow and thereby save his life, then Henry Fonda ought to do so. (AP)

35. It is not necessarily the case that if Henry Fonda need only cross a room to put his hand on X's brow and thereby save X's life that X has a right against him that he do so. (AP)

36. [So] it is not necessarily the case that if X ought to treat Y in a given way, that Y is treated unjustly if he has not been so treated. (31–33)(34,35)

37. [So] it is not necessarily the case that if X ought to treat Y in a given way that Y has a right to be treated in that way. (36)

Paragraphs 38–42

To develop the above point, Thomson cites the Biblical account of the Good Samaritan and points out that we often characterize conduct as above and beyond the call of duty. Just how much above and beyond the call of duty a given act is a matter of degree. From a moral perspective, we might well hold, as Thomson does, that we ought often to treat others in a given way even if we believe that the other has no right to be treated in that way. We are often appalled when people, as in the Kitty Genovese case, stand by and watch another person being assaulted. On the other hand, we do not think that an individual is morally obligated to risk his life, or even to risk severe injury, to interfere in such cases. We think it morally obligatory to be at most a Minimally Decent Samaritan. To use our own example, we might well think that we ought to give a stranger directions when she asks for them, even though we would deny that she has a right to our giving her directions. By the same token, Thomson points out that, legally speaking, the United States generally does not even require Minimally Decent Samaritanism. Thus her argument continues as follows:

38. A Minimally Decent Samaritan renders minimal assistance above and beyond the call of duty. (AP)

39. A Good Samaritan renders considerable assistance above and beyond the call of duty. (AP)

40. A Splendid Samaritan renders an exceptional amount of assistance above and beyond the call of duty. (AP)

41. At most, it is morally obligatory to be a Minimally Decent Samaritan. (AP)

42. In the United States of America, it is generally not even required that one be a Minimally Decent Samaritan. (AP)

43. Some urge making it illegal for a woman to refuse use of her body to persons (fetuses) who have no special right to use her body. (AP)

44. In most cases in which the fetus has no right to use the woman's body, if she carries to term, she does more than is required of a Minimally Decent Samaritan. (AP)

45. [So] some urge that women be legally required to be more than Minimally Decent Samaritans in a legal context that does not usually require even Minimally Decent Samaritanism. (42–44)

46. [So] it is morally unjustifiable so to urge. (41,45)

Paragraph 42

Finally, Thomson returns to the issue of third parties. Her argument is as follows:

47. If X is a third party who knows that Y is threatening Z's life, then X may interfere on behalf of Z. (AP)

48. If X is a third party who knows that Y is seriously imposing on Z and that Y has no special right to do so, then X may aid in extricating Z. (AP)

49. [So] if X is a third party who knows that a given abortion is not morally forbidden, then X may aid the woman who seeks the abortion. (47,48)

Paragraphs 44–48

What follows is a summary and a pair of observations. Thomson points out that she considers it a strength of her position that it does not yield the conclusion that abortion is always permissible. The permissibility depends on the circumstances. The judgment to be made concerns the extent of the demand made by the fetus on the woman. Unless the woman has given the fetus a right to the use of her body, the fetus, of course, never has a right to that use. Nevertheless, sometimes the woman ought to continue the pregnancy. Finally, no one ever has a right to demand the death of the fetus. While one may indeed have the right to extricate oneself from the violinist, one does not have the right to demand his death.

Argument Outline

Main Argument

1. Human organisms are persons from the moment of conception. (AP)

2. [So] the fetus has a right to life. (1)

3. All women are persons. (AP)

4. [So] women have a right to decide what happens in and to their bodies. (3)

5. Unless a person has given another a right to the use of her body, having a right to life does not entail having either a right to use or a right to continue to use that person's body—even if one *needs* it for life itself. (P)

6. [So] unless a woman gives a fetus prior consent to use her body, the woman does the fetus no injustice by refusing it use of her body even if the fetus needs it for life itself. (4,5)

7. In many pregnancies, the woman has not given the fetus consent to use her body. (P)

8. [So] in many pregnancies, the woman does the fetus no injustice by refusing it use of her body. (6,7)

9. At most, it is morally obligatory to be a Minimally Decent Samaritan.[3]

10. In most cases in which the fetus has no right to use the woman's body, if the woman carries to term, she does more than is required of a Minimally Decent Samaritan. (AP)

11. [So] abortion is morally permissible in most such cases.[4] (10)

12. There are many cases of this sort. (AP)

13. In some cases, either a woman has given prior consent or not more than Minimally Decent Samaritanism is required to bring the baby to term. (P)

14. [So] in some cases, abortion is morally impermissible. (13)

15. If a third party knows that a given abortion is morally permissible, that party may aid the woman seeking the abortion. (P)

16. **[So] even if the fetus is a person, abortion is permissible in many cases.** (8,11,12,15)

Argument for line 5

17. It is not necessarily the case that if X is dying and the only thing that will save X's life is the touch of Henry Fonda's hand then X has a right to be given that touch. (AP)

18. If, without one's consent, one were attached to another such that to detach oneself would entail the death of the other, then in many circumstances, one may detach oneself. (AP)

---

[3]Thomson claims that American law does not even require one to be a Minimally Decent Samaritan.

[4]As for the law, Thomson infers that either we should permit abortion in cases where the woman has not permitted the fetus to use her body or we should adopt Minimally Decent Samaritan laws.

5. [So] having a right to life does not entail having either a right to use or a right to continue to use another person's body—even if one *needs* it for life itself. (17)(18)

Argument for line 7

19. In the case of rape, the woman has not given the fetus the right to use her body. (AP)

20. If X opens a window to air a room and a burglar climbs in, X has not consented to the burglar's use of her house even though she is partially responsible for his presence, having voluntarily done what enabled him to get in, in full knowledge that there are burglars, and that burglars burgle. (AP)

21. If X has bars installed outside her windows to prevent burglars, and a burglar gets in because of a defect in the bars, X has not consented to the burglar's use of her house. (AP)

22. Suppose people-seeds drift about like pollen and if X opens her windows, a seed may take root in her carpets. X doesn't want children, so she installs fine mesh screens. But it happens that one of the screens is defective and a seed drifts in and takes root. The person-plant who now develops does not have a right to the use of X's house. (AP)

23. The examples cited in 18–21 are analogous to many pregnancies. (AP)

7. [So] in many pregnancies, the woman has not given the fetus consent to use her body.[5] (19–23*)

Argument for line 13[6]

24. The fetus has been given a right to use its mother's body if her pregnancy results from a voluntary act, undertaken in full knowledge that pregnancy will probably result. (AP)

---

[5]The force of these analogical arguments can be appreciated only if the reader thinks of the fetus as an *independent* person in its own right and therefore as a being who has no greater claim on the woman than any other. That it is growing in a woman's body need generate no greater psychological or moral commitment than one might have to a violinist attached to her body. While Thomson provides no overriding principle on the basis of which we can decide whether in a given case consent has been given or not, she points to many cases in which she believes that such consent has not been given.

[6]Since Thomson is primarily concerned to show that there are numerous cases in which abortion is permissible even if the fetus is a person, she does not pursue a lengthy defense of line 13. However, she does count it as a strength of her argument that is does not yield the conclusion that abortion is always permissible.

25. If continuing the pregnancy entails little dislocation of a woman's life (as measured in terms of danger, pain, or hardship), then only Minimally Decent Samaritanism is required. (AP)

13. **[So] in some cases, either a woman has given prior consent or not more than Minimally Decent Samaritanism is required to bring the baby to term.** **(24,25)**

Argument for line 15

26. If X is a third party who knows that Y is threatening Z's life, then X may interfere on behalf of Z. (AP)

27. If X is a third party who knows that Y is seriously imposing on Z and that Y has no special right to do so, then X may aid in extricating Z. (AP)

15. **[So] if a third party knows that a given abortion is morally permissible, that party may aid the woman seeking the abortion.** **(26,27)**

Some Implications

First, Thomson refutes the conservatives' argument that since fetuses are persons abortion is never (or rarely) permissible is unsound. The conservatives' argument proceeds as follows:

[1. Human organisms are persons at the moment of conception.] [AP]

[2. Every person has a right to life.] [AP]

[3. So, the fetus has a right to life.] [1,2]

[4. A woman has a right to decide what happens in and to her body.] [AP]

[5. A person's right to life is stronger and more stringent than a person's right to decide what happens in and to his or her body.] [AP]

[6. So, the fetus's right to life outweighs the woman's right to decide what happens in and to her body.] [3–5]

[7. So, unless the woman's life is at stake, a fetus may not be aborted.] [6]

Thomson's key objection concerns the reasoning that leads from line 6 to line 7, which seems to rest on a suppressed premiss such as the following:

6a: If something has a right to life, then it may never intentionally be deprived of its life or may only be intentionally deprived of its life in cases in which it threatens the life of another. (SP)

Thomson suggests, however, that the correct premiss would be as follows:

> 6b: If something has a right to life, then it may not be intentionally
> deprived of its life unjustly.   (AP)

It simply turns out that there are many more instances in which physically dependent persons may not unjustly be deprived of their lives than may physically independent persons.

Second, Thomson claims from the fact that X ought to treat Y in a given way it neither follows that Y has a right to be treated in that way nor that Y has been treated unjustly if not treated in that way. Similarly, it does not follow from the fact that X does not violate Y's rights by treating Y in a given way that it is morally permissible for X to treat Y in that way. Thomson's arguments for these claims are as follows:

> 28. If, of two siblings, X and Y, X is given a box of chocolates and X
>   eats them all and refuses to share with Y, then X is greedy but
>   not unjust to Y.   (AP)
>
> 29. If two siblings, X and Y, are given a box of chocolates and X eats
>   them all and refuses to share with Y, then X is both greedy and
>   unjust.   (AP)
>
> 30. One ought not be greedy.   (AP)
>
> 31. Again, if Y need only cross the room to put his hand on X's brow
>   to save X's life, then Y ought to do so.   (AP)
>
> 32. But X does not have a right to have Y cross the room to save
>   X's life.   (AP)
>
> 33. [So] it is not necessarily the case that if X ought to treat Y
>   in a given way, that Y is treated unjustly if Y has not been so
>   treated.   (28–30)(31,32)
>
> 34. [So] it is not necessarily the case that if X ought to treat Y in a
>   given way that Y has a right to be treated in that way.   (33)

Is an Embryo a Person?

Charles A. Gardner

1   In the familiar polemics on the subject of abortion one side argues in support of women's rights, the other side in support of babies' rights. But so far only one side of the debate has attempted to engage a question that should be intrinsic to the abortion issue: What is the embryo?

2   To Dr. Jack Wilkie, President of the National Right to Life Committee, the embryo is a human being from the moment of conception. His definition of a human being depends on the forty-six chromosomes first present in the fertilized egg. "Contained within the single cell who I once was," he says, "was the totality of everything I am today."

3   Judges and state legislators across the United States seem inclined to accept the argument about chromosomes and totality. In *Webster v. Reproductive Health Services* the Supreme Court upheld a Missouri fetal rights law that asserts "life begins at conception." In September a Tennessee court ruled that seven frozen embryos at the center of a bitter divorce suit are children, that they are "human beings existing as embryos." Judge W. Dale Young gave "custody" of the embryos to their "mother," and, basing his decision entirely upon the testimony of one geneticist, concluded that "a man is a man; that upon fertilization, the entire constitution of the man is clearly, unequivocally spelled-out, including arms, legs, nervous systems, and the like; that upon inspection via DNA manipulation, one can see the life codes for each of these otherwise unobservable elements of the unique individual."

4   The "biological" argument that a human being is created at fertilization is increasingly used by antiabortion forces in their effort to back up

Reprinted with permission from *The Nation* (Nov. 13, 1989), pp. 557–559. © 1989 The Nation Company, Inc.

religious arguments based on church tradition. This purportedly scientific argument comes as a surprise to most embryologists, however, for it contradicts all that they have learned in the past few decades. The benefit of that knowledge, more sophisticated, subtle and complete than ever before, has been notably missing from most public discussions of abortion and from all the legal decisions that have created so much recent publicity.

5   The embryo exists utterly beyond our normal means of understanding. We are accustomed to trust our eyes. A thing has bark around a thick column, limbs, branches and bunches of green leaves. It must be a tree. While the early embryo bears no physical resemblance to anything we think of as human, later, at three months, it has fingers, legs, a nose and eyes. But the first conclusion one draws from even those appearances may have to be revised.

6   The fertilized egg knows nothing about how to make a finger, a nose or eyes. It knows only how to divide into two cells, which then know how to divide to make four. How, then, does the fertilized egg give rise to a baby?

7   The fertilized egg contains all the DNA necessary for the embryo to develop. Half the DNA has been supplied by the egg and the other half by a single sperm cell. We often read in textbooks and the press that this DNA is the "blueprint of life." But an analogy between a blueprint and the DNA is misleading. If a human being were a house, then the DNA would specify doorknobs, hinges, lumber and nails, window panes, wires, switches, fuses and a thousand other individual parts. But it would not tell how to put those parts together in the right order and at the right time. It is unfortunate that biologists have contributed to the belief that DNA represents some sort of essence or "life force." Rather, it is only part of the information necessary for the correct formation of the embryo.

8   In fact there does not seem to be any blueprint for embryonic development. Each step toward greater complexity depends instead upon the pattern of cells and molecules just reached in the preceding step. The information required to make an eye or a finger does not exist in the fertilized egg. It exists in the positions and interactions of cells and molecules that will be formed only at a later time.

9   But if the individual does not arise out of the DNA then from where does he or she come? The fertilized egg clearly has potential. Perhaps if we consider the fertilized egg as a whole, poised as it seems to be to follow a present pathway (blueprint or no), then we can discern the incipient individual.

10   We must ask, Is there a present pathway? Is there only one road for the fertilized egg to travel? Embryologists have always been impressed by the ability of the embryo to adjust to alterations in its normal path of development. They have studied the embryos of fish, frogs, chickens and mice because these closely resemble human embryos. In fact, when early human and mouse embryos are compared, the process of development is so similar that these embryos are not distinguishable from each other in any significant way. Let us, therefore, consider one experiment.

11   If a fertilized mouse egg from two white-furred parents goes through four cell divisions, the embryo will have reached the sixteen-cell stage. If this embryo is then brought together with a sixteen-cell embryo from two black-furred parents, a ball of thirty-two cells is formed. The ball of cells will go on to make a single individual with mixed black and white fur. Any particular cell of its body has come from either the one set of parents or the other. A similar event sometimes occurs naturally in humans when two sibling embryos combine into one. The resultant person may be completely normal.

12   If the two original embryos were determined to become particular individuals, such a thing could not happen. The embryos would recognize themselves to be different people, and would not unite. But here the cells seem unaware of any distinction between themselves. They seem to recognize each other as early embryonic cells and nothing more. The only explanation is that the individual is not fixed or determined at this early stage. In fact the body pattern has not even begun to form.

13   The early human embryo, like the mouse, is a ball of cells. The body pattern of the embryo will be established only very gradually by these cells, and not in a way that one might intuitively expect. The fertilized egg does not divide into one cell destined to make the head, one to make an arm, another a leg. There is no program to specify the fate of each cell. Rather, a cell's behavior is influenced at each stage by its location within the developing body pattern of the embryo. Each stage brings new information, information that will change as the body pattern changes. And each cell will respond to this new information in a somewhat random way. For example, one cell of the sixteen-cell embryo may contribute randomly to the formation of many different organs or structures of the body. Later on a descendant of that cell may find itself restricted to the brain but will still be able to contribute to a wide variety of cell types there. It may make different types of nerve cells or non-nerve cells. And because of the extremely complex cell migrations that take place during the development of the brain, the cell's progeny may function in many regions of the brain.

14   With this layering of chance event upon chance event the embryo gradually evolves its form. The mixture of chance and planning that goes into every step of the process is what makes each person unique. Even the distinct pattern of ridges and swirls that make up a fingerprint is not present in the fertilized egg. Identical twins grow from the same egg, have exactly the same DNA and develop in the same maternal environment, yet they have different fingerprints. If something so relatively simple and superficial as a fingerprint arises out of chance events, then what of an organ as complex as the human brain?

15   The fertilized egg is clearly not a prepackaged human being. There is no body plan, no blueprint, no tiny being pre-formed and waiting to unfold. It is not "complete" or "the totality" of a person. The fertilized egg may follow many different paths; the route will be penned in only as the paths are taken; the particular person that it might become is not yet there. Our genes give us a propensity for certain characteristics, but it is the enactment of the complex

process of development that gives us our individual characteristics. So how can an embryo be a human being?

16   Of course, the embryo is always human; it is of human origin, but so is every egg and sperm cell. The problem is in the definition of the word "human." It may be either an adjective or a noun. As an adjective it carries no particular moral weight. We have human hair, human fingernails; the human cells in our saliva all have forty-six chromosomes, but they have no special significance. The noun, however, does have a moral dimension. Its synonym "human being" connotes individuality or personhood. It may also be associated with human thoughts and feelings. With respect to the embryo, then, its use may relate to the development of the brain.

17   In the early embryo, a structure forms that biologists call the neural tube. It is a hollow cord of cells that runs along the central axis of the body, complete from head to tail after the first month (human embryos have tails for a while). One end of this tube bulges like the far tip of a long thin balloon being inflated. This area is called the brain, although until the second month of development the cells there do not become nerves; there are no special connections among them and there can be no thoughts. During the third and fourth months, nerve cells appear. Simple reflexes form first. The largest and most complex area of the brain, the cerebrum, develops last of all. In its decision in the *Webster* case, the Supreme Court majority took up the issue of "viability"—the point at which the fetus can survive outside the womb—and suggested that this stage might be reached as early as the twentieth week. Apart from the question of whether the lungs could function at this point, which in itself is doubtful, there is the more compelling matter of the brain, whose qualities ultimately distinguish us as human beings. In the cerebrum, the mature brain cell pattern is not seen until the sixth or seventh month.

18   The conscious mind is dauntingly complex, and its workings are just now beginning to be understood. We do know that the structure of the brain—the types and locations of the nerve cells and their interconnections—is intimately related to the function of the brain. The higher faculties must develop very late. Thoughts and feelings must arise very gradually. Thus, an embryo may have fingers, hands, a nose and eyes, even reflex movements, but still have no mind.

19   The early embryo, before development of the mature human brain, has only one quality to distinguish it from all other living things: It has the potential to become a human being. But it is a strange kind of potential, having no determined path or blueprint to follow. The fertilized egg cell does not contain its fate, just as a grape seed does not contain wine.

20   Of course we know the potential of the fertilized egg and the early embryo because we have awareness, thoughts and feelings. But the early embryo has none of these things. This group of cells cannot know its fate or want to become anything. Still each of us must struggle with the philosophical and moral implications of this type of potential. It may help to remember that potential here is very tenuous and dependent upon the influence of many extrinsic factors. And the very question of potential presents us with a

"chicken or the egg" kind of problem. Every egg and every sperm cell in our bodies could contribute to the formation of a human being. Obviously, an egg or sperm cell is not a "complete" human being, but then neither is the fertilized egg. Fertilization, the injection of sperm DNA into the egg, is just one of the many small steps toward full human potential. It seems arbitrary to invest this biological event with any special moral significance. As we have seen, we are more than the sum of our chromosomes; DNA is not destiny.

21   There will always be arguments based on spiritual or ethical beliefs to convince an individual of the rightness or wrongness of abortion, but each person should first understand the biology to which those beliefs refer. State-imposed restrictions on abortion would clearly take away individual choice in the matter. But the state may not act on the basis of religious tradition. It must recognize the fundamental difference between an embryo and a human being. The nature of embryonic development makes it impossible to think of an egg or a cluster of cells as a person. Time itself must be woven into the fabric of the embryo before it becomes a baby. And most abortions in the United States are performed well before the pattern of the weave is recognizable. Ninety-one percent are performed within three months of fertilization. It would be a great tragedy if, in ignorance of the *process* that is the embryo, state legislators pass laws restricting individual freedom of choice and press them upon people. The embryo is not a child. It is not a baby. It is not yet a human being.

Outline

of Charles A. Gardner's
"Is an Embryo a Person?"

Main Argument

    1. Some people argue (call it A):   (AP)

    [1. The fertilized human egg contains forty-six human chromosomes.]   [AP]

    [2. If something contains forty-six human chromosomes, then it contains the entire genetic code of a person.]   [AP]

    [3. If something contains the entire genetic code of a person, then its entire human constitution is clearly, unequivocally spelled-out, including arms, legs, nervous system, and so on.]   [AP]

    [4. If something's entire human constitution is spelled-out, then it is a person.]   [SP]

    [5. So, all fertilized human eggs are persons.]   [1–4]

    2. But statement 1.3 is false.   (P)

    3. [So] A is unsound.   (1,2)

Arguments for line 2

A.

    4. If a sixteen-cell mouse-zygote from two white-furred parents is brought together with a sixteen-cell mouse-zygote from two

black-furred parents, the ball of thirty-two cells will make a single individual with mixed black and white fur. (AP)

5. Similar events sometimes occur between two human sibling embryos. (AP)

6. The resultant person may be completely normal. (AP)

7. If the two original cell clusters were determined to be specific individuals, no such thing could happen.[1] (AP)

2. [So] statement 1.3 is false. (4–7)

B.

8. The early human embryo, like the embryo of a mouse, is a ball of cells. (AP)

9. A cell's behavior is influenced at each stage by its position within the developing body pattern of the embryo. (AP)

10. A cell's position is, to some extent, determined by chance. (AP)

11. [So] there is no program to specify the fate of each cell. (8–10)

2. [So] statement 1.3 is false. (11)

C.

12. Identical twins have identical chromosomes. (AP)

13. Identical twins have nonidentical fingerprints. (AP)

14. If identical twins have nonidentical fingerprints, it is likely that they have nonidentical brains. (AP)

15. [So] it is likely that identical twins have nonidentical brains. (13,14)

16. The nature of an individual's brain significantly affects the individual's character. (SP)

2. [So] statement 1.3 is false. (12–16)

17. [So] it is likely that identical twins have nonidentical characters. (15,16)

2. [So] (it is likely that) statement 1.3 is false. (17)

---

[1]Note also that the occurrence of such events raises difficulty for the immediate ensoulment theory. For if each sixteen-celled embryo has a soul, then the resultant thirty-two-celled embryo either has two souls or one of the souls must disappear.

Further Considerations

18. In the cerebrum, the mature brain-cell pattern does not develop until the sixth or seventh month. (AP)

19. The conscious mind is dependent on the cerebrum. (AP)

20. [So] thoughts and feelings develop very late. (18–19)

21. [So] embryos are not aware of their potential. (20)

22. [So] embryos cannot want or desire anything. (20)

23. A necessary condition for being a human being is that one be able to want or desire something. (SP)

24. [So] the embryo is not yet a human being. (22,23)

Abortion and Human Rights

Norman C. Gillespie

Philosophical and popular thinking about abortion is influenced by the belief that the fundamental issue in settling the morality of abortion is whether a fetus is a person (is a human being, has a right to life, or has passed the point at which "life begins"). Despite widespread disagreement over "where to draw the line," many people believe (a) that there is a point somewhere between conception and adulthood that is morally significant, and (b) that the morality of a particular abortion depends upon whether it occurs before or after that point. These assumptions are widely shared: ardent antiabortionists insist that the significant point is conception; at least one philosopher thinks that the Supreme Court, in permitting abortions during the first two trimesters of pregnancy, has ". . . for all practical purposes . . . resolve[d] the difficult question of when life begins;"[1] and more than one philosopher has searched for criteria for determining whether or not a being is a person in order to settle the morality of abortion—the basic idea being that if a fetus is not a person, then abortion is morally permissible. All of these ideas, I shall argue, rest upon mistaken assumptions, and after explicating briefly some of the principles that determine the distribution of human rights, I shall argue on the basis of those principles that (a) and (b) are false.

Reprinted from *Ethics,* vol. 87, no. 3 (April 1977, © by The University of Chicago), pp. 237–243. Used by permission of The University of Chicago Press and the author.

I

2   In many philosophic discussions of abortion, the problem arises: if an early abortion is morally permissible, why not a late abortion or even, as one philosopher has suggested, infanticide?[2] What is the morally relevant difference between them? These questions rely upon some standard principles of moral reasoning; yet, as we shall see, their full implications have not been recognized by most participants in such discussions. According to the principle of universalizability (U), if an act is morally right for one person, then it is morally right for all relevantly similar persons, and this principle can be restated as: (R) If one person has a right to x, then all relevantly similar persons have the same right to x. In analyzing these principles and the role of relevant similarities and relevant differences in moral reasoning, one finds, as Alan Gewirth puts it, that "according to the universalizability thesis, a singular moral judgment, which says that some individual subject S has some moral predicate P, is based on a reason according to which (a) S has some nonmoral property Q and (b) having Q is a sufficient justifying condition for having P, so that if one accepts the judgment and the reason then one must accept the generalization that every subject that has Q has P."[3] In short, moral properties are supervenient upon nonmoral ones; individuals are relevantly similar or relevantly different in virtue of their nonmoral properties; and whatever moral properties one has, all relevantly similar individuals share the same moral properties.

3   In the abortion dispute, the relevant nonmoral properties are thought to be viability, brain activity, independence, memory, and desires; and on that basis it is argued that human beings have rights.

4   Some philosophers have argued that universalizability is trivial in that there can be unique nonmoral properties in virtue of which only one individual, or only one class of individuals, has certain moral properties. In responding to this criticism, Gewirth points out that "in all these cases . . . the justifying [nonmoral] properties in question [may] involve an important *comparative* element. . . . The point is that even when a reason for a right or duty directly applies only to one person, where that reason logically involves a comparative element it applies in a comparative or proportional way to other persons. The logical form of that proportionality is [L] if x units of some property Q justify that one have x units of some right or duty E, then y units of Q justify that one have y units of E. Such proportionality is a pervasive feature of traditional doctrines of distributive justice."[4]

5   Now, whatever nonmoral properties one selects as a basis for determining human rights, it seems likely that those properties will be comparative and thus involve (L) in any assessment of whether a being has any rights. Indeed, as is true of most people, even if someone does not know on what basis we say that adult human beings have rights, he can appreciate that children are sufficiently like adults to have some rights, that the same is true of small children, that about-to-be-born babies are comparatively like infants, and that fetuses are comparatively similar to about-to-be-born babies.

6   This line of reasoning is familiar. When it is used with 'bald' and the number of hairs on one's head (or 'poor' and the number of pennies one has), it is called "the Sorites paradox." Yet, on the basis of (L) it is not paradoxical at all, it is instead, what reason would demand in dealing with such continuums. That 'bald,' 'poor,' and 'person' are vague is widely recognized; what is not so widely appreciated is how to deal with such terms, especially in moral argument. Insisting upon "drawing the line" in applying such terms is irrational; it only produces such paradoxical remarks as "it is not true that the fetus is a human being—but it is not false either," and "the indeterminateness of the fetus' humanity . . . means that, whatever you believe, it's not true—but neither is it false."[5]

7   The rational thing to do is to treat such cases on a *comparative* basis: to say that A is poorer (balder) than B, and, in the abortion dispute, that small children are not full-fledged, responsible adults, that infants are further from adulthood than small children, and fetuses further still removed from adulthood than infants. Given our awareness of the spectrum from poverty to riches, from baldness to a full head of hair, and from conception to adulthood, we can specify quite precisely where an individual falls along any of those spectrums. So precision is possible without drawing any lines; and in determining the rights of a being we can proceed in exactly the same fashion. Thus, when an adult requests an abortion, if it is seen as a conflict of rights case, the comparative strength of the rights of the being to be aborted is determined by its stage of development. A conceptus would have a minimal right to live (supposing that an unfertilized ovum has none), whereas an almost full term fetus would have considerably more of a right, but still less than its mother. So that one morally relevant difference between an early and a late abortion is the degree of development of the fetus.

8   It is this reasoning, I find, that influences our moral thinking about abortion. It explains (1) why no one favors infanticide, since with infants there is no comparable conflict of rights, (2) why we think one should save the life of the mother if it is necessary to choose between her life and that of the unborn, (3) why we find it impossible to draw a line (say, at six months of fetal development) and insist that abortions a few minutes earlier are significantly morally different, (4) why "we are more and more reluctant [as we go back in the life of a fetus] to say that this is a human being and must be treated as such,"[6] and (5) why the use of the "morning-after pill" seems to so many people to be morally unobjectionable. On this reasoning, a fetus has a right to life, but that right is less than that of its mother. A fetus is, as the Supreme Court put it, "less than a full person," which implies that its rights are less than full—*not that it has no rights at all*. Thus, given the facts of human development, (L) explains why abortion is a genuine moral problem, why it is the sort of problem it is, and why it troubles us in the way it does. An abortion cannot be dismissed as simply "elective surgery," but neither is an early abortion equivalent to murder. Furthermore, (L) renders consistent the assignment of fetal rights (as some courts have done) with the Supreme Court decision

that a fetus is not a person in the full legal sense of that term: one does not have to be a full-fledged person in order to have rights, or to be treated immorally.

II

9   The most serious distortion that affects moral discussions of abortion is the idea that abortion presents a "line-drawing problem." In introducing a series of essays on abortion, Joel Feinberg characterizes the views implicit in many of those essays when he writes, "I do not wish to suggest that 'the status of the unborn' problem is insoluble, but only that it is a problem, and a difficult one, for liberal, moderate and conservative alike, insofar as they seek principled, and not merely arbitrary solutions to line-drawing problems."[7] If one thinks he must be able to "draw a line" in order to defend early abortions, no wonder the "status of the unborn problem" seems insoluble. Yet, Feinberg's remarks overlook entirely, as do many philosophic essays on abortion, the *principled* solution provided by (L) to the problem and the question of whether the unborn have any rights.

10   In his remarks, Feinberg embraces an assumption that is at the heart of the antiabortionist position, namely, (c) if a being has a right to life, it is the same right to life that an adult human being has. In accepting (c), Feinberg considerably increases the burden which any liberal or moderate on abortion must bear. For an antiabortionist can argue: (d) an infant has a right to life, (e) there is no reasonable place to "draw the line" between conception and birth, therefore, a conceptus has the same right to life as an infant. The inference from (d) and (e) to (f) is common; yet it depends crucially upon (c). If (c) is false, (f) does not follow from (d) and (e), and the antiabortionist must argue for (c) in order to defend his position. Too often, this requirement is overlooked—as Feinberg overlooks it—and liberals and moderates are left with the impression that their respective positions are unreasonable because they are unable to reasonably "draw the line." Yet, anyone who favors early abortions can emphasize the very facts about human development that are crucial for the antiabortionist position, and, in doing so maintain that the right to life of a conceptus or zygote are minimal, while those of infants and about-to-be-born babies are considerable. Once one sees this possibility, the "line drawing problem" and the intellectual burden it imposes disappear.

11   In other philosophical discussions of abortion, one finds such remarks as, "What properties must something have to be a person, i.e., to have a serious right to life?"[8] Here, the mistake is: (g) If something is not a person, it does not have a serious right to life. And, in another discussion, the claim is made that "to stabilize his position [on abortion] the moderate would have to *invent* a new set of moral categories and principles . . . because our principles of justice apply solely to the relations between persons."[9] Here the fallacy is: (h) If something is not a person, our principles of justice do not apply to it. Position (g) is fallacious because being a person is a sufficient, but not a

necessary condition, for having rights; and (h) is false because, as (L), which is a principle of justice, makes plain, less than full persons can have rights, and these rights can be unjustly violated.

III

12 More than any other position on abortion, it is the moderate position—that early abortions generally, and some late abortions, are morally justified—that has been misunderstood by failing to appreciate the role of (L) in our moral reasoning. Roger Wertheimer finds the moderate position popular, but problematic.[10] What are its problems? First, it complicates specific moral decisions: there is a great variety of possible cases, and a difference in details—especially for mid-term abortions—often requires a difference in moral judgment. Second, Wertheimer claims that a moderate, to support his position, must invent new categories and moral principles. Any moderate would grant the first point, perhaps even insist upon it as a true account of the nature of the problem, but the second criticism is simply bizarre. After all, if the moderate position is popular, are all its adherents simply relying upon their own invented moral categories and moral principles? A much more likely explanation of its popularity is that it relies upon such standard moral principles as (U), (R), and (L).

13   Wertheimer notes that most liberals and conservatives on abortion are really only extreme moderates, since they agree that while abortion is not simply elective surgery, a fetus is not a fellow adult who must be treated as such. In short, the fetus occupies a special, intermediate place in our moral thinking. In Wertheimer's words, "it has a separate moral status, just as animals do," and he apparently infers from that claim that if the fetus has a separate status, our ordinary principles of justice do not apply to it. He argues that "our principles of justice apply solely to relations between persons," hence they do not apply to a fetus, and that argument is simply fallacious. For (L) is a principle of justice (which Wertheimer ignores), and it makes it plain that fetuses as well as animals can be treated unjustly. (Indeed, in trying to understand our moral thinking about animals, (L) would seem to be indispensable, since they, like fetuses, are like persons in some ways, but not in others. To treat them as sticks or stones would be to ignore that fact and to violate (L).)

14   If one adopts a moderate position on abortion, then one requires a reason to abort a fetus, and the strength of the requisite reason is proportional to the facts of the situation and the comparative rights of the parties involved. In "A Defense of Abortion,"[11] Judith Thomson supposes, for the sake of argument, that the right to life of a fetus is the same as that of its mother, and then examines several analogous conflict of rights cases in order to determine whether it is always morally wrong to kill, or let die, an innocent person. Many women would reject the supposition that their rights are on a par with those of a fetus and resent antiabortionists who make that supposition the cornerstone of their position. Since that supposition is mistaken, according to (L), their rejection of it is well founded. Yet, in Thomson's cases, the conclusion that the rights of a fetus are less than those of a normal adult only strengthens

her conclusion that some abortions are morally permissible. For if it is sometimes morally permissible to let an innocent person die, or to cause his death, then the reasons required to do so with a being that is less than a full person are proportionally less. Hence the moral principles (U), (R), and (L), the supervenience analysis of the attribution of human rights, and the categories 'person' and 'less than a full person' provide the basis for the moderate position on abortion.

IV

15 Two important criticisms might be made of the position I have argued. The first is that while (L) requires a proportionality in our moral assessments based on claims of human rights, unless one knows for certain what the nonmoral or natural characteristics are for determining human rights, one cannot be certain that fetuses and infants possess such characteristics in any proportional or comparative degree. This criticism seems accurate. We do not know for certain that a fetus is less than a full person in a morally significant sense unless we know those characteristics upon which we base the attribution of human rights. Yet, how would one establish what those natural characteristics are? Only, it seems, by analyzing our moral thinking about human beings and why *we think* that persons have rights. If one so proceeds, I think it is evident, or at least extremely likely, fetuses will be found to occupy the "in-between" status I have attributed to them. That intuition, after all, is one datum that any analysis of 'person' or 'has rights' would have to take into account. So if not certain, the moderate position on abortion is reasonably secure.

16 The second criticism objects to the idea of "partial rights" or "less than full rights." A right, one might insist, is not something that grows or diminishes, or something you can have more or less of. You either have it or you do not, in the way that a statement is either true or false. But one has only to substitute 'person' for 'rights' in that claim to argue against it. If there is a certain symmetry between being a person and having rights, then if persons can grow and develop, why should their rights not do the same? The idea that a child acquires more rights as it develops is not incoherent; it is, instead, the way most parents raise their children. And it is not simply that a child acquires more rights of different kinds as it develops; it also acquires more of the same right, such as the right to self-determination. One reply to this argument might be that, while a *child* grows and develops, *a person* does not—that is, a child becomes a person at some point and remains so from then on. So "personhood" is not elastic in the way that my position requires.

17 The trouble with that reply is that, if it is granted, it loses its force. Any "line-drawing" definition of 'person' which insists that only those beings who satisfy the definition have any rights is simply unrealistic. For once so defined, 'person' and 'has rights' would be inadequate to handle the moral problems we confront in dealing with abortion. It is not the definition of 'person,' but the reality to which that term applies, that is crucial for moral assessments. So if someone defines 'person' in such a way that a fetus, an

infant, and even a small child is not a person, the continuum of human development and the moral problems it presents are still before us. It is not as if a "line-drawing" definition of 'person' makes those problems disappear. So even if my use of 'person' and 'has rights' is revisionary, the facts of the situation require it, if those terms are to be adequate for discussing the morality of abortion. The alternative "line-drawing" approach only produces intellectual confusion and paradox.

V

18 Two assumptions, (a) there is a point somewhere between conception and adulthood that is morally significant, and (b) the morality of particular abortions depends on whether they occur before or after that point, underlie many discussions of the morality of abortion. In this paper, I have pointed out that if the properties in virtue of which persons have rights are comparative, then (b) is false and there is no reason to think that (a) is true. There are morally significant differences between early and late abortions, but these do not entail the conclusion that there is a point somewhere between the two at which one can draw a line and demarcate the morally right from the morally wrong abortions. Instead, mid-term and late abortions are morally complicated. Their correct resolution depends upon numerous factors, some peculiar to the individual case, and not the discovery of that point at which "life begins." There are many biological reasons for doubting that there is such a point, and I have argued that it is not morally necessary that we find or create it.

Notes

1. Daniel Callahan, "Remarks on the Supreme Court's Ruling on Abortion," in *The Problem of Abortion* [first ed.], ed. Joel Feinberg (Belmont, Calif., 1973), p. 194.

2. Michael Tooley, "In Defense of Abortion and Infanticide," in *The Problem of Abortion*, ed. Joel Feinberg. Reprinted in this book on pages 83–96.

3. Alan Gewirth, "The Non-Trivializability of Universalizability," *Australasian Journal of Philosophy* 47, no. 2 (1969): 123, n. 2.

4. Ibid., p. 126 (cf. Aristotle Nichomachean Ethics 5. 3. 1131a. 18 ff).

5. Roger Wertheimer, "Understanding the Abortion Argument," *Philosophy and Public Affairs* 1, no. 1 (1971): 86, 88–89.

6. Phillipa Foot, "The Problem of Abortion and the Doctrine of Double Effect" *Oxford Review,* no. 5 (1967); reprinted in *Moral Problems,* ed. James Rachels (New York, 1971), p. 29.

7. Feinberg [first ed.], p. 4.

8. Tooley, [*infra,* p. 83].

9. Wertheimer, p. 90.

10. Ibid, pp. 89–91.

11. Judith Jarvis Thomson, "A Defense of Abortion," *Philosophy and Public Affairs* 1, no. 1 (1971): 47–66. Reprinted in this book on pages 113–127.

Outline

of Norman C. Gillespie's
"Abortion and Human Rights"

Main Argument

1. Every claim that S has some moral property P must be based on claims that S has some nonmoral property Q and that having Q is a sufficient justifying reason for having P.   (AP)

2. Whatever moral properties one has, all relevantly similar individuals share the same moral properties.   (1)

3. Whenever Q is a "comparative property,"[1] then, if having x units of some nonmoral property Q justify one's having x units of some moral property P, then y units of Q justify one's having y units of P.   (1)

4. To attribute personhood is to attribute some moral property.   (AP)

5. Personhood is attributed on the basis of such nonmoral properties as sentience, rationality, autonomy.   (AP)

6. Such properties as sentience, rationality, and autonomy are comparative.   (AP)

7. [So] individuals may be more or less persons.   (3–6)

---

[1] That is, a property that admits of degrees.

8. [So] normal adults are full persons; children are less persons; infants are less still; and fetuses even less. (7)

9. [So] it is not the case that there is a morally significant point somewhere between conception and adulthood that divides persons from nonpersons. (8)

10. [So] normal adults have full rights; children have some rights; infants fewer; fetuses fewer still; and so on. (See Section II, below.) (8)

11. Abortion problems are conflict of interest problems. (AP)

12. [So] a zygote's interests count less than an embryo's; an embryo's less than a fetus's; and a fetus's less than a neonate's. (10,11)

13. [So] abortion is never merely elective surgery. (12)

14. [So] early abortion is never murder. (12)

15. The moral results arrived at by this argument do not depend on solving the line-drawing problem. (SP)

16. [So] the morality of abortion does not depend on whether it occurs before or after some morally significant cutoff point that occurs somewhere between conception and birth. (13–15)

17. [So] both the claim that there is a morally significant point somewhere between conception and adulthood that divides persons from nonpersons and the claim that the morality of a particular abortion depends upon whether it occurs before or after that point are mistaken. (9,16)

Implications of line 10

A. The extreme conservatives' argument is unsound.

18. Conservatives argue (call it A): (AP)

   [1. An infant has a right to life.] [AP]

   [2. There is no reasonable place to draw a line between conception and birth.] [AP]

   [3. So, a conceptus has the same right to life as an infant.] [1,2]

19. But A assumes P: If a being has a right to life, then it has the same right to life as an adult human being. (AP)

20. P is not true. (10)

21. [So] the conservatives' argument is unsound. (18–20)

B. The extreme liberals' position is unsound.

22. Liberals argue (call it B): (AP)

[1. Something has a serious right to life only if it is of such and such a sort (for example, person, sentient being, conceptual being).] [AP]

[2. Zygotes, fetuses, and so on, are not those sorts of things.] [AP]

[3. So, zygotes, fetuses, and so on, do not have a serious right to life.] [1,2]

23. But B assumes P. (AP)

24. P is not true. (10)

25. [So] the extreme liberals' argument is unsound. (22–24)

Abortion and the Concept of a Person

Jane English

1   The abortion debate rages on. Yet the two most popular positions seem to be clearly mistaken. Conservatives maintain that a human life begins at conception and that therefore abortion must be wrong because it is murder. But not all killings of humans are murders. Most notably, self defense may justify even the killing of an innocent person.

2   Liberals, on the other hand, are just as mistaken in their argument that since a fetus does not become a person until birth, a woman may do whatever she pleases in and to her own body. First, you cannot do as you please with your own body if it affects other people adversely.[1] Second, if a fetus is not a person, that does not imply that you can do to it anything you wish. Animals, for example, are not persons, yet to kill or torture them for no reason at all is wrong.

3   At the center of the storm has been the issue of just when it is between ovulation and adulthood that a person appears on the scene. Conservatives draw the line at conception, liberals at birth. In this paper I first examine our concept of a person and conclude that no single criterion can capture the concept of a person and no sharp line can be drawn. Next I argue that if a fetus is a person, abortion is still justifiable in many cases; and if a fetus is not a person, killing it is still wrong in many cases. To a large extent, these two solutions are in agreement. I conclude that our concept of a person cannot and need not bear the weight that the abortion controversy has thrust upon it.

Reprinted from *Canadian Journal of Philosophy,* vol. 5, no. 2 (October 1975), pp. 233–243. Used by permission of the *Canadian Journal of Philosophy* and the Estate of Jane English.

I

4   The several factions in the abortion argument have drawn battle lines around various proposed criteria for determining what is and what is not a person. For example, Mary Anne Warren[2] lists five features (capacities for reasoning, self-awareness, complex communication, etc.) as her criteria for personhood and argues for the permissibility of abortion because a fetus falls outside this concept. Baruch Brody[3] uses brain waves. Michael Tooley[4] picks having-a-concept-of-self as his criterion and concludes that infanticide and abortion are justifiable, while the killing of adult animals is not. On the other side, Paul Ramsey[5] claims a certain gene structure is the defining characteristic. John Noonan[6] prefers conceived-of-humans and presents counterexamples to various other candidate criteria. For instance, he argues against viability as the criterion because the newborn and infirm would then be non-persons, since they cannot live without the aid of others. He rejects any criterion that calls upon the sorts of sentiments a being can evoke in adults on the grounds that this would allow us to exclude other races as non-persons if we could just view them sufficiently unsentimentally.

5   These approaches are typical: foes of abortion propose sufficient conditions for personhood which fetuses satisfy, while friends of abortion counter with necessary conditions for personhood which fetuses lack. But these both presuppose that the concept of a person can be captured in a straight jacket of necessary and/or sufficient conditions.[7] Rather, "person" is a cluster of features, of which rationality, having a self-concept and being conceived of humans are only part.

6   What is typical of persons? Within our concept of a person we include, first, certain biological factors: descended from humans, having a certain genetic makeup, having a head, hands, arms, eyes, capable of locomotion, breathing, eating, sleeping. There are psychological factors: sentience, perception, having a concept of self and of one's own interests and desires, the ability to use tools, the ability to use language or symbol systems, the ability to joke, to be angry, to doubt. There are rationality factors: the ability to reason and draw conclusions, the ability to generalize and to learn from past experience, the ability to sacrifice present interests for greater gains in the future. There are social factors: the ability to work in groups and to respond to peer pressure, the ability to recognize and consider as valuable the interests of others, seeing oneself as one among "other minds," the ability to sympathize, encourage, love, the ability to evoke from others the responses of sympathy, encouragement, love, the ability to work with others for mutual advantage. Then there are legal factors: being subject to the law and protected by it, having the ability to sue and enter contracts, being counted in the census, having a name and citizenship, the ability to own property, inherit, and so forth.

7   Now the point is not that this list is incomplete, or that you can find counterinstances to each of its points. People typically exhibit rationality, for instance, but someone who was irrational would not thereby fail to qualify as a person. On the other hand, something could exhibit the majority of these

features and still fail to be a person, as an advanced robot might. There is no single core of necessary and sufficient features which we can draw upon with the assurance that they constitute what really makes a person; there are only features that are more or less typical.

8   This is not to say that no necessary or sufficient conditions can be given. Being alive is a necessary condition for being a person, and being a U.S. Senator is a sufficient condition. But rather than falling inside a sufficient condition or outside a necessary one, a fetus lies in the penumbra region where our concept of a person is not so simple. For this reason I think a conclusive answer to the question whether a fetus is a person is unattainable.

9   Here we might note a family of simple fallacies that proceed by stating a necessary condition for personhood and showing that a fetus has that characteristic. This is a form of the fallacy of affirming the consequent. For example, some have mistakenly reasoned from the premise that a fetus is human (after all, it is a human fetus rather than, say, a canine fetus), to the conclusion that it is *a* human. Adding an equivocation on "being," we get the fallacious argument that since a fetus is something both living and human, it is a human being.

10   Nonetheless, it does seem clear that a fetus has very few of the above family of characteristics, whereas a newborn baby exhibits a much larger proportion of them—and a two-year-old has even more. Note that the traditional anti-abortion argument has centered on pointing out the many ways in which a fetus resembles a baby. They emphasize its development ("It already has ten fingers . . .") without mentioning its dissimilarities to adults (it still has gills and a tail). They also try to evoke the sort of sympathy on our part that we only feel toward other persons ("Never to laugh . . . or feel the sunshine?"). This all seems to be a relevant way to argue, since its purpose is to persuade us that a fetus satisfies so many of the important features on the list that it ought to be treated as a person. Also note that a fetus near the time of birth satisfies many more of these factors than a fetus in the early months of development. This could provide reason for making distinctions among the different stages of pregnancy, as the U. S. Supreme Court has done.[8]

11   Historically, the time at which a person has been said to come into existence has varied widely. Muslims date personhood from fourteen days after conception. Some medievals followed Aristotle in placing ensoulment at forty days after conception for a male fetus and eighty days for a female fetus.[9] In European common law since the Seventeenth Century, abortion was considered the killing of a person only after quickening, the time when a pregnant woman first feels the fetus move on its own. Nor is this variety of opinions surprising. Biologically, a human being develops gradually. We shouldn't expect there to be any specific time or sharp dividing point when a person appears on the scene.

12   For these reasons I believe our concept of a person is not sharp or decisive enough to bear the weight of a solution to the abortion controversy. To use it to solve that problem is to clarify *obscurum per obscurius* [the obscure by the obscure].

II

13 Next let us consider what follows if a fetus is a person after all. Judith Jarvis Thomson's landmark article, "A Defense of Abortion"[10] correctly points out that some additional argumentation is needed at this point in the conservative argument to bridge the gap between the premise that a fetus is an innocent person and the conclusion that killing it is always wrong. To arrive at this conclusion, we would need the additional premise that killing an innocent person is always wrong. But killing an innocent person is sometimes permissible, most notably in self defense. Some examples may help draw out our intuitions or ordinary judgments about self defense.

14   Suppose a mad scientist, for instance, hypnotized innocent people to jump out of the bushes and attack innocent passers-by with knives. If you are so attacked, we agree you have a right to kill the attacker in self defense, if killing him is the only way to protect your life or to save yourself from serious injury. It does not seem to matter here that the attacker is not malicious but himself an innocent pawn, for your killing of him is not done in a spirit of retribution but only in self defense.

15   How severe an injury may you inflict in self defense? In part this depends upon the severity of the injury to be avoided: you may not shoot someone merely to avoid having your clothes torn. This might lead one to the mistaken conclusion that the defense may only equal the threatened injury in severity; that to avoid death you may kill, but to avoid a black eye you may only inflict a black eye or the equivalent. Rather, our laws and customs seem to say that you may create an injury somewhat, but not enormously, greater than the injury to be avoided. To fend off an attack whose outcome would be as serious as rape, a severe beating or the loss of a finger, you may shoot; to avoid having your clothes torn, you may blacken an eye.

16   Aside from this, the injury you may inflict should only be the minimum necessary to deter or incapacitate the attacker. Even if you know he intends to kill you, you are not justified in shooting him if you could equally well save yourself by the simple expedient of running away. Self defense is for the purpose of avoiding harms rather than equalizing harms.

17   Some cases of pregnancy present a parallel situation. Though the fetus is itself innocent, it may pose a threat to the pregnant woman's well-being, life prospects or health, mental or physical. If the pregnancy presents a slight threat to her interests, it seems self defense cannot justify abortion. But if the threat is on a par with a serious beating or the loss of a finger, she may kill the fetus that poses such a threat, even if it is an innocent person. If a lesser harm to the fetus could have the same defensive effect, killing it would not be justified. It is unfortunate that the only way to free the woman from the pregnancy entails the death of the fetus (except in very late stages of pregnancy). Thus a self defense model supports Thomson's point that the woman has a right only to be freed from the fetus, not a right to demand its death.[11]

18   The self defense model is most helpful when we take the pregnant woman's point of view. In the pre-Thomson literature, abortion is often framed as a question for a third party: do you, a doctor, have a right to choose between the life of the woman and that of the fetus? Some have claimed that if you were a passer-by who witnessed a struggle between the innocent hypnotized attacker and his equally innocent victim, you would have no reason to kill either in defense of the other. They have concluded that the self defense model implies that a woman may attempt to abort herself, but that a doctor should not assist her. I think the position of the third party is somewhat more complex. We do feel some inclination to intervene on behalf of the victim rather than the attacker, other things equal. But if both parties are innocent, other factors come into consideration. You would rush to the aid of your husband whether he was attacker or attackee. If a hypnotized famous violinist were attacking a skid row bum, we would try to save the individual who is of more value to society. These considerations would tend to support abortion in some cases.

19   But suppose you are a frail senior citizen who wishes to avoid being knifed by one of these innocent hypnotics, so you have hired a bodyguard to accompany you. If you are attacked, it is clear we believe that the bodyguard, acting as your agent, has a right to kill the attacker to save you from a serious beating. Your rights of self defense are transferred to your agent. I suggest that we should similarly view the doctor as the pregnant woman's agent in carrying out a defense she is physically incapable of accomplishing herself.

20   Thanks to modern technology, the cases are rare in which pregnancy poses as clear a threat to a woman's bodily health as an attacker brandishing a switchblade. How does self defense fare when more subtle, complex and long-range harms are involved?

21   To consider a somewhat fanciful example, suppose you are a highly trained surgeon when you are kidnapped by the hypnotic attacker. He says he does not intend to harm you but to take you back to the mad scientist who, it turns out, plans to hypnotize you to have a permanent mental block against all your knowledge of medicine. This would automatically destroy your career which would in turn have a serious adverse impact on your family, your personal relationships and your happiness. It seems to me that if the only way you can avoid this outcome is to shoot the innocent attacker, you are justified in so doing. You are defending yourself from a drastic injury to your life prospects. I think it is no exaggeration to claim that unwanted pregnancies (most obviously among teenagers) often have such adverse life-long consequences as the surgeon's loss of livelihood.

22   Several parallels arise between various views on abortion and the self defense model. Let's suppose further that these hypnotized attackers only operate at night, so that it is well known that they can be avoided completely by the considerable inconvenience of never leaving your house after dark. One view is that since you could stay home at night, therefore if you go out and are selected by one of these hypnotized people, you have no right to defend yourself. This parallels the view that abstinence is the only acceptable way to avoid pregnancy. Others might hold that you ought to take along some defense such

as Mace which will deter the hypnotized person without killing him, but that if this defense fails, you are obliged to submit to the resulting injury, no matter how severe it is. This parallels the view that contraception is all right but abortion is always wrong, even in cases of contraceptive failure.

23   A third view is that you may kill the hypnotized person only if he will actually kill you, but not if he will only injure you. This is like the position that abortion is permissible only if it is required to save a woman's life. Finally we have the view that it is all right to kill the attacker, even if only to avoid a very slight inconvenience to yourself and even if you knowingly walked down the very street where all these incidents have been taking place without taking along any Mace or protective escort. If we assume that a fetus is a person, this is the analogue of the view that abortion is always justifiable, "on demand."

24   The self defense model allows us to see an important difference that exists between abortion and infanticide, even if a fetus is a person from conception. Many have argued that the only way to justify abortion without justifying infanticide would be to find some characteristic of personhood that is acquired at birth. Michael Tooley, for one, claims infanticide is justifiable because the really significant characteristics of person are acquired some time after birth. But all such approaches look to characteristics of the developing human and ignore the relation between the fetus and the woman. What if, after birth, the presence of an infant or the need to support it posed a grave threat to the woman's sanity or life prospects? She could escape this threat by the simple expedient of running away. So a solution that does not entail the death of the infant is available. Before birth, such solutions are not available because of the biological dependence of the fetus on the woman. Birth is the crucial point not because of any characteristics the fetus gains, but because after birth the woman can defend herself by a means less drastic than killing the infant. Hence self defense can be used to justify abortion without necessarily thereby justifying infanticide.

III

25 On the other hand, supposing a fetus is not after all a person, would abortion always be morally permissible? Some opponents of abortion seem worried that if a fetus is not a full-fledged person, then we are justified in treating it in any way at all. However, this does not follow. Non-persons do get some consideration in our moral code, though of course they do not have the same rights as persons have (and in general they do not have moral responsibilities), and though their interests may be overridden by the interests of persons. Still, we cannot just treat them in any way at all.

26   Treatment of animals is a case in point. It is wrong to torture dogs for fun or to kill wild birds for no reason at all. It is wrong Period, even though dogs and birds do not have the same rights persons do. However, few people think it is wrong to use dogs as experimental animals, causing them considerable suffering in some cases, provided that the resulting research will probably bring discoveries of great benefit to people. And most of us think it all

right to kill birds for food or to protect our crops. People's rights are different from the consideration we give to animals, then, for it is wrong to experiment on people, even if others might later benefit a great deal as a result of their suffering. You might volunteer to be a subject, but this would be supererogatory; you certainly have a right to refuse to be a medical guinea pig.

27 But how do we decide what you may or may not do to non-persons? This is a difficult problem, one for which I believe no adequate account exists. You do not want to say, for instance, that torturing dogs is all right whenever the sum of its effects on people is good—when it doesn't warp the sensibilities of the torturer so much that he mistreats people. If that were the case, it would be all right to torture dogs if you did it in private, or if the torturer lived on a desert island or died soon afterward, so that his actions had no effect on people. This is an inadequate account, because whatever moral consideration animals get, it has to be indefeasible, too. It will have to be a general proscription of certain actions, not merely a weighing of the impact on people on a case-by-case basis.

28 Rather, we need to distinguish two levels on which consequences of actions can be taken into account in moral reasoning. The traditional objections to Utilitarianism focus on the fact that it operates solely on the first level, taking all the consequences into account in particular cases only. Thus Utilitarianism is open to "desert island" and "lifeboat" counterexamples because these cases are rigged to make the consequences of actions severely limited.

29 Rawls' theory could be described as a teleological sort of theory, but with teleology operating on a higher level.[12] In choosing the principles to regulate society from the original position, his hypothetical choosers make their decisions on the basis of the total consequences of various systems. Furthermore, they are constrained to choose a general set of rules which people can readily learn and apply. An ethical theory must operate by generating a set of sympathies and attitudes toward others which reinforces the functioning of that set of moral principles. Our prohibition against killing people operates by means of certain moral sentiments including sympathy, compassion and guilt. But if these attitudes are to form a coherent set, they carry us further: we tend to perform supererogatory actions, and we tend to feel similar compassion toward person-like non-persons.

30 It is crucial that psychological facts play a role here. Our psychological constitution makes it the case that for our ethical theory to work, it must prohibit certain treatment of non-persons which are significantly person-like. If our moral rules allowed people to treat some person-like non-persons in ways we do not want people to be treated, this would undermine the system of sympathies and attitudes that makes the ethical system work. For this reason, we would choose in the original position to make mistreatment of some sorts of animals wrong in general (not just wrong in the cases with public impact), even though animals are not themselves parties in the original position. Thus it makes sense that it is those animals whose appearance and behavior are most like those of people that get the most consideration in our moral scheme.

31   It is because of "coherence of attitudes," I think, that the similarity of a fetus to a baby is very significant. A fetus one week before birth is so much like a newborn baby in our psychological space that we cannot allow any cavalier treatment of the former while expecting full sympathy and nurturative support for the latter. Thus, I think that anti-abortion forces are indeed giving their strongest arguments when they point to the similarities between a fetus and a baby, and when they try to evoke our emotional attachment to and sympathy for the fetus. An early horror story from New York about nurses who were expected to alternate between caring for six-week premature infants and disposing of viable 24-week aborted fetuses is just that—a horror story. These beings are so much alike that no one can be asked to draw a distinction and treat them so very differently.

32   Remember, however, that in the early weeks after conception, a fetus is very much unlike a person. It is hard to develop these feelings for a set of genes which doesn't yet have a head, hands, beating heart, response to touch or the ability to move by itself. Thus it seems to me that the alleged "slippery slope" between conception and birth is not so very slippery. In the early stages of pregnancy, abortion can hardly be compared to murder for psychological reasons, but in the latest stages it is psychologically akin to murder.

33   Another source of similarity is the bodily continuity between fetus and adult. Bodies play a surprisingly central role in our attitudes toward persons. One has only to think of the philosophical literature on how far physical identity suffices for personal identity or Wittgenstein's remark that the best picture of the human soul is the human body. Even after death, when all agree the body is no longer a person, we still observe elaborate customs of respect for the human body; like people who torture dogs, necrophiliacs are not to be trusted with people.[13] So it is appropriate that we show respect to a fetus as the body continuous with the body of a person. This is a degree of resemblance to persons that animals cannot rival.

34   Michael Tooley also utilizes a parallel with animals. He claims that it is always permissible to drown newborn kittens and draws conclusions about infanticide.[14] But it is only permissible to drown kittens when their survival would cause some hardship. Perhaps it would be a burden to feed and house six more cats or to find other homes for them. The alternative of letting them starve produces even more suffering than the drowning. Since the kittens get their rights second-hand, so to speak, *via* the need for coherence in our attitudes, their interests are often overridden by the interests of full-fledged persons. But if their survival would be no inconvenience to people at all, then it is wrong to drown them, *contra* Tooley.

35   Tooley's conclusions about abortion are wrong for the same reason. Even if a fetus is not a person, abortion is not always permissible, because of the resemblance of a fetus to a person. I agree with Thomson that it would be wrong for a woman who is seven months pregnant to have an abortion just to avoid having to postpone a trip to Europe. In the early months of pregnancy when the fetus hardly resembles a baby at all, then, abortion is permissible whenever it is in the interests of the pregnant woman or her family. The

reasons would only need to outweigh the pain and inconvenience of the abortion itself. In the middle months, when the fetus comes to resemble a person, abortion would be justifiable only when the continuation of the pregnancy or the birth of the child would cause harms—physical, psychological, economic or social—to the woman. In the late months of pregnancy, even on our current assumption that a fetus is not a person, abortion seems to be wrong except to save a woman from significant injury or death.

36   The Supreme Court has recognized similar gradations in the alleged slippery slope stretching between conception and birth. To this point, the present paper has been a discussion of the moral status of abortion only, not its legal status. In view of the great physical, financial and sometimes psychological costs of abortion, perhaps the legal arrangement most compatible with the proposed moral solution would be the absence of restrictions, that is, so-called abortion "on demand."

37   So I conclude, first, that application of our concept of a person will not suffice to settle the abortion issue. After all, the biological development of a human being is gradual. Second, whether a fetus is a person or not, abortion is justifiable early in pregnancy to avoid modest harms and seldom justifiable late in pregnancy except to avoid significant injury or death.[15]

Notes

1. We also have paternalistic laws which keep us from harming our own bodies even when no one else is affected. Ironically, anti-abortion laws were originally designed to protect pregnant women from a dangerous but tempting procedure.

2. Mary Anne Warren, "On the Moral and Legal Status of Abortion," *Monist* 57 (1973), p. 55.

3. Baruch Brody, "Fetal Humanity and the Theory of Essentialism," in Robert Baker and Frederick Elliston, eds., *Philosophy and Sex* (Buffalo, N.Y., 1975).

4. Michael Tooley, "Abortion and Infanticide," *Philosophy and Public Affairs* 2 (1971).

5. Paul Ramsey, "The Morality of Abortion," in James Rachels, ed., *Moral Problems* (New York, 1971).

6. John Noonan, "Abortion and the Catholic Church: A Summary History," *Natural Law Forum* 12 (1967), pp. 125–131.

7. Wittgenstein has argued against the possibility of so capturing the concept of a game, *Philosophical Investigations* (New York, 1958), paragraphs 66–71.

8. Not because the fetus is partly a person and so has some of the rights of persons, but rather because of the rights of person-like non-persons. This I discuss in part III below.

9. Aristotle himself was concerned, however, with the different question of when the soul takes form. For historical data, see Jimmye Kimmey, "How the Abortion Laws Happened," *Ms.* 1 (April, 1973), pp. 48ff, and John Noonan, loc. cit.

10. J.J.Thomson, "A Defense of Abortion," *Philosophy and Public Affairs* 1 (19, 1).

11. Ibid.

12. John Rawls, *A Theory of Justice* (Cambridge, Mass., 1971), Paragraphs 3–4.

13. On the other hand, if they can be trusted with people, then our moral customs are mistaken. It all depends on the facts of psychology.

14. Op. cit., pp. 40, 60–61.

15. I am deeply indebted to Larry Crocker and Arthur Kuflik for their constructive comments.

Outline

of Jane English's
"Abortion and the Concept of a Person"

Main Argument

1. We (probably) cannot use the concept of a person to solve the abortion issue. (P)

2. Even if early fetuses are innocent persons, aborting them is morally permissible in many cases. (P)

3. If late fetuses are innocent persons, aborting them is not morally permissible in many cases. (P)

4. Even if late fetuses are not persons, aborting them is not morally permissible in many cases. (P)

5. If early fetuses are not persons, aborting them is morally permissible in many cases. (P)

6. Whether fetuses are or are not persons, aborting early fetuses is permissible in many cases and aborting late fetuses is not permissible in many cases. (2–5)

7. [So] the concept of a person need not bear the weight of the abortion controversy. (6)

8. [So] the concept of a person cannot and need not bear the weight of the abortion controversy. (1,7)

Argument for line 1

9. A variety of features—biological, psychological, rational, social, and legal—are typical of persons. (AP)

10. Conceptuses lack many of the typical features of persons. (AP)

11. In general, the sufficient conditions conservatives propose for applying the term 'person' entail that many things that have few typical features of persons would be called persons. (AP)

12. Proposed sufficient conditions for applying a term that entail that many things that have few of the typical features of things normally called by that term are unsatisfactory. (SP)

13. [So] in general, conservatives' criteria for identifying persons are unacceptable. (9–12)

14. Adult human beings often lack one or more of the typical features of persons. (AP)

15. In general, the necessary conditions liberals propose for personhood entail that the term would not apply to many things that have many typical features of persons. (AP)

16. Proposed necessary conditions for applying a term that entail that the term would not apply to many things that possess many of the typical features of things normally called by that term are unacceptable. (SP)

17. [So] in general, liberals' criteria are unacceptable. (1,13–16)

18. Criteria of personhood employed through history have varied. (AP)

19. [So] we (probably) cannot provide a satisfactory set of necessary and sufficient conditions of personhood. (13,17,18)

1. [So] we (probably) cannot use the concept of a person to solve the abortion issue. (19)

Argument for line 2

20. If one is attacked by an innocent person who threatens serious physical, mental, or economic harm, one may kill that person in self-defense. (AP)

21. [So] one may sometimes kill innocent persons. (20)

22. In self-defense, one may not inflict more than somewhat greater harm than is threatened. (AP)

23. In self-defense, one may only inflict the minimum harm necessary to prevent the threatened harm. (AP)

24. Many nonviable fetuses threaten serious physical, emotional, or economic harm to the woman. (AP)

25. The minimum harm that one can inflict on a nonviable fetus to prevent its harming the woman is to abort it and thus destroy it. (AP)

2. [So] even if early fetuses are innocent persons, aborting them is morally permissible in many cases. (20–25)

Argument for line 3

26. If fetuses are persons, then even if a viable fetus threatens serious harm to the woman, it can often be delivered and put up for adoption. (AP)

27. [So] if fetuses are persons, to abort viable fetuses is to inflict an injury greater than that necessary to prevent the threatened injury to the woman. (26)

3. [So] if late fetuses are innocent persons, aborting them is not morally permissible in many cases. (21,22,27)

Argument for line 4

28. One may not torture dogs. (AP)

29. Dogs are nonpersons. (AP)

30. [So] it is not the case that one may do whatever one wishes to nonpersons. (28,29)

31. Moral systems must employ rules that people can readily use. (AP)

32. Moral systems can work only if they generate a set of sympathies and attitudes toward others that reinforces the rules. (AP)

33. If moral rules do not prohibit some (cruel) treatment of animals and person-like nonpersons, then psychological incoherence results. (AP)

34. [So] moral systems that prohibit most killing of human beings must extend some protection against killing to animals and to person-like nonpersons. (31–33)

35. Late fetuses resemble persons. (AP)

36. There exists bodily continuity between fetus and adult. (AP)

37. Physical identity is a significant factor in personal identity. (AP)

38. Even after death, we still respect the human body. (AP)

39. [So] it is appropriate that we show respect to fetuses. (36–38)

40. [So] late fetuses are to be treated much like people are treated. (39)

4. [So] even if late fetuses are not persons, aborting them is not morally permissible in many cases. (30,34,35)(40)

Argument for line 5

41. Fetuses at early states are unlike persons. (AP)

42. Moral systems that prohibit most killing of human beings need not extend protection against killing of animals and nonperson-like nonpersons. (SP)

43. [So] excluding early fetuses from the prohibition against killing does not generate psychological incoherence in our sympathies and attitudes toward persons. (41,42)

5. [So] if early fetuses are not persons, aborting them is morally permissible in many cases. (43)

Part III

Supplementary Essays

Coming to Grips
with Abortion

Jodi L. Jacobson

Among the first actions taken by Romania's provisional government following the execution of dictator Nicolae Ceausescu in December 1989 was the repeal of a ban on abortion. The 14-year-old edict, created by Ceausescu in a fruitless attempt to raise the nation's birth rate, outlawed contraceptives and made abortion a criminal offense punishable in some instances by death. Despite the harsh law, data show that in the eighties the country outranked virtually all other European nations in rates of abortion and abortion-related maternal mortality.[1]

In legalizing abortion, Romania joined 35 other countries that have made similar changes since the late seventies. In fact, a 30-year tide of liberalization in laws governing access to family planning—contraceptives and abortion—reduced the relative number of unintended pregnancies and deaths due to illegal abortion in many countries, leading to vast improvements in public health and lower fertility worldwide. Today, however, abortion is at the center of an intense public controversy over religious and moral beliefs about the status of the fetus and a woman's right to make choices about pregnancy and motherhood.[2]

From the standpoint of public policy, few would disagree that reducing the number of unintended pregnancies and terminations worldwide is a desirable goal. A growing body of evidence suggests that dealing with abortion

An expanded version of this chapter appeared as Worldwatch Paper 97:
The Global Politics of Abortion. Reprinted from *State of the World, 1991*,
Lester Brown et al., eds., pp. 113–131. Used by permission of World
Watch Institute.

as part of a comprehensive strategy of public health and family planning, rather than making it illegal, is the most direct route to this end.

But abortion politics has become deadlocked in a no-win dispute over the ideology and criminality of various procedures, yielding a tug-of-war over laws that do not even begin to address the complexity of this social phenomenon. This stalemate postpones the day when the energies spent fighting over reproductive freedom can be directed fully toward improving the health and welfare of women and children worldwide.

A dispassionate debate on abortion seems a remote possibility. But the current polemic reflects scant understanding of its real place in demographic and public health trends, or of the social forces that influence abortion rates. Important questions go unasked: How many abortions are there and how many are legal? Where are the rates climbing, where falling? Who has this procedure, and why? What role does abortion play in social change? What are the costs to society of illegal abortions? How can the number of abortions be reduced without forcing women to carry unwanted pregnancies to term?

Irrefutable evidence remains unconsidered. Abortions are carried out in every country, no matter the law. History has shown that women determined to exercise control over the number of children they bear will do so, even if it means having dangerous illegal procedures. Worldwide, perhaps 50 million abortions are performed each year, nearly half of them illegal. Romania's experience is only one illustration that, irrespective of restrictive laws and religious doctrines and in spite of financial, logistical, and social obstacles, women everywhere continue to terminate unwanted pregnancies.[3]

It is the number of maternal deaths, not abortions, that is most affected by legal codes. Criminalizing abortion makes one of the safest of all surgical procedures highly dangerous by driving it into the hands of unskilled and often unscrupulous practitioners. High rates of maternal death and even higher rates of permanent physical impairment, along with exorbitant fees, fear of discovery, ostracism, and loss of vital income due to illness, are only a few of the realities of life for women who seek to end unwanted pregnancies in societies with restricted access to abortion. Where the incidence of illegal procedures is high, a disproportionate share of scarce medical resources goes to treating complications. Moreover, because abortion—whether legal or illegal—plays a significant role in the move from high to low fertility, policies that restrict access actually delay the demographic transition.

Looking beyond the rhetoric to the reality of abortion—its incidence, its social and health costs when illegal, its place in the fertility transition, the way it fits in with the broader struggle for human equity and equality—makes crystal clear the urgency of moving the abortion debate from the realm of crime to common sense.

The Pace of Liberalization

Liberalization of abortion laws began full force in the fifties, as recognition of the need to reduce maternal mortality and increase reproductive choices became widespread. Social justice was also an issue. Bringing abortion into the public domain narrowed the difference between those who could afford adequate medical care and those forced to resort to unsafe practitioners.

The strategy worked. France, Poland, Tunisia, the United Kingdom, and the United States are a few examples of countries where the relative number of births due to unintended pregnancies and deaths due to illegal procedures fell following liberalization. Between 1970 and 1976, for instance, abortion-related mortality among women in the United States fell from 30 per 100,000 live births to 5. And in Poland, an analysis by the Commission on Health and Physical Culture concluded that legalization had, among other things, contributed to the elimination of infanticide and of suicides by pregnant women, and had initiated a fall in abortion-related deaths.[4]

The term "liberal" is generally applied to policies that recognize the rights of a pregnant woman to terminate an unwanted pregnancy under various conditions to be greater than those of a developing embryo or fetus . . . up to a point. In countries with the most liberal laws, that point is legally set at "viability," the gestational stage at which a fetus can first reasonably be expected to live outside the womb, albeit with intensive medical assistance.

The crucial stages in the development of brain, heart, and lungs—the organs central to life, and hence to the question of viability—begin around the 20th week of pregnancy and proceed rapidly through birth. In medical circles, viability is generally recognized to occur at between 24 and 28 weeks of pregnancy. For this reason, most countries that use the viability framework severely circumscribe abortion rights after the 24th week, the end of the second trimester. The United Kingdom passed a law in early 1990 reducing the legal limit on abortion from 28 to 24 weeks.[5]

Abortion laws are usually grouped according to "indications," the circumstances traditionally used to justify legal terminations. These categories are broad, representing a diverse set of statutes. (See Table 1 for examples of countries in each category.)

Countries with the narrowest laws either completely ban abortions or restrict them to cases where pregnancy poses a risk to the woman's life; some allow the operation in the case of rape and incest. Other laws consider risks to physical and mental health; still others, the case of a severely impaired fetus. Some societies allow the operation for what are known as "social" reasons, as in the case where an additional child will bring undue burdens to an existing family. The broadest category is that recognizing contraceptive failure as a sound basis for abortion, or allowing procedures on request (usually within the first trimester).[6]

Most governments leave specific interpretations to the discretion of the medical community. The definition of "health," for example, is flexible. In some countries, doctors follow the broad definition of the World Health Organization (WHO): "a state of complete physical, mental, and social well being and not merely the absence of disease or infirmity."[7]

According to Rebecca Cook, professor of law at the University of Toronto, several of the 35 countries that liberalized their laws since 1977 created

Table 1. Conditions Under Which Abortions Are Allowed,
          Selected Countries, 1989

Life Endangerment[1]	Other Maternal Health Reasons[2]	Social and Socio-Medical Reasons[3]	No Mandated Conditions[4]
Bangladesh	Costa Rica	Argentina	Canada
Brazil	Egypt	India	China
Chile	Ghana	Peru	Czechoslovakia
Colombia	Israel	Poland	Italy
Indonesia	Kenya	United Kingdom	France
Ireland	Morocco	West Germany	Netherlands
Lebanon	Zimbabwe		Soviet Union
Mexico			Sweden
Nigeria			Tunisia
Pakistan			United States
Philippines			
Sudan			

[1]When a woman's life would be endangered by carrying the child to term; some countries in this category prohibit abortion without exception. [2]Such as a threat to the woman's overall health, and sometimes in the case of fetal abnormality, rape, or incest. [3]Social factors, such as insufficient income, poor housing, or marital status, may be considered in evaluating a "threat" to the woman's health, or may be deemed sufficient conditions in and of themselves to warrant termination of a pregnancy. [4]Countries in this category have liberal abortion laws, commonly known as "on request," which indicates the lack of legal obstacles to abortion but not necessarily the lack of social or administrative ones.

Source: Rebecca J. Cook, "Abortion Laws and Policies: Challenges and Opportunities," *International Journal of Gynecology and Obstetrics*, Supplement 3, 1989.

new categories, such as adolescence, advanced maternal age, or infection with the AIDS virus, as a basis for legal abortion. Cyprus, Italy, and Taiwan, for instance, all broadened their regulations to consider "family welfare," while Hong Kong included adolescence as a valid consideration.[8]

France and the Netherlands added clauses pertaining to pregnancy-related distress. In Hungary, one of the first East European countries to liberalize its laws (in 1956), abortion rights have been extended to women who are single or who have been separated from their husbands for up to six months, to women over 35 who have had at least three previous deliveries, and to women caught in economic hardship, such as the lack of appropriate housing.[9]

Most people in the world now live in countries that have moved from blanket prohibition of abortion to a more reasoned acceptance of its role as a backup to contraceptive failure and unwanted pregnancy. The

Table 2. Abortion Laws Worldwide, by Number of Countries and Share of World Population

Legal Conditions	Countries[1]	Share of World Population
	(number)	(percent)
Life Endangerment[2]	53	25
Other Maternal Health Reasons	42	12
Social and Socio-Medical Reasons	14	23
No Mandated Conditions[3]	23	40

[1]Countries with populations of at least 1 million. [2]Technically, in some countries in this category abortion is prohibited without exception. [3]Includes some of the world's most populous countries (China, the Soviet Union, and the United States).

Source: Stanley K. Henshaw, "Induced Abortion: A World Review, 1990," *Family Planning Perspectives*, March/April 1990.

Alan Guttmacher Institute (AGI) indicates that about 40 percent of the world's population in theory has access to induced abortion on request. (See Table 2.)

Again, laws in countries grouped in the same category vary widely. In Tunisia—one of the few Muslim countries with liberalized laws—abortion is legally available on request until viability, while in France abortions on request are sanctioned only through the first trimester. Other countries with similar on-request status through varying stages of gestation are Canada, China, the Soviet Union, the United States, and virtually all of Eastern and Western Europe.[10]

Adding the share of the world covered by social or maternal health indications—including India, with its 835 million people—brings the total to 75 percent (nearly 4 billion people) who are governed by laws that permit abortion on medical or broader social and economic grounds. Included in this second group, it should be noted, however, are countries like Ethiopia and Costa Rica, where abortion is legal only in cases of risk to the woman's health.[11]

Another 20 percent of the world lives in 49 countries that have resisted liberalization and still totally prohibit abortion, except in some cases to save the woman's life, while the remaining 5 percent (in four other countries) is governed by laws that add rape and incest to this restrictive set of conditions. One in four women in the world, therefore, has little access to abortion—and she is likely to live in Africa, Latin America, or Muslim Asia, where she also has the least access to safe, affordable means of contraception to prevent unwanted pregnancy.[12]

Roadblocks to Access

Access to abortion and other family planning services, like health care in general, is determined by four variables: laws, policies and the way they are interpreted, the commitment of public funds to provide services, and personal resources, particularly money. Control over many of these factors—from the enforced shortage of available facilities to the personal views of physicians— is used by opponents of abortion rights to limit access to services.

Interpretations of laws are often as important as the statutes themselves in determining the availability of abortions. Stanley K. Henshaw, deputy director of research at AGI, finds that "in most Muslim countries, and in Latin America and Africa, few legal abortions are performed under the health exception, while in Israel, New Zealand and South Korea, the legal abortion rates [under the health indication] are comparable to those in countries that allow abortion on request."[13]

In many countries where women should be able to get an abortion on demand, they find it difficult to exercise their legal rights for a variety of reasons, including stricter-than-usual medical regulations, burdensome administrative requirements, lack of public funds for services, lack of information or referral networks, lack of trained providers, extreme centralization of services, and local opposition or reluctance to enforce national laws.

Access is determined in part by medical regulations governing how, where, and by whom services can be provided. In most countries with liberal laws, abortions must generally be performed by licensed providers (though not necessarily physicians), a regulation that safeguards public health. Some countries take this one step further, however, by requiring that the operations be carried out only in designated hospitals or centers, or by highly trained specialists.

These and other laws often work against the goal of ensuring that abortions are carried out at the earliest possible point. New laws in Bermuda, Qatar, and the Seychelles, while more liberal than the former ones, include hospital committee authorization requirements before an abortion can be performed. In most cases, these regulations, strongly supported by opponents of abortion rights, act only to delay abortion until later stages of pregnancy— when procedures are riskier and the fetus more developed. Unfortunately, several American states are considering such restrictions.[14]

These institutional and third-party authorization requirements have come under legal attack in many countries, and have been overturned in the courts or defeated in legislatures in several, including Canada and Czechoslovakia. In 1988, the Canadian Supreme Court struck down that nation's standing abortion law, which required that terminations be performed only in hospitals and that women receive the permission of a hospital authorization committee. Among other findings, the Court stated that the delays in procuring abortions resulting from these administrative requirements interfered with "a woman's right to physical and bodily integrity."[15]

The lack of a government or public commitment to provide or fund services can severely undermine legal rights. Abortion became legal on broad grounds in India in 1971. But because registered practitioners are clustered in urban areas, rural women have little access to services. Survey data from 1984 showed that only about 1,000 out of a total of 15,000 physicians trained to perform abortions were living in rural areas, although 78 percent of the country's population falls in this category.[16]

Not surprisingly, just 388,000 of the estimated 4 million to 6 million abortions in India were carried out legally in government-regulated facilities. Were the Indian government to commit funds to expanding the number of outlets for reproductive health care, literally millions of women could avoid the dangers of illegal terminations.[17]

In Turkey, abortion is in theory available on request through the 10th week of pregnancy. But Turkish law states that an abortion may be carried out only by or under the supervision of a gynecological specialist trained in such procedures, as opposed to, say, a general practitioner or a trained paramedic.[18]

The scarcity of trained specialists even in urban areas limits access. In rural Turkey, where medical services of any kind are generally hard to come by, such services are virtually nonexistent. Many potential outlets—health clinics staffed by medical personnel but without a trained specialist—are excluded from delivering services. Rural women without the information and financial resources to reach a doctor in a city are left with the choice of having an illegal abortion or carrying the pregnancy to term.

The many roadblocks to access are illustrated by the situation in Zambia, a country with one of the most liberal laws in Africa. Abortions are legal through the 12th week of pregnancy on broad grounds, but they may only be performed in a hospital setting. What is more, to get permission for a legal abortion a woman must obtain the signatures of three physicians (one of them a specialist) on a form that lists her previous births and abortions. The physicians must agree on one of three grounds for termination of the pregnancy—a medical condition of either the woman or the fetus or a nonmedical condition that justifies termination.[19]

Despite the relatively liberal law, illegal abortions far outnumber legal ones in Zambia. First, the administrative requirements are neither widely known nor understood, especially among rural women. In fact, several Zambian doctors interviewed by Renee Holt, a nurse and lawyer who studies abortion trends, believe that "many Zambian women are not [even] aware of their right to an abortion and visit backstreet abortionists rather than a hospital." Second, the requirements themselves are virtually impossible to fulfill: Only three specialists in the entire country—one of whom now lives in Kenya—are legally empowered to sign the forms. Only one hospital in Lusaka performs the operation; sanctioned facilities—and hence legal abortions—virtually do not exist elsewhere.[20]

Holt reports that "obstetricians and gynecologists at the University Teaching Hospital (UTH) did not have enough operating time to perform all abortions requested. They were turning away half of the requests each day, and these were returning to UTH as incomplete or septic [infected] abortions, which then demanded their time [to save the woman's life], setting up a vicious cycle." Small wonder, then, that even Zambian women aware of their legal rights resort to illegal practitioners.[21]

Conversely, in some countries where abortion is illegal in principle it is carried out quite freely in practice. Such "lapsed law" countries include Brazil, Egypt, Indonesia, Mexico, Nigeria, and Thailand. In Colombia, abortions are technically legal only in cases where the woman's life is in danger. Observers note, however, that safe, dependable, and affordable services are available in most urban areas, and are freely advertised in local newspapers and on billboards. In Bogotá, private clinics provide comprehensive reproductive health services, including prenatal care, contraceptive counseling, and abortion. In fact, in at least one area local policewomen are on hand to escort neighborhood clients to a clinic.[22]

Access to abortion in Colombia is enhanced by the tacit or active willingness of a government to overlook restrictive legislation, which serves to placate opponents of legal abortion. It is essential to note, however, that in Colombia—as in several other countries where a blind eye is similarly turned—extreme inequalities persist in who can get safe services, and the incidence of illegal abortion remains high. Low-income rural women are particularly disadvantaged in not having the resources—the connections, education, money—to gain access to or information on safe abortions.[23]

Money is among the most critical factors in securing safe abortions, especially where laws are prohibitive. In Mexico, for example, access to safe procedures is restricted even when legally indicated under the country's narrow but ambiguous law. Safe services can be obtained in urban areas—for a price. The cost for medical abortions ranges from $215 to $644. Even the lower estimate is more than twice the monthly minimum wage of $103. According to one report, "many experts believe that safe medical abortion is now beyond the reach of the middle class."[24]

The resolution of a number of issues now under debate throughout the world could have a negative effect on abortion rights by restricting access. Those being considered are when and to what extent government health care programs should cover the costs of legal procedures, whether a husband's consent or notification should be required before a married woman can obtain an abortion, and whether laws should require parental notification or consent in the case of adolescents. Placing limits on access is only one part of a broader attack on legalized abortion. A glance beneath the surface waters of liberalization reveals a strong undertow tugging at recently codified reproductive rights.

Opponents of abortion rights, dismayed at the extent of legalization, have devised a three-pronged strategy. First, they seek to reinstate restrictive policies in countries where they have been liberalized—Canada, France, Italy, Poland, Spain, the United States, and Germany, to name a few. Second, they aim to maintain or reinstate restrictions in the Third World by supporting the growth of parallel movements there. Third, they are using legal and economic stoppers to plug every hole in the dam restricting access to services. This movement has scored some significant successes since 1977, most notably in countries where laws have been made considerably more restrictive.

Finland and Israel, for example, made their liberal laws more restrictive, while Iran and Ireland have forbidden abortions altogether. A Honduran law permitting abortions in cases where they would protect the life and health of the mother and in cases of rape and fetal deformity was rejected because it was perceived to conflict with constitutional provisions stating that the "right to life is inviolable." Changes in the constitutions of Ecuador (1978) and the Philippines (1986) incorporated provisions giving the right to life "from the moment of conception."[25]

In July 1989, the United States—a country with one of the world's most liberal policies—took a step backward on reproductive rights. The U.S. Supreme Court's ruling in *Webster v. Reproductive Services* in effect gave the green light to those states seeking to regulate abortion procedures strictly. In *Webster,* the court threw out the trimester framework of viability established in the landmark 1973 *Roe v. Wade* decision, which permitted states to regulate abortions only after the first trimester and to ban them only in the last.[26]

The case upheld the State of Missouri's law that physicians must carry out extensive tests for viability before performing abortions after 20 weeks. Furthermore, *Webster* severely curtailed access to services in that state by upholding Missouri's ban on the use of public facilities for the operation. Since then, restrictive laws of various shades have been introduced in a number of state legislatures, although only a few have been passed.

Global trends in abortion politics are both reflected in and fueled by events in the United States. The U.S. decision in *Webster,* a major success of the so-called pro-life movement, sent shock waves through ranks of activists in Western Europe. The abortion debate there has been far less emotional than in the United States but is becoming more polarized. Europeans from both camps have described the decision as a "wind from the west."[27]

The struggle over abortion rights is now an international affair, with money and anti-abortion protestors crossing the Atlantic from the United States. Moreover, a broader global effort to repeal or restrict abortion rights is being coordinated by the U.S.-based umbrella group Human Life International, which has set up branch offices in 31 countries. Its agenda in developing countries focuses on restricting abortion rather than providing couples with the means to prevent unintended pregnancies. Yet studies show that millions of Third World couples still lack access to contraceptives. Not surprisingly, poor women in these countries already suffer the highest rates of death due to complications of pregnancy and illegal abortion.

A Sense of Scale

Broadly speaking, abortion rates are governed by the cultural and economic pressures about family size in a given society and the mix of laws and policies that determine access to family planning. The numbers of illegal versus legal procedures in a given country, the degree to which pregnancy termination is used to regulate fertility, and the demographic makeup of the groups relying most heavily on this method are all shaped by social and economic pressures to limit or delay childbearing, by the availability and reliability of contraceptives, and by the legal, cultural, and political climate that surrounds abortion services.[28]

Abortion rates tend to be low where desired family size is large and fertility rates are limited only by traditional practices such as heavy reliance on breastfeeding and postpartum abstinence. In rapidly modernizing societies, however, changes in the status of women, in levels of education and income, and in the composition of the work force, among other things, lead to equally rapid changes in desired family size.

As the number of children that they prefer falls, couples look for ways to avoid or terminate unwanted pregnancies. Abortion rates then tend to rise rapidly (irrespective of the legal status), especially if there is no strong tradition of contraceptive use or if contraceptives are not widely available. It is at this point in the transition that abortion's effect on birth rates is highest.

Although rates of contraceptive use and abortion may rise together for a while, eventually the latter peaks and begins to decline. In South Korea, for instance, both rates rose rapidly from the late sixties throughout the seventies, reflecting an increasing desire for smaller families. But between 1979 and 1985, the rate of adoption of contraceptives continued to climb, while the abortion rate fell back to the level of 1973. Induced abortion clearly played a major role in South Korea's fertility transition: without it birth rates would have been some 22 percent higher in that period.[29]

In this way, abortion has played an integral though varied role in the transition from high to low fertility in virtually every country that has to date achieved replacement-level fertility (approximately two children per family). The transition to lower abortion rates and birth rates is slowed wherever access to family planning information and supplies is limited.

True to the pattern, the incidence of abortion has declined most rapidly in those countries where legalized abortion has been included as part of truly comprehensive voluntary family planning services—among the few to note are Denmark, France, Iceland, Italy, and the Netherlands. But in contrast, in societies on the cusp or in the process of this transition throughout Africa, Asia, and Latin America, illegal abortion is now widely relied upon to limit famiy size, though at a tremendous price in women's lives and health.[30]

Based on available data about legal procedures, abortion appears to rank fourth in terms of birth control methods used, behind female sterilization, intra-uterine devices, and oral contraceptives. Use of these other methods, however, is heavily concentrated in China, India, and the industrial nations, whereas abortion is relied on everywhere.[31]

Estimates of the number of illegal abortions and maternal deaths for individual developing countries are generally drawn from hospital- or community-based studies that offer but a fragmented picture of the real situation.

In both Bangladesh and Brazil, for example, demographic studies indicate that 20–35 percent of all pregnancies are aborted. Yet because of legal restrictions, bureaucratic indifference, and social disapproval, abortion in these countries is largely undocumented and clandestine.[32]

In fact, so few countries keep accurate statistics on abortion that the omission itself has political implications of tremendous import. If society remains ignorant of the number of legal versus illegal procedures, if the number of women who die or are physically impaired due to illegal abortions remains unknown, if the costs in terms of health and productivity (not to mention individual freedom) remain untallied, then there is no empirical basis on which to challenge opponents of abortion rights. In effect, the pathetically poor quality of data narrows the debate on which set of societal and individual priorities should prevail.

Despite the lack of hard numbers, several researchers have made estimates based on available evidence, from which a number of conclusions about trends at the global and regional level can be drawn. Demographers calculate that from a third to half of all women of reproductive age undergo at least one induced abortion in their lifetimes. According to calculations by Stanley Henshaw of the Alan Guttmacher Institute, some 36–51 million abortions were performed worldwide in 1987. He estimates the annual number of illegal procedures at 10–20 million, leaving from 26–31 million legal ones. Other estimates put the total number at between 40 million and 60 million. Using either set of figures implies close to one induced abortion for every two to three births worldwide.[33]

Comparisons of trends within and between countries are made using abortion rates, the number of procedures per 1,000 women of reproductive age. Again, lack of data for many countries makes true comparisons difficult. But by using figures from countries with reliable statistics as well as figures adjusted for illegal abortions in those without data, a sketch can be drawn of regional and national trends.

In many countries, abortion has become the primary method of family planning as a direct result of government policies (or lack of them) that result in limited access to contraception. The connection is made plain by the situation in Eastern Europe and the Soviet Union, where a "contraceptive iron curtain" has hung for decades.[34]

With the exceptions of Albania (which retains restrictive policies) and of the former East Germany and Yugoslavia (which liberalized their laws in the seventies), abortion laws were changed in most of Eastern Europe in the fifties, making legal a practice that was already widespread. Few of these governments, however, concurrently made the availability of contraceptive information or supplies a priority; consequently, couples continued to rely on less effective methods, such as withdrawal, using abortion as a backup.[35]

This pattern held as social ills, economic hardship—evident in housing shortages and long lines for basic rations—and environmental deterioration reinforced the strong desire of East Europeans to limit the size of their families. With virtually only one way to achieve this goal, throughout the

Table 3. **Legal Abortion Rates, Selected East European Countries, 1987**

Country	Abortions
	(per thousand women aged 15–44)
Bulgaria	65
Czechoslovakia	47
East Germany[1]	27
Hungary	38
Romania[2]	91
Yugoslavia[1]	71

[1]1984 data. [2]Includes official estimates of illegal abortion.

Source: Stanley K. Henshaw, "Induced Abortion: A World Review, 1990," *Family Planning Perspectives*, March/April 1990.

sixties and seventies rates of induced abortion in the region were the highest recorded in the world. Even today, abortion rates in most of Eastern Europe are high for women throughout their reproductive years. (See Table 3.)[36]

The lack of effective contraceptives in the Soviet Union has led to heavy reliance on abortion there. The nation has some 70 million women of childbearing age yet not a single factory producing modern contraceptives, except the poor-quality condoms widely disparaged as "galoshes." Writing in the Soviet magazine *Ogonyok*, medical researcher Andrei Popov states that "the way out [of unwanted pregnancies] is well-known—abortions . . . child abandonment [and] infanticide."[37]

Abortions are available throughout the Soviet Union on demand and at low cost. And the average Soviet woman, who terminates between five and seven pregnancies during her reproductive years, will likely take advantage of the system at some time. Still, administrative and technological barriers combined with public disapproval drive the majority of women to obtain what are essentially illegal procedures that they must pay for out of pocket. Many are reluctant to request state-funded abortions because, by law, the procedure must be recorded in work and health documents.[38]

It is clear the Soviet Union's share of total abortions worldwide is large; what is less clear is just what that share is. Official statistics put the number of terminations in 1987 at nearly 7 million, well in excess of the 6 million recorded live births; official rates were 100 per 1,000 women of reproductive age in 1985. Estimates made by independent researchers imply the true numbers are far higher. Henshaw calculates that possibly 11 million abortions are performed annually. Demographer Tomas Frejka, citing estimates of 13 million unauthorized procedures, claims the number could approach 20 million, a figure close to one put forward by Murray Feshbach, a researcher on Soviet health at Georgetown University.[39]

Three East European countries—Czechoslovakia, the former East Germany, and Hungary—apparently kept their abortion rates relatively low by encouraging widespread contraceptive practice. Hungary, for example, relied on a campaign that included dissemination and education on the use of modern contraceptives. Between 1966 and the late seventies, the share of Hungarian women using modern contraceptives increased dramatically, leading to a substantial decline in terminations. In the words of Henry David, Director of the U.S.-based Transnational Family Research Institute, Hungary went from being "an abortion culture" to one relying on education and modern contraception.[40]

In Latin America, abortion rates have been consistently high for over two decades, despite quite restrictive laws and the firm opposition of the Catholic church to any kind of modern family planning. Indeed, there is evidence of a long tradition of induced abortion in the region. In 1551, the King of Spain was notified that the indigenous population in his Venezuelan colony practiced induced abortion, through the use of medicinal herbs, to prevent their children from being born into slavery.[41]

During the seventies, the International Planned Parenthood Federation estimated that abortion rates in Latin America and the Caribbean were higher than in any other developing region: an estimated one fourth of all pregnancies in Latin America were intentionally aborted in that period, compared with estimates of less than 10 percent in Africa and 15–20 percent in South and Southeast Asia.[42]

Fertility rates have fallen since the sixties, but the desire for even smaller families is strong throughout the region. Data from the World Fertility Survey in the seventies showed that while the average family contained at least four children, over half the women interviewed wanted to have only two to four. And over half the women with three children in all Latin American countries except Paraguay wanted no more.[43]

Because political and religious opposition has kept contraceptive outlets to a minimum, the number of illegal abortions is high and shows no signs of falling in the near future. Experts put the total in excess of 5 million, but some claim the number in Brazil alone may surpass 4 million.[44]

Tracking illegal abortions in Latin America is difficult at best. Tomas Frejka reports that "a large proportion of the induced abortions are performed in violation of existing laws and [providers] have a vested interest not to report them. Even after the fact, women tend to deny having had an abortion, and health personnel who treat abortion complications will under-report cases . . . to avoid involvement with the law." A hospital study in Campinas, Brazil, for instance, found maternal deaths due to abortion were underreported by 40 percent.[45]

Today, induced abortion continues to account for about one fourth of total fertility control in Latin America. Although use of contraceptives has been increasing steadily since the sixties, it is still relatively low and supplies remain unevenly distributed throughout the region. Access to services is unequal: those most at risk of unwanted pregnancy—teens, the unmarried, and low-income women—are those for whom contraceptives and safe abortion services are most out of reach. Rates of contraceptive failure are still high, too. Frejka claims that "the incidence of induced abortion in Latin America will remain high, at least through the 1990s, even if its legislation continues to be restrictive. [This] situation implies serious reproductive health, and economic as well as social, problems for a large number of women and their families."[46]

A similar picture is developing in Africa, where the number of induced abortions and the related health and social costs of illegal or clandestine procedures are likely to continue rising for at least the next decade. The predominantly young population is characterized by high fertility and low rates of contraceptive use. Access to both contraceptives and safe abortion services is limited geographically and by income. Although fertility rates in Africa are among the highest in the world, the desire to limit family size is growing.

Yet laws circumscribing reproductive rights in Africa, inherited from colonial governments, remain largely intact. Among the former British colonies, for instance, only Zambia has liberalized its law. Francophone Africa lags even further behind in this regard. In addition to criminalizing abortion, the French law of 1920 outlawed the sale, distribution, and advertisement of all contraceptives. Only Burundi, Togo, and the Seychelles among the Francophone countries have liberalized their laws enough to allow abortions for social indications.[47]

Social and cultural limitations on women in Africa are an equally important factor, and may be much harder to change than laws. Nolwandle Nozipo Mashalaba, a private family practitioner in Botswana, sees the lack of communication between African couples on matters of sexuality and the desire to maintain male dominance within the household as the primary roadblocks to preventing pregnancies that women themselves may not want. She notes that where "men migrate . . . for work, they keep the wife in a continuous state of pregnancy and lactation as a way to keep her (possible) infidelity to a minimum."[48]

Studies show that these and other constraints can hamper contraceptive use even where knowledge of modern methods is high. A 1984 survey in Botswana found that more than 70 percent of women in both rural and urban areas knew at least one modern method of family planning; a more recent survey in Zimbabwe indicated that 9 out of 10 knew at least one method and the majority were familiar with five or more. But a number of factors—including the inaccessibility of clinics, fear and anxiety over side effects, ineffective counseling, and the lack of programs for men—keep rates of contraceptive use well under 15 percent throughout most of Africa. Illegal abortion, in Mashalaba's words, is "the only solution."[49]

In Asia, abortion rates are high regardless of the law. Indonesia provides a classic example of the inevitable clash between rapidly changing social values and restrictive legal codes. According to Indonesian researchers Ninuk Widyantoro and Sarsanto W. Sarwono, rates of both abortion and contraceptive use in the country are climbing rapidly, indicating that "couples desire much smaller families than traditionally prevailed." They estimate that between 750,000 and 1 million abortions are performed annually.[50]

The legal status of the procedure has long been cloudy in Indonesia. A profusion of laws and morals concerning abortion and other family planning methods reflects the country's diverse national heritage, drawn from the traditions of indigenous ethnic groups melded together with the mores and practices of Buddhism, Christianity, Hinduism, Islam, and former Dutch colonizers. In the seventies, high rates of maternal illness and death from unsafe procedures prompted the members of the medical community to seek clarification of the welter of statutes from the Indonesian High Court.[51]

Although abortion was not then technically liberalized, nor has its status changed since, the court's decision that "procedures could not be regarded as illegal if they were carried out within the framework of normal medical practice by specialists and doctors" paved the way for an increase in trained providers. Since then, access to safe services has improved. Many doctors, although mainly in urban areas, have been trained in the use of and provided with vacuum aspiration equipment. Moreover, the Indonesian government has made a major commitment to increasing access to contraceptive information and supplies. Still, Widyantoro and Sarwono estimate that due to unequal access, social ambivalence about abortion, and lack of information on services, perhaps as many as 800,000 illegal abortions are carried out each year, "with many more unsuccessful attempted terminations going unnoticed." As a result, complication and fatality rates remain high.[52]

Looking at the pattern of induced abortions in various nations according to age, marital status, educational level, and current family size provides an indication of which demographic groups have the greatest numbers of unwanted pregnancies, and even suggests who has least access to effective, affordable, and acceptable contraceptives. In most industrial countries, for example, as in Canada and the United States, abortion rates tend to be highest among teenagers and women aged 20–24, groups that seek to delay childbearing either because of their marital status (single) or for other reasons, such as the desire to complete their education. (See Table 4.)

Making sex education and contraceptives more available to these groups lowers their abortion rates. The Transnational Family Research Institute compared approaches to family planning in Denmark and the United States to see how different strategies can result in different rates of unintended pregnancy and abortion among particular demographic groups.[53]

The Institute found that inability to pay limits access to contraceptives more often in the United States than in Denmark, especially among those groups most at risk of unwanted pregnancy. In the absence of national health insurance, women rely largely on private physicians to obtain contraceptives, and many are disadvantaged by cost constraints, their ineligibility for public assistance, or their place of residence.[54]

Data show that 17 percent of American women with low incomes lack health insurance of any kind; this group includes one fourth of women under

Table 4. Legal Abortion Rates by Age of Woman, Selected Countries, Most Recent Year

Country	19 or Younger	20–24	25–29	30–34	35–39	40 or Older
	(legal abortions per thousand women in age group)					
Canada	15	19	12	8	5	2
East Germany	17	26	31	31	24	11
England/Wales	21	24	16	11	7	3
Hungary	26	45	47	46	41	22
Tunisia	1	13	27	36	31	16
United States	46	52	31	18	10	3

Source: Stanley K. Henshaw, "Induced Abortion: A World Review, 1990," *Family Planning Perspectives*, March/April 1990.

25, one fourth of unmarried women, and one third of women whose incomes fell below 150 percent of the federal poverty level—all groups with the highest rates of unwanted pregnancy and abortion. Many of these women cannot afford to purchase contraceptives. In Denmark, by contrast, national health insurance provides contraceptives, counseling, and pre- and postpregnancy health care for everyone, regardless of income.[55]

Federally funded family planning clinics do exist in the United States, but a lack of political commitment has kept their budgets spare, leading to limited hours, long waits for appointments, and a narrower menu of services offered. Moreover, services have been declining in the wake of recent budget cuts: less than half as much funding was made available to these clinics in fiscal year 1989 than in 1981.[56]

Danish family planning programs focus on preventing unwanted pregnancies to the greatest extent possible by making contraceptive services universally available, even to teenagers. The results are clear. Today, pregnancy rates among Danish teens are less than half those in the United States. Abortion rates among women age 15–19 fell by nearly half between 1977 and 1985. (See Table 5.)

The situation regarding teen access to contraceptives in the United States is vastly different. Proposals for starting U.S. programs similar to those in Denmark are hotly contested. As a result, rates of teenage pregnancy and of abortion in the United States well exceed those of other industrial countries, even though the ages at which teens first experience sex are comparable.[57]

The growing disparity between low rates of contraceptive use and increasing desires to limit family size—the unmet need for family planning that is evident throughout the Third World—is a sure prescription for even higher rates of illegal abortion. Regional surveys suggest that 50–60 percent of couples in Latin America, 60–80 percent in low-income Asian countries

Table 5.   Teen Abortion Rates, United States and Denmark,
           1977–85

Year	United States	Denmark
	(abortions per thousand women aged 15–19)	
1977	37	25
1978	40	24
1979	42	22
1980	43	23
1981	43	20
1982	43	18
1983	43	18
1984	43	17
1985	44	16

Source: Henry P. David et al., "United States and Denmark: Different Approaches to Health Care and Family Planning," *Studies in Family Planning*, January/February 1990.

(except China), 75 percent in the Middle East and North Africa, and 90 percent of sub-Saharan Africa do not use any form of modern contraception. On the other hand, the same studies show that a majority of couples in Latin America and Asia—and a growing percentage throughout the Middle East and Africa—wish to space the timing or limit the number of their children.[58]

In most developing countries, abortion rates are highest among married women with several children who have little means of preventing additional, unwanted pregnancies. In Latin America, abortion rates among women over 35 are twice those for women age 20–34; the rate among women with five or more children is more than twice that for women with only one. A clinic-based study from Allahabad, India, found that a large majority of women seeking abortions were married, between 20 and 29, and that most had several children already. Studies in Indonesia documented almost identical results—the majority of clients were married, had two to three children, and were over 25.[59]

It is commonly believed that abortion in Africa is used primarily by women in their teens and early twenties who want to delay childbearing. This fits with the social and demographic makeup of urban areas, for example, where higher levels of education and broader opportunities for women encourage a desire to delay marriage and childbearing. Data from Nairobi bear this out: 79 percent of the induced abortion patients in one hospital study were young, single women.[60]

But additional data point to the growing reliance on abortion here as well of older women with several children, especially in rural areas. In Tunisia, for instance, rates are highest among women age 25–39. A sample in Nigeria showed that 30 percent of complications from abortion in one hospital were reported in women over 25; of all the women, 52 percent had two or more children.[61]

Likewise, a Kenyan study found that 46 percent of abortion patients had one to three children, 22 percent had four to six, and 7 percent had seven or more. Under increasing social and economic stress, more married women are turning to abortion as their primary means of birth control. The striking implication of this finding is that the unmet need for family planning in Africa may be far higher than is currently assumed. If this is true, then the need to improve access to contraceptives, the safety of abortion services, and general reproductive health care throughout Africa—especially to stave off a precipitous rise in illegal operations not to mention to reduce fertility—is far more urgent than the spending and policy priorities of most African governments indicate.[62]

Abortion trends throughout the developing world could be predicted from what is known about the downward pressure on birth rates created by economic growth and rising incomes. But evidence is mounting that quite a different process is at work. A growing share of the world's population lives in poverty, and inequalities in income, housing, and access to social services are increasing. These trends have been exacerbated by consistently high levels of international debt, widespread environmental degradation, and a pattern of development that has relentlessly ignored the needs and priorities of women.

The Invisible Plague

Each year, according to WHO, at least a half-million women worldwide die from pregnancy-related causes. Of these, roughly 200,000 lose their lives as a result of an illegal abortion, most of which are performed by unskilled attendants under unsanitary conditions or are self-inflicted with hangers, knitting needles, toxic herbal teas, and the like. In terms of sheer numbers, more than half the abortion-related deaths worldwide occur in South and Southeast Asia, followed by sub-Saharan Africa, and then Latin America and the Caribbean. And for every woman who dies, 30–40 more suffer serious, often lifelong health problems—among them hemorrhaging, infection, abdominal or intestinal perforations, kidney failure, and permanent infertility—that affect their ability to provide for themselves and for any children they already have.[63]

Here again, simple public recognition of problems related to women's health is stymied by lack of accurate data to assess and publicize the true extent of the problem. Reliable statistics on the incidence of induced abortion and related maternal mortality rates are available from only a handful of countries—the United States and most European countries are among those keeping accurate statistics. Even data from WHO are incomplete.

Perhaps the most distressing fact about abortion-related deaths and illnesses is that the vast majority of complications that lead to these outcomes are totally preventable. What consigns so many women around the world to death or physical impairment is not a deficiency in technology, but a deficiency in the value placed on women's lives. Technologically simple, inexpensive, easy-to-use tools for safe early abortion are well known, and widely used in some countries. But social intransigence, religious intolerance, economic self-interest, and political apathy all narrow the options for millions of women. Society's message to these women is, in effect, "carry this unwanted pregnancy or risk your life to end it."

Because of the social stigma of abortion, the dispersion of medical technologies for safe procedures is held back even while progress is made on other forms of health care. According to Julie DeClerque of the International Projects Assistance Services (IPAS), "data on infant mortality and hospital admissions for abortion complications in Santiago, Chile over a 20-year period show that while infant mortality dropped by over half, hospitalization from abortion complications increased by over 60 percent."[64]

Equally disturbing is the resounding silence on the part of international bodies concerned with health and development—the World Bank and the U.S. Agency for International Development, to name two—about the human and economic costs of illegal abortion. Abortion-related deaths and illness are to them an invisible plague.

The number of abortion deaths is a direct reflection of access to safe services. WHO studies in various settings indicate that the share of maternal deaths caused by induced abortion ranges from 7 percent to more than 50. On average, between 20 and 25 percent of maternal mortality is attributable to illegal or clandestine abortion. In Latin America, complications of illegal abortion are thought to be the main cause of death in women between the ages of 15 and 39.[65]

Abortion-related deaths are estimated to reach 1,000 per 100,000 illegal abortions in some parts of Africa, as opposed to less than 1 death per 100,000 legal procedures in the United States. Hospital admissions in African cities, virtually the only available indicator of abortion trends, are rising in tandem with reliance on abortion as a method of birth control. Khama Rogo, a medical doctor and faculty member at the University of Nairobi, indicates that admissions of women suffering from complications of illegal abortions have risen 600–800 percent at Nairobi's Kenyatta National Hospital over the past decade. He estimates that in 1990 more than 74,000 African women may have died following an illegal termination.[66]

Rogo notes that in East and Central Africa at least 20 percent of all maternal deaths are due to complications of induced abortion, and that the share has reached 54 percent in Ethiopia. He suspects that "gross underreporting" of abortion cases may be responsible for the fact that studies in several West African hospitals imply overall maternal death rates from abortion of only 10 percent.[67]

Hospitals in many developing countries are literally inundated with women seeking treatment for complications of illegal abortion. Over 30 percent of the beds in the gynecological and obstetric wards of most urban hospitals in Latin America are filled with women suffering abortion complications. At Mama Yemo hospital in Kinshasa, Zaire, and at the Kenyatta National Hospital in Nairobi, Kenya, some 60 percent of all gynecological cases fall in this same category. And at a hospital in Accra, Ghana, between 60 and 80 percent of all minor surgery performed relates to the after-effects of illegal abortions; in 1977, half that hospital's blood supply was allocated to related transfusions.[68]

From a fifth to half of all maternal deaths worldwide could be prevented by providing access to safe abortion services. No international effort to accomplish this is on the horizon, but in a few countries individual groups are working to furnish the technical means and training to deal more efficiently, at least, with complications. IPAS, for one, has been working in sub-Saharan Africa to train clinicians in safe use of the manual vacuum aspiration technique. Use of this in the treatment of incomplete abortions has reduced the time needed to treat women suffering from poorly executed operations, and lowered their risk of hemorrhage and infection. Pilot projects at hospitals in both Kenya and Nigeria have yielded "a great savings in health resources," according to Ann Leonard of IPAS.[69]

Each roadblock to safe abortion raises the social costs of illegal procedures severalfold. Illegal abortions drain health resources. Complications from them require treatments that are in short supply. A study of 617 women suffering abortion complications who were admitted to 10 hospitals in Zaire found that 95 percent required antibiotics, 62 percent anesthetics, and 17 percent transfusions. Oftentimes, hospital supplies in Africa are so scarce that women must go to the local pharmacy and provide their own antibiotics—or not receive treatment. The increased competition for health resources posed by the growing numbers of illegal abortions in Africa will make coping with another health crisis there—AIDS—that much more difficult.[70]

A recent accounting by the Alan Guttmacher Institute of U.S. national and state expenditures on contraceptive counseling and supplies hints at the broad social costs of unwanted births. AGI estimated that every dollar spent to provide contraceptive services to women who might otherwise find it difficult or impossible to obtain them without help saved $4.40. In 1987, a total of $412 million was spent by federal and state governments for family planning. The study's authors calculated that without this funding about 1.2 million more unintended pregnancies would have occurred nationwide, leading to 509,000 mistimed or unwanted births and 516,000 abortions. Averting these unwanted pregnancies saved $1.8 billion that would otherwise have been spent on medical and nutritional services and on welfare payments.[71]

From Crime to Common Sense

The impact of unwanted pregnancy embraces but extends beyond the individual to encompass broader objectives, including the struggle for women to become equal partners in society and efforts to improve health among women and children. Less well recognized but equally important is the role that abortion plays in the transition from high to low fertility.

An international consensus among a diverse body of policymakers already exists on the adverse effects of rapid population growth on economic performance, the environment, family welfare, health, and political stability. For reasons of politics, many of these same leaders shy away from or ignore the role played by abortion in slowing birth rates. Yet as public health researchers Stephen Mumford and Elton Kessel note, "no nation wanting to reduce its growth to less than 1 percent can expect to do so without the widespread use of abortion." Policymakers who call for slower population growth while remaining silent on the issue of access to safe abortion are willing to achieve this goal at a high price in women's lives.[72]

The tremendous social gains to be reaped from eliminating illegal abortions cannot be ignored. First among them is a reduction in abortion-related maternal mortality of at least 25 percent and in related illnesses of far more. Reductions in illegal abortions and unwanted pregnancies would save billions in social and health care costs, freeing these resources for other uses.

Only by increasing access to family planning information and supplies, offering couples a wider and safer array of contraceptives, and improving the delivery of comprehensive reproductive health care services can the number of abortions be reduced. Some countries have already chosen this commonsense approach. Italy, for instance, now requires local and regional health authorities to promote contraceptive services and other measures to reduce the demand for abortion, while Czech law aims to prevent terminations through sex education in schools and health facilities and through the provision of free contraceptives and associated care. Some countries now require postabortion contraceptive counseling and education; some mandate programs for men as well.[73]

Many of these efforts register success quickly. On the Swedish Island of Gotland, for example, abortions were nearly halved in an intensive three-year program to provide information and improved family planning services. Similar results have been seen in France and elsewhere.[74]

The steps needed to make these gains universal are plain. Decriminalization and clarification of laws governing abortion would secure the rights of couples around the world to plan the size and spacing of their families safely. Policies that put abortion into the context of public health and family planning would immediately reduce the incidence of illegal operations. Removal of the administrative, financial, and geographic roadblocks to access both to safe abortions and to family planning services in general would reduce overall abortion rates and further improve public health.

While the way is evident, the will is lacking. The missing ingredient is political commitment. Natural allies—representatives of groups concerned with women's rights, environmental degradation, family planning, health, and population growth—have failed to mount a concerted effort to dispel abortion myths. And despite the overwhelming evidence of the high human and social costs incurred by restrictive laws, abortion politics remains dominated by narrowly drawn priorities that reflect only one set of beliefs and attitudes. Respect for both ethical diversity and factual accuracy is a precondition for a truly "public" policy on the question of abortion.

Reforming restrictive laws may stir opposition. Failing to do so exacts an emotional and economic toll on society—and sentences countless women around the world to an early grave.

Notes

1. Henry David, Director, Transnational Family Research Institute, Bethesda, Md., private communication, February 28, 1990.

2. Since January 1990, several other countries have liberalized their abortion laws, including Belgium, Bulgaria (which made abortion available on request in the first trimester), and Malaysia; Stanley K. Henshaw, Deputy Director of Research, Alan Guttmacher Institute, New York, private communication, June 7, 1990.

3. Stanley K. Henshaw, "Induced Abortion: A World Review, 1990," *Family Planning Perspectives,* March/April 1990.

4. Abortion-related mortality rates in the United States from W. Cates et al., "Legalized Abortion: Effect on National Trends of Maternal and Abortion-Related Mortality," *American Journal of Obstetricians and Gynecologists,* Vol. 132, 1978; Marek Okolski, "Abortion and Contraception in Poland," *Studies in Family Planning,* November 1983.

5. Henshaw, private communication.

6. A comprehensive discussion of abortion laws and trends worldwide can be found in Henshaw, "Induced Abortion," and in Rebecca J. Cook, "Abortion Laws and Policies: Challenges and Opportunities," *International Journal of Gynecology and Obstetrics,* Supplement 3, 1989; see also Rebecca J. Cook and Bernard M. Dickens, "International Developments in Abortion Laws: 1977–88," *American Journal of Public Health,* October 1988.

7. Ruth Dixon-Mueller, "Abortion Policy and Women's Health in Developing Countries," *International Journal of Health Services,* Vol. 20, No. 2, 1990.

8. Cook, "Abortion Laws and Policies."

9. Ibid.; Henshaw, "Induced Abortion."

10. Cook, "Abortion Laws and Policies"; Henshaw, "Induced Abortion."

11. Cook, "Abortion Laws and Policies"; Henshaw, "Induced Abortion"; India's population from Population Reference Bureau, *1990 World Population Data Sheet* (Washington, D.C.: 1990).

12. Henshaw, "Induced Abortion."

13. Ibid.

14. Cook, "Abortion Laws and Policies"; National Abortion Rights Action League, "Post-*Webster* Anti-Choice Legislative Activity," Washington, D.C., memorandums, March 29 and July 31, 1990.

15. D.K. Piragoff, Canadian Department of Justice, Ottawa, Canada, private communication, June 7, 1990.

16. Dixon-Mueller, "Abortion Policy and Women's Health in Developing Countries"; "Deaths from Abortion," in Erica Royston and Sue Armstrong, eds., *Preventing Maternal Deaths* (Geneva: World Health Organization (WHO), 1989).

17. "Deaths from Abortion," in Royston and Armstrong, *Preventing Maternal Deaths*.

18. Katie McLaurin, "Issues of Access to Abortion: Policy, Law and Reality," presentation at the American Public Health Association Annual Meeting, Chicago, October 22–26, 1989.

19. Ibid.; Renee Holt, "Abortion: Law, Practice, and Project Possibilities in Zambia," prepared for Columbia University Center for Population and Family Health, New York, September 25, 1989.

20. Holt, "Abortion in Zambia."

21. Julie DeClerque, "Unsafe Abortion Practices in Subsaharan Africa and Latin America: A Call to Policymakers," presentation at Panel on Culture, Public Policy, and Reproductive Health, Association for Women in Development Conference, Washington, D.C., November 17–19, 1989; Holt, "Abortion in Zambia."

22. Tomas Frejka, Senior Representative, Population Council Latin America Region, private communication, March 12, 1990; Dixon-Mueller, "Abortion Policy and Women's Health in Developing Countries"; DeClerque, "Unsafe Abortion Practices."

23. Royston and Armstrong, *Preventing Maternal Deaths*.

24. Mary O'Keefe, "Abortion: Law, Practice, and Project Possibilities in Mexico," prepared for Columbia University Center for Population and Family Health, New York, September 25, 1989.

25. Cook, "Abortion Laws and Policies"; Henshaw, private communication.

26. Al Kamen, "5–4 Ruling Stops Short of Overturning Roe," *Washington Post*, July 4, 1989; for in-depth analyses of the *Webster* decision, see "The Fight Over *Roe v. Wade*: The *Webster* Briefs," *Family Planning Perspectives*, May/June 1989, and Jeannie I. Rosoff, "The *Webster* Decision: A Giant Step Backwards," *Family Planning Perspectives*, July/August 1989.

27. Howard LaFranchi, "Wind from the West: Europe Gears for Abortion Battle," *Christian Science Monitor*, August 17, 1989.

28. For a discussion of these trends, see Tomas Frejka, "Induced Abortion and Fertility," *International Family Planning Perspectives*, December 1985.

29. Henshaw, "Induced Abortion"; Frejka, "Induced Abortion and Fertility."

30. Henshaw, "Induced Abortion."

31. John Paxman, "Abortion in Latin America" (draft), prepared for Population Council meeting in Bogotá, Colombia, October 1988.

32. Adrienne Germain, *Reproductive Health and Dignity: Choices By Third World Women* (New York: International Women's Health Coalition, 1987).

33. Henshaw, "Induced Abortion"; Frejka, "Induced Abortion and Fertility."

34. Tomas Frejka, *Induced Abortion and Fertility: A Quarter Century of Experience in Eastern Europe,* Center for Policy Studies, Working Paper No. 99 (New York: Population Council, 1983); Henry P. David, *Abortion Research Notes* (Transnational Family Research Institute, Bethesda, Md.), various issues.

35. Frejka, *Induced Abortion and Fertility: Eastern Europe*; Henshaw, "Induced Abortion."

36. "Poland's Hard Life Finds More Women Choosing Abortion," *New York Times,* May 23, 1983; John Tagliabue, "Abortion Issue in Poland Splits the Opposition," *New York Times,* May 29, 1989.

37. Frejka, *Induced Abortion and Fertility: Eastern Europe*; Popov as quoted in Michael Dobbs, "90% of 1st Pregnancies Said Aborted in USSR," *Washington Post,* January 20, 1989.

38. Henshaw, "Induced Abortion"; Frejka, *Induced Abortion and Fertility: Eastern Europe.*

39. Frejka, *Induced Abortion and Fertility: Eastern Europe*; Statisticheskiy Spornik, *Naseleniye SSR,* Moscow, 1987; Feshbach quoted in Dobbs, "90% of 1st Pregnancies Said Aborted in USSR."

40. Frejka, *Induced Abortion and Fertility: Eastern Europe*; David, private communication.

41. Tomas Frejka and Lucille Atkin, "The Role of Induced Abortion in the Fertility Transition of Latin America," prepared for IUSSP/CELADE/CENEP Seminar on the Fertility Transition, Buenos Aires, Argentina, April 3, 1990.

42. IPPF cited in Tomas Frejka et al., *Program Document: Research Program for the Prevention of Unsafe Induced Abortion and Its Adverse Consequences in Latin America and the Caribbean,* Center for Policy Studies, Working Paper No. 23 (Mexico City: Population Council, 1989).

43. Frejka and Atkin, "The Role of Induced Abortion in the Fertility Transition of Latin America."

44. Paxman, "Abortion in Latin America"; Mary O'Keefe, "Abortion: Law, Practice, and Project Possibilities in Brazil," prepared for Columbia University Center for Population and Family Health, September 25, 1989.

45. Frejka et al., *Program Document: Research Program for the Prevention of Unsafe Induced Abortion*; O'Keefe, "Abortion in Brazil."

46. Frejka and Atkin, "The Role of Induced Abortion in the Fertility Transition of Latin America."

47. Khama Rogo, "Induced Abortion in Africa" (unpublished draft), prepared for Population Association of America Annual Meeting, Toronto, Canada, May 2–3, 1990.

48. N.N. Mashalaba, "Commentary on the Causes and Consequences of Unwanted Pregnancy from an African Perspective," *International Journal of Gynecology and Obstetrics,* Supplement 3, 1989.

49. Ibid.

50. Ninuk Widyantoro et al., "Induced Abortion: The Indonesian Experience," prepared for the Population Association of America Annual Meeting, Toronto, Canada, May 3, 1990.

51. Ibid.; Renee Holt, "Abortion: Law, Practice, and Project Possibilities in Indonesia," paper prepared for Columbia University Center for Population and Family Health, September 25, 1989.

52. Widyantoro et al., "Induced Abortion: The Indonesian Experience"; Holt, "Abortion in Indonesia."

53. Henry P. David et al., "United States and Denmark: Different Approaches to Health Care and Family Planning," *Studies in Family Planning,* January/February 1990.

54. Ibid.

55. Ibid.

56. Ibid.

57. Ibid.

58. Germain, *Reproductive Health and Dignity.*

59. "Deaths from Abortion," in Royston and Armstrong, *Preventing Maternal Deaths*; Holt, "Abortion in Indonesia."

60. Rogo, "Induced Abortion in Africa."

61. Ibid.; Francine M. Coeytaux, "Induced Abortion in sub-Saharan Africa: What We Do and Do Not Know," *Studies in Family Planning,* May/June 1988.

62. Rogo, "Induced Abortion in Africa."

63. DeClerque, "Unsafe Abortion Practices"; Royston and Armstrong, *Preventing Maternal Deaths*; Henshaw, "Induced Abortion"; data on numbers of women whose health is impaired as a result of illegal abortion from DeClerque, "Unsafe Abortion Practices."

64. DeClerque, "Unsafe Abortion Practices."

65. Fred T. Sai and Janet Nassim, "The Need for a Reproductive Health Approach," *International Journal of Gynecology and Obstetrics,* Supplement 3, 1989; Royston and Armstrong, *Preventing Maternal Deaths*; Frejka and Atkin, "The Role of Induced Abortion in the Fertility Transition of Latin America."

66. Rogo, "Induced Abortion in Africa."

67. Ibid.

68. Irene Figa-Talamanca et al., "Illegal Abortion: An Attempt to Assess its Cost to the Health Services and Its Incidence in the Community," *International Journal of Health Services,* Vol. 16, No. 3, 1986; Rogo, "Induced Abortion in Africa"; Royston and Armstrong, *Preventing Maternal Deaths.*

69. Ann Leonard and Francine Coeytaux, "Abortion Complications in Subsaharan Africa" (internal document), International Projects Assistance Services, Chapel Hill, N.C., undated.

70. "Determinants and Consequences of Pregnancy Wastage in Zaire: A Study of Patients with Complications Requiring Hospital Treatment in Kinshasa, Matadi and Bukavu" (draft), prepared by Family Health International, Research Triangle Park, N.C., and Comite National des Naissances Desirables, Kinshasa, Zaire, undated.

71. Jacqueline Darroch Forrest and Susheela Singh, "Public Sector Savings Resulting from Expenditures for Contraceptive Services," *Family Planning Perspectives*, January/February 1990.

72. Stephen D. Mumford and Elton Kessel, "Is Wide Availability of Abortion Essential to National Population Growth Control Programs? Experiences of 116 Countries," *American Journal of Obstetrics and Gynecology*, July 15, 1984.

73. Cook, "Abortion Laws and Policies."

74. Ibid.

Why Abortion Is Immoral

Donald Marquis

The view that abortion is, with rare exceptions, seriously immoral has received little support in the recent philosophical literature. No doubt most philosophers affiliated with secular institutions of higher education believe that the anti-abortion position is either a symptom of irrational religious dogma or a conclusion generated by seriously confused philosophical argument. The purpose of this essay is to undermine this general belief. This essay sets out an argument that purports to show, as well as any argument in ethics can show, that abortion is, except possibly in rare cases, seriously immoral, that it is in the same moral category as killing an innocent adult human being.

The argument is based on a major assumption. Many of the most insightful and careful writers on the ethics of abortion—such as Joel Feinberg, Michael Tooley, Mary Anne Warren, H. Tristram Engelhardt, Jr., L. W. Sumner, John T. Noonan, Jr., and Philip Devine[1]—believe that whether or not abortion is morally permissible stands or falls on whether or not a fetus is the sort of being whose life it is seriously wrong to end. The argument of this essay will assume, but not argue, that they are correct.

Also, this essay will neglect issues of great importance to a complete ethics of abortion. Some anti-abortionists will allow that certain abortions, such as abortion before implantation or abortion when the life of a woman is threatened by a pregnancy or abortion after rape, may be morally permissible. This essay will not explore the casuistry of these hard cases. The purpose of this essay is to develop a general argument for the claim that the overwhelming majority of deliberate abortions are seriously immoral.

Reprinted from *The Journal of Philosophy* LXVIII (April 1989), pp. 183–202. Used by permission of the *Journal of Philosophy* and the author.

I

A sketch of standard anti-abortion and pro-choice arguments exhibits how those arguments possess certain symmetries that explain why partisans of those positions are so convinced of the correctness of their own positions, why they are not successful in convincing their opponents, and why, to others, this issue seems to be unresolvable. An analysis of the nature of this standoff suggests a strategy for surmounting it.

Consider the way a typical anti-abortionist argues. She will argue or assert that life is present from the moment of conception or that fetuses look like babies or that fetuses possess a characteristic such as a genetic code that is both necessary and sufficient for being human. Anti-abortionists seem to believe that (1) the truth of all of these claims is quite obvious, and (2) establishing any of these claims is sufficient to show that abortion is morally akin to murder.

A standard pro-choice strategy exhibits similarities. The pro-choicer will argue or assert that fetuses are not persons or that fetuses are not rational agents or that fetuses are not social beings. Pro-choicers seem to believe that (1) the truth of any of these claims is quite obvious, and (2) establishing any of these claims is sufficient to show that an abortion is not a wrongful killing.

In fact, both the pro-choice and the anti-abortion claims do seem to be true, although the "it looks like a baby" claim is more difficult to establish the earlier the pregnancy. We seem to have a standoff. How can it be resolved?

As everyone who has taken a bit of logic knows, if any of these arguments concerning abortion is a good argument, it requires not only some claim characterizing fetuses, but also some general moral principle that ties a characteristic of fetuses to having or not having the right to life or to some other moral characteristic that will generate the obligation or the lack of obligation not to end the life of a fetus. Accordingly, the arguments of the anti-abortionist and the pro-choicer need a bit of filling in to be regarded as adequate.

Note what each partisan will say. The anti-abortionist will claim that her position is supported by such generally accepted moral principles as "It is always prima facie seriously wrong to take a human life" or "It is always prima facie seriously wrong to end the life of a baby." Since these are generally accepted moral principles, her position is certainly not obviously wrong. The pro-choicer will claim that her position is supported by such plausible moral principles as "Being a person is what gives an individual intrinsic moral worth" or "It is only seriously prima facie wrong to take the life of a member of the human community." Since these are generally accepted moral principles, the pro-choice position is certainly not obviously wrong. Unfortunately, we have again arrived at a standoff.

Now, how might one deal with this standoff? The standard approach is to try to show how the moral principles of one's opponent lose their plausibility under analysis. It is easy to see how this is possible. On the one hand, the anti-abortionist will defend a moral principle concerning the wrongness of killing which tends to be broad in scope in order that even fetuses at an early stage of pregnancy will fall under it. The problem with broad principles is that they often embrace too much. In this particular instance, the principle "It is always prima facie wrong to take a human life" seems to entail that it is wrong to end the existence of a living human cancer-cell culture, on the grounds that the culture is both living and human. Therefore, it seems that the anti-abortionist's favored principle is too broad.

On the other hand, the pro-choicer wants to find a moral principle concerning the wrongness of killing which tends to be narrow in scope in order that fetuses will *not* fall under it. The problem with narrow principles is that they often do not embrace enough. Hence, the needed principles such as "It is prima facie seriously wrong to kill only persons" or "It is prima facie wrong to kill only rational agents" do not explain why it is wrong to kill infants or young children or the severely retarded or even perhaps the severely mentally ill. Therefore, we seem again to have a standoff. The anti-abortionist charges, not unreasonably, that pro-choice principles concerning killing are too narrow to be acceptable; the pro-choicer charges, not unreasonably, that anti-abortionist principles concerning killing are too broad to be acceptable.

Attempts by both sides to patch up the difficulties in their positions run into further difficulties. The anti-abortionist will try to remove the problems in her position by reformulating her principle concerning killing in terms of human beings. Now we end up with: "It is always prima facie seriously wrong to end the life of a human being." This principle has the advantage of avoiding the problem of the human cancer-cell culture counterexample. But this advantage is purchased at a high price. For although it is clear that a fetus is both human and alive, it is not at all clear that a fetus is a human *being*. There is at least something to be said for the view that something becomes a human being only after a process of development, and that therefore first trimester fetuses and perhaps all fetuses are not yet human beings. Hence, the anti-abortionist, by this move, has merely exchanged one problem for another.[2]

The pro-choicer fares no better. She may attempt to find reasons why killing infants, young children, and the severely retarded is wrong which are independent of her major principle that is supposed to explain the wrongness of taking human life, but which will not also make abortion immoral. This is no easy task. Appeals to social utility will seem satisfactory only to those who resolve not to think of the enormous difficulties with a utilitarian account of the wrongness of killing and the significant social costs of preserving the lives of the unproductive.[3] A pro-choice strategy that extends the definition of 'person' to infants or even to young children seems just as arbitrary as an anti-abortion strategy that extends the definition of 'human being' to fetuses. Again, we find symmetries in the two positions and we arrive at a standoff.

There are even further problems that reflect symmetries in the two positions. In addition to counterexample problems, or the arbitrary application problems that can be exchanged for them, the standard anti-abortionist principle "It is prima facie seriously wrong to kill a human being," or one of its variants, can be objected to on the grounds of ambiguity. If 'human being' is taken to be a *biological* category, then the anti-abortionist is left with the problem of explaining why a merely biological category should make a moral difference. Why, it is asked, is it any more reasonable to base a moral conclusion on the number of chromosomes in one's cells than on the color of one's skin?[4] If 'human being', on the other hand, is taken to be a *moral* category, then the claim that a fetus is a human being cannot be taken to be a premise in the anti-abortion argument, for it is precisely what needs to be established. Hence, either the anti-abortionist's main category is a morally irrelevant, merely biological category, or it is of no use to the anti-abortionist in establishing (noncircularly, of course) that abortion is wrong.

Although this problem with the anti-abortionist position is often noticed, it is less often noticed that the pro-choice position suffers from an analogous problem. The principle "Only persons have the right to life" also suffers from an ambiguity. The term 'person' is typically defined in terms of psychological characteristics, although there will certainly be disagreement concerning which characteristics are most important. Supposing that this matter can be settled, the pro-choicer is left with the problem of explaining why *psychological* characteristics should make a *moral* difference. If the pro-choicer should attempt to deal with this problem by claiming that an explanation is not necessary, that in fact we do treat such a cluster of psychological properties as having moral significance, the sharp-witted anti-abortionist should have a ready response. We do treat being both living and human as having moral significance. If it is legitimate for the pro-choicer to demand that the anti-abortionist provide an explanation of the connection between the biological character of being a human being and the wrongness of being killed (even though people accept this connection), then it is legitimate for the anti-abortionist to demand that the pro-choicer provide an explanation of the connection between psychological criteria for being a person and the wrongness of being killed (even though that connection is accepted).[5]

Feinberg has attempted to meet this objection (he calls psychological personhood "commonsense personhood"):

> The characteristics that confer commonsense personhood are not arbitrary bases for rights and duties, such as race, sex or species membership; rather they are traits that make sense out of rights and duties and without which those moral attributes would have no point or function. It is because people are conscious; have a sense of their personal identities; have plans, goals, and projects; experience emotions; are liable to pains, anxieties, and frustrations; can reason and bargain, and so on—it is because of these attributes that people have values and interests, desires and expectations of their own, including a stake in their own futures, and a personal well-being of a sort we cannot ascribe to unconscious or nonrational beings. Because of their developed capacities they can assume duties and responsibilities and can have and make claims on one another. Only because of their sense of self, their life plans, their value hierarchies, and their stakes

in their own futures can they be ascribed fundamental rights. There is nothing arbitrary about these linkages (*op. cit.,* p. 270).

The plausible aspects of this attempt should not be taken to obscure its implausible features. There is a great deal to be said for the view that being a psychological person under some description is a necessary condition for having duties. One cannot have a duty unless one is capable of behaving morally, and a being's capability of behaving morally will require having a certain psychology. It is far from obvious, however, that having rights entails consciousness or rationality, as Feinberg suggests. We speak of the rights of the severely retarded or the severely mentally ill, yet some of these persons are not rational. We speak of the rights of the temporarily unconscious. The New Jersey Supreme Court based their decision in the Quinlan case on Karen Ann Quinlan's right to privacy, and she was known to be permanently unconscious at that time. Hence, Feinberg's claim that having rights entails being conscious is, on its face, obviously false.

Of course, it might not make sense to attribute rights to a being that would never in its natural history have certain psychological traits. This modest connection between psychological personhood and moral personhood will create a place for Karen Ann Quinlan and the temporarily unconscious. But then it makes a place for fetuses also. Hence, it does not serve Feinberg's prochoice purposes. Accordingly, it seems that the pro-choicer will have as much difficulty bridging the gap between psychological personhood and personhood in the moral sense as the anti-abortionist has bridging the gap between being a biological human being and being a human being in the moral sense.

Furthermore, the pro-choicer cannot any more escape her problem by making person a purely moral category than the anti-abortionist could escape by the analogous move. For if person is a moral category, then the pro-choicer is left without the resources for establishing (noncircularly, of course) the claim that a fetus is not a person, which is an essential premise in her argument. Again, we have both a symmetry and a standoff between pro-choice and anti-abortion views.

Passions in the abortion debate run high. There are both plausibilities and difficulties with the standard positions. Accordingly, it is hardly surprising that partisans of either side embrace with fervor the moral generalizations that support the conclusions they preanalytically favor, and reject with disdain the moral generalizations of their opponents as being subject to inescapable difficulties. It is easy to believe that the counterexamples to one's own moral principles are merely temporary difficulties that will dissolve in the wake of further philosophical research, and that the counterexamples to the principles of one's opponents are as straightforward as the contradiction between *A* and *O* propositions in traditional logic. This might suggest to an impartial observer (if there are any) that the abortion issue is unresolvable.

There is a way out of this apparent dialectical quandary. The moral generalizations of both sides are not quite correct. The generalizations hold for the most part, for the usual cases. This suggests that they are all *accidental* generalizations, that the moral claims made by those on both sides of the dispute do not touch on the *essence* of the matter.

This use of the distinction between essence and accident is not meant to invoke obscure metaphysical categories. Rather, it is intended to reflect the rather atheoretical nature of the abortion discussion. If the generalization a partisan in the abortion dispute adopts were derived from the reason why ending the life of a human being is wrong, then there could not be exceptions to that generalization unless some special case obtains in which there are even more powerful countervailing reasons. Such generalizations would not be merely accidental generalizations; they would point to, or be based upon, the essence of the wrongness of killing, what it is that makes killing wrong. All this suggests that a necessary condition of resolving the abortion controversy is a more theoretical account of the wrongness of killing. After all, if we merely believe, but do not understand, why killing adult human beings such as ourselves is wrong, how could we conceivably show that abortion is either immoral or permissible?

II

In order to develop such an account, we can start from the following unproblematic assumption concerning our own case: it is wrong to kill *us*. Why is it wrong? Some answers can be easily eliminated. It might be said that what makes killing us wrong is that a killing brutalizes the one who kills. But the brutalization consists of being inured to the performance of an act that is hideously immoral; hence, the brutalization does not explain the immorality. It might be said that what makes killing us wrong is the great loss others would experience due to our absence. Although such hubris is understandable, such an explanation does not account for the wrongness of killing hermits, or those whose lives are relatively independent and whose friends find it easy to make new friends.

A more obvious answer is better. What primarily makes killing wrong is neither its effect on the murderer nor its effect on the victim's friends and relatives, but its effect on the victim. The loss of one's life is one of the greatest losses one can suffer. The loss of one's life deprives one of all the experiences, activities, projects, and enjoyments that would otherwise have constituted one's future. Therefore, killing someone is wrong, primarily because the killing inflicts (one of) the greatest possible losses on the victim. To describe this as the loss of life can be misleading, however. The change in my biological state does not by itself make killing me wrong. The effect of the loss of my biological life is the loss to me of all those activities, projects, experiences, and enjoyments which would otherwise have constituted my future personal life. These activities, projects, experiences, and enjoyments are either valuable for their own sakes or are means to something else that is valuable for its own sake. Some parts of my future are not valued by me now, but will come to be valued by me as I grow older and as my values and capacities change. When I am killed, I am deprived both of what I now value which would have been part of my future personal life, but also what I would come to value. Therefore, when I die, I am deprived of all of the value of my future. Inflicting this loss on me is ultimately what makes killing me wrong. This being the case, it would seem that what makes killing *any* adult human being prima facie seriously wrong is the loss of his or her future.[6]

How should this rudimentary theory of the wrongness of killing be evaluated? It cannot be faulted for deriving an 'ought' from an 'is', for it does not. The analysis assumes that killing me (or you, reader) is prima facie seriously wrong. The point of the analysis is to establish which natural property ultimately explains the wrongness of the killing, given that it is wrong. A natural property will ultimately explain the wrongness of killing, only if (1) the explanation fits with our intuitions about the matter and (2) there is no other natural property that provides the basis for a better explanation of the wrongness of killing. This analysis rests on the intuition that what makes killing a particular human or animal wrong is what it does to that particular human or animal. What makes killing wrong is some natural effect or other of the killing. Some would deny this. For instance, a divine-command theorist in ethics would deny it. Surely this denial is, however, one of those features of divine-command theory which renders it so implausible.

The claim that what makes killing wrong is the loss of the victim's future is directly supported by two considerations. In the first place, this theory explains why we regard killing as one of the worst of crimes. Killing is especially wrong, because it deprives the victim of more than perhaps any other crime. In the second place, people with AIDS or cancer who know they are dying believe, of course, that dying is a very bad thing for them. They believe that the loss of a future to them that they would otherwise have experienced is what makes their premature death a very bad thing for them. A better theory of the wrongness of killing would require a different natural property associated with killing which better fits with the attitudes of the dying. What could it be?

The view that what makes killing wrong is the loss to the victim of the value of the victim's future gains additional support when some of its implications are examined. In the first place, it is incompatible with the view that it is wrong to kill only beings who are biologically human. It is possible that there exists a different species from another planet whose members have a future like ours. Since having a future like that is what makes killing someone wrong, this theory entails that it would be wrong to kill members of such a species. Hence, this theory is opposed to the claim that only life that is biologically human has great moral worth, a claim which many anti-abortionists have seemed to adopt. This opposition, which this theory has in common with personhood theories, seems to be a merit of the theory.

In the second place, the claim that the loss of one's future is the wrong-making feature of one's being killed entails the possibility that the futures of some actual nonhuman mammals on our own planet are sufficiently like ours that it is seriously wrong to kill them also. Whether some animals do have the same right to life as human beings depends on adding to the account of the wrongness of killing some additional account of just what it is about my future or the futures of other adult human beings which makes it wrong to kill us. No such additional account will be offered in this essay. Undoubtedly, the provision of such an account would be a very difficult matter. Undoubtedly, any such account would be quite controversial. Hence, it surely should not reflect badly on this sketch of an elementary theory of the wrongness of killing that it is indeterminate with respect to some very difficult issues regarding animal rights.

In the third place, the claim that the loss of one's future is the wrong-making feature of one's being killed does not entail, as sanctity of human life theories do, that active euthanasia is wrong. Persons who are severely and incurably ill, who face a future of pain and despair, and who wish to die will not have suffered a loss if they are killed. It is, strictly speaking, the value of a human's future which makes killing wrong in this theory. This being so, killing does not necessarily wrong some persons who are sick and dying. Of course, there may be other reasons for a prohibition of active euthanasia, but that is another matter. Sanctity-of-human-life theories seem to hold that active euthanasia is seriously wrong even in an individual case where there seems to be good reason for it independently of public policy considerations. This consequence is most implausible, and it is a plus for the claim that the loss of a future of value is what makes killing wrong that it does not share this consequence.

In the fourth place, the account of the wrongness of killing defended in this essay does straightforwardly entail that it is prima facie seriously wrong to kill children and infants, for we do presume that they have futures of value. Since we do believe that it is wrong to kill defenseless little babies, it is important that a theory of the wrongness of killing easily account for this. Personhood theories of the wrongness of killing, on the other hand, cannot straightforwardly account for the wrongness of killing infants and young children.[7] Hence, such theories must add special ad hoc accounts of the wrongness of killing the young. The plausibility of such ad hoc theories seems to be a function of how desperately one wants such theories to work. The claim that the primary wrong-making feature of a killing is the loss to the victim of the value of its future accounts for the wrongness of killing young children and infants directly; it makes the wrongness of such acts as obvious as we actually think it is. This is a further merit of this theory. Accordingly, it seems that this value of a future-like-ours theory of the wrongness of killing shares strengths of both sanctity-of-life and personhood accounts while avoiding weaknesses of both. In addition, it meshes with a central intuition concerning what makes killing wrong.

The claim that the primary wrong-making feature of a killing is the loss to the victim of the value of its future has obvious consequences for the ethics of abortion. The future of a standard fetus includes a set of experiences, projects, activities, and such which are identical with the futures of adult human beings and are identical with the futures of young children. Since the reason that is sufficient to explain why it is wrong to kill human beings after the time of birth is a reason that also applies to fetuses, it follows that abortion is prima facie seriously morally wrong.

This argument does not rely on the invalid inference that, since it is wrong to kill persons, it is wrong to kill potential persons also. The category that is morally central to this analysis is the category of having a valuable future like ours; it is not the category of personhood. The argument to the conclusion that abortion is prima facie seriously morally wrong proceeded independently of the notion of person or potential person or any equivalent. Someone may wish to start with this analysis in terms of the value of a human future, conclude that abortion is, except perhaps in rare circumstances, seriously morally wrong, infer that fetuses have the right to life, and then call fetuses "persons" as a result of their having the right to life. Clearly, in this case, the category of person is being used to state the *conclusion* of the analysis rather than to generate the *argument* of the analysis.

The structure of this anti-abortion argument can be both illuminated and defended by comparing it to what appears to be the best argument for the wrongness of the wanton infliction of pain on animals. This latter argument is based on the assumption that it is prima facie wrong to inflict pain on me (or you, reader). What is the natural property associated with the infliction of pain which makes such infliction wrong? The obvious answer seems to be that the infliction of pain causes suffering and that suffering is a misfortune. The suffering caused by the infliction of pain is what makes the wanton infliction of pain on me wrong. The wanton infliction of pain on other adult humans causes suffering. The wanton infliction of pain on animals causes suffering. Since causing suffering is what makes the wanton infliction of pain wrong and since the wanton infliction of pain on animals causes suffering, it follows that the wanton infliction of pain on animals is wrong.

This argument for the wrongness of the wanton infliction of pain on animals shares a number of structural features with the argument for the serious prima facie wrongness of abortion. Both arguments start with an obvious assumption concerning what it is wrong to do to me (or you, reader). Both then look for the characteristic or the consequence of the wrong action which makes the action wrong. Both recognize that the wrong-making feature of these immoral actions is a property of actions sometimes directed at individuals other than postnatal human beings. If the structure of the argument for the wrongness of the wanton infliction of pain on animals is sound, then the structure of the argument for the prima facie serious wrongness of abortion is also sound, for the structure of the two arguments is the same. The structure common to both is the key to the explanation of how the wrongness of abortion can be demonstrated without recourse to the category of person. In neither argument is that category crucial.

This defense of an argument for the wrongness of abortion in terms of a structurally similar argument for the wrongness of the wanton infliction of pain on animals succeeds only if the account regarding animals is the correct account. Is it? In the first place, it seems plausible. In the second place, its major competition is Kant's account. Kant believed that we do not have direct duties to animals at all, because they are not persons. Hence, Kant had to explain and justify the wrongness of inflicting pain on animals on the grounds that "he who is hard in his dealings with animals becomes hard also in his dealing with men."[8] The problem with Kant's account is that there seems to be no reason for accepting this latter claim unless Kant's account is rejected. If the alternative to Kant's account is accepted, then it is easy to understand why someone who is indifferent to inflicting pain on animals is also indifferent to inflicting pain on humans, for one is indifferent to what makes inflicting pain wrong in both cases. But, if Kant's account is accepted, there is no intelligible reason why one who is hard in his dealings with animals (or crabgrass or stones) should also be hard in his dealings with men. After all, men are persons: animals are no more persons than crab grass or stones. Persons are Kant's crucial moral category. Why, in short, should a Kantian accept the basic claim in Kant's argument?

Hence, Kant's argument for the wrongness of inflicting pain on animals rests on a claim that, in a world of Kantian moral agents, is demonstrably false. Therefore, the alternative analysis, being more plausible anyway, should be accepted. Since this alternative analysis has the same structure as the anti-abortion argument being defended here, we have further support for the argument for the immorality of abortion being defended in this essay.

Of course, this value of a future-like-ours argument, if sound, shows only that abortion is prima facie wrong, not that it is wrong in any and all circumstances. Since the loss of the future to a standard fetus, if killed, is, however, at least as great a loss as the loss of the future to a standard adult human being who is killed, abortion, like ordinary killing, could be justified only by the most compelling reasons. The loss of one's life is almost the greatest misfortune that can happen to one. Presumably abortion could be justified in some circumstances, only if the loss consequent on failing to abort would be at least as great. Accordingly, morally permissible abortions will be rare indeed unless, perhaps, they occur so early in pregnancy that a fetus is not yet definitely an individual. Hence, this argument should be taken as showing that abortion is presumptively very seriously wrong, where the presumption is very strong—as strong as the presumption that killing another adult human being is wrong.

III

How complete an account of the wrongness of killing does the value of a future-like-ours account have to be in order that the wrongness of abortion is a consequence? This account does not have to be an account of the necessary conditions for the wrongness of killing. Some persons in nursing homes may lack valuable human futures, yet it may be wrong to kill them for other reasons. Furthermore, this account does not obviously have to be the sole reason killing is wrong where the victim did have a valuable future. This analysis claims only that, for any killing where the victim did have a valuable future like ours, having that future by itself is sufficient to create the strong presumption that the killing is seriously wrong.

One way to overturn the value of a future-like-ours argument would be to find some account of the wrongness of killing which is at least as intelligible and which has different implications for the ethics of abortion. Two rival accounts possess at least some degree of plausibility. One account is based on the obvious fact that people value the experience of living and wish for that valuable experience to continue. Therefore, it might be said, what makes killing wrong is the discontinuation of that experience for the victim. Let us call this the *discontinuation account.*[9] Another rival account is based upon the obvious fact that people strongly desire to continue to live. This suggests that what makes killing us so wrong is that it interferes with the fulfillment of a strong and fundamental desire, the fulfillment of which is necessary for the fulfillment of any other desires we might have. Let us call this the *desire account.*[10]

Consider first the desire account as a rival account of the ethics of killing which would provide the basis for rejecting the anti-abortion position. Such an account will have to be stronger than the value of a future-like-ours account of the wrongness of abortion if it is to do the job expected of it. To entail the wrongness of abortion, the value of a future-like-ours account has only to provide a sufficient, but not a necessary, condition for the wrongness of killing. The desire account, on the other hand, must provide us also with a necessary condition for the wrongness of killing in order to generate a pro-choice conclusion on abortion. The reason for this is that presumably the argument from the desire account moves from the claim that what makes killing wrong is interference with a very strong desire to the claim that abortion is not wrong because the fetus lacks a strong desire to live. Obviously, this inference fails if someone's having the desire to live is not a necessary condition of its being wrong to kill that individual.

One problem with the desire account is that we do regard it as seriously wrong to kill persons who have little desire to live or who have no desire to live or, indeed, have a desire not to live. We believe it is seriously wrong to kill the unconscious, the sleeping, those who are tired of life, and those who are suicidal. The value-of-a-human-future account renders standard morality intelligible in these cases; these cases appear to be incompatible with the desire account.

The desire account is subject to a deeper difficulty. We desire life, because we value the goods of this life. The goodness of life is not secondary to our desire for it. If this were not so, the pain of one's own premature death could be done away with merely by an appropriate alteration in the configuration of one's desires. This is absurd. Hence, it would seem that it is the loss of the goods of one's future, not the interference with the fulfillment of a strong desire to live, which accounts ultimately for the wrongness of killing.

It is worth noting that, if the desire account is modified so that it does not provide a necessary, but only a sufficient, condition for the wrongness of killing, the desire account is compatible with the value of a future-like-ours account. The combined accounts will yield an anti-abortion ethic. This suggests that one can retain what is intuitively plausible about the desire account without a challenge to the basic argument of this paper.

It is also worth noting that, if future desires have moral force in a modified desire account of the wrongness of killing, one can find support for an anti-abortion ethic even in the absence of a value of a future-like-ours account. If one decides that a morally relevant property, the possession of which is sufficient to make it wrong to kill some individual, is the desire at some future time to live—one might decide to justify one's refusal to kill suicidal teenagers on these grounds, for example—then, since typical fetuses will have the desire in the future to live, it is wrong to kill typical fetuses. Accordingly, it does not seem that a desire account of the wrongness of killing can provide a justification of a pro-choice ethic of abortion which is nearly as adequate as the value of a human-future justification of an anti-abortion ethic.

The discontinuation account looks more promising as an account of the wrongness of killing. It seems just as intelligible as the value of a future-like-ours account, but it does not justify an anti-abortion position. Obviously, if it is the continuation of one's activities, experiences, and projects, the loss of which makes killing wrong, then it is not wrong to kill fetuses for that reason, for fetuses do not have experiences, activities, and projects to be continued or discontinued. Accordingly, the discontinuation account does not have the anti-abortion consequences that the value of a future-like-ours account has. Yet, it seems as intelligible as the value of a future-like-ours account, for when we think of what would be wrong with our being killed, it does seem as if it is the discontinuation of what makes our lives worthwhile which makes killing us wrong.

Is the discontinuation account just as good an account as the value of a future-like-ours account? The discontinuation account will not be adequate at all, if it does not refer to the *value* of the experience that may be discontinued. One does not want the discontinuation account to make it wrong to kill a patient who begs for death and who is in severe pain that cannot be relieved short of killing. (I leave open the question of whether it is wrong for other reasons.) Accordingly, the discontinuation account must be more than a bare discontinuation account. It must make some reference to the positive value of the patient's experiences. But, by the same token, the value of a future-like-ours account cannot be a bare future account either. Just having a future surely does not itself rule out killing the above patient. This account must make some reference to the value of the patient's future experiences and projects also. Hence, both accounts involve the value of experiences, projects, and activities. So far we still have symmetry between the accounts.

The symmetry fades, however, when we focus on the time period of the value of the experiences, etc., which has moral consequences. Although both accounts leave open the possibility that the patient in our example may be killed, this possibility is left open only in virtue of the utterly bleak future for the patient. It makes no difference whether the patient's immediate past contains intolerable pain, or consists in being in a coma (which we can imagine is a situation of indifference), or consists in a life of value. If the patient's future is a future of value, we want our account to make it wrong to kill the patient. If the patient's future is intolerable, whatever his or her immediate past, we want our account to allow killing the patient. Obviously, then, it is the value of that patient's future which is doing the work in rendering the morality of killing the patient intelligible.

This being the case, it seems clear that whether one has immediate past experiences or not does no work in the explanation of what makes killing wrong. The addition the discontinuation account makes to the value of a human future account is otiose. Its addition to the value-of-a-future account plays no role at all in rendering intelligible the wrongness of killing. Therefore, it can be discarded with the discontinuation account of which it is a part.

IV

The analysis of the previous section suggests that alternative general accounts of the wrongness of killing are either inadequate or unsuccessful in getting around the anti-abortion consequences of the value of a future-like-ours argument. A different strategy for avoiding these anti-abortion consequences involves limiting the scope of the value of a future argument. More precisely, the strategy involves arguing that fetuses lack a property that is essential for the value-of-a-future argument (or for any anti-abortion argument) to apply to them.

One move of this sort is based upon the claim that a necessary condition of one's future being valuable is that one values it. Value implies a valuer. Given this one might argue that, since fetuses cannot value their futures, their futures are not valuable to them. Hence, it does not seriously wrong them deliberately to end their lives.

This move fails, however, because of some ambiguities. Let us assume that something cannot be of value unless it is valued by someone. This does not entail that my life is of no value unless it is valued by me. I may think, in a period of despair, that my future is of no worth whatsoever, but I may be wrong because others rightly see value—even great value—in it. Furthermore, my future can be valuable to me even if I do not value it. This is the case when a young person attempts suicide, but is rescued and goes on to significant human achievements. Such young people's futures are ultimately valuable to them, even though such futures do not seem to be valuable to them at the moment of attempted suicide. A fetus's future can be valuable to it in the same way. Accordingly, this attempt to limit the anti-abortion argument fails.

Another similar attempt to reject the anti-abortion position is based on Tooley's claim that an entity cannot possess the right to life unless it has the capacity to desire its continued existence. It follows that, since fetuses lack the conceptual capacity to desire to continue to live, they lack the right to life. Accordingly, Tooley concludes that abortion cannot be seriously prima facie wrong (*op. cit.*, pp. 46/7).

What could be the evidence for Tooley's basic claim? Tooley once argued that individuals have a prima facie right to what they desire and that the lack of the capacity to desire something undercuts the basis of one's right to it (*op. cit.*, pp. 44/5). This argument plainly will not succeed in the context of the analysis of this essay, however, since the point here is to establish the fetus's right to life on other grounds. Tooley's argument assumes that the right to life cannot be established in general on some basis other than the desire for life. This position was considered and rejected in the preceding section of this paper.

One might attempt to defend Tooley's basic claim on the grounds that because a fetus cannot apprehend continued life as a benefit, its continued life cannot be a benefit or cannot be something it has a right to or cannot be something that is in its interest. This might be defended in terms of the general proposition that, if an individual is literally incapable of caring about or taking an interest in some X, then one does not have a right to X or X is not a benefit or X is not something that is in one's interest.[11]

Each member of this family of claims seems to be open to objections. As John C. Stevens[12] has pointed out, one may have a right to be treated with a certain medical procedure (because of a health insurance policy one has purchased), even though one cannot conceive of the nature of the procedure. And, as Tooley himself has pointed out, persons who have been indoctrinated, or drugged, or rendered temporarily unconscious may be literally incapable of caring about or taking an interest in something that is in their interest or is something to which they have a right, or is something that benefits them. Hence, the Tooley claim that would restrict the scope of the value of a future-like-ours argument is undermined by counterexamples.[13]

Finally, Paul Bassen[14] has argued that, even though the prospects of an embryo might seem to be a basis for the wrongness of abortion, an embryo cannot be a victim and therefore cannot be wronged. An embryo cannot be a victim, he says, because it lacks sentience. His central argument for this seems to be that, even though plants and the permanently unconscious are alive, they clearly cannot be victims. What is the explanation of this? Bassen claims that the explanation is that their lives consist of mere metabolism and mere metabolism is not enough to ground victimizability. Mentation is required.

The problem with this attempt to establish the absence of victimizability is that both plants and the permanently unconscious clearly lack what Bassen calls "prospects" or what I have called "a future life like ours." Hence, it is surely open to one to argue that the real reason we believe plants and the permanently unconscious cannot be victims is that killing them cannot deprive them of a future life like ours; the real reason is not their absence of present mentation.

Bassen recognizes that his view is subject to this difficulty, and he recognizes that the case of children seems to support this difficulty for "much of what we do for children is based on prospects." He argues, however, that, in the case of children and in other such cases "potentiality comes into play only where victimizability has been secured on other grounds" (*ibid.*, p. 333).

Bassen's defense of his view is patently question-begging, since what is adequate to secure victimizability is exactly what is at issue. His examples do not support his own view against the thesis of this essay. Of course, embryos can be victims: when their lives are deliberately terminated, they are deprived of their futures of value, their prospects. This makes them victims, for it directly wrongs them.

The seeming plausibility of Bassen's view stems from the fact that paradigmatic cases of imagining someone as a victim involve empathy, and empathy requires mentation of the victim. The victims of flood, famine, rape, or child abuse are all persons with whom we can empathize. That empathy seems to be part of seeing them as victims.[15]

In spite of the strength of these examples, the attractive intuition that a situation in which there is victimization requires the possibility of empathy is subject to counterexamples. Consider a case that Bassen himself offers: "Posthumous obliteration of an author's work constitutes a misfortune for him only if he had wished his work to endure" (*op cit.*, p. 318). The conditions Bassen wishes to impose upon the possibility of being victimized here seem far too strong. Perhaps this author, due to his unrealistic standards of excellence and his low self-esteem, regarded his work as unworthy of survival, even though it possessed genuine literary merit. Destruction of such work would surely victimize its author. In such a case, empathy with the victim concerning the loss is clearly impossible.

Of course, Bassen does not make the possibility of empathy a necessary condition of victimizability; he requires only mentation. Hence, on Bassen's actual view, this author, as I have described him, can be a victim. The problem is that the basic intuition that renders Bassen's view plausible is missing in the author's case. In order to attempt to avoid counterexamples, Bassen has made his thesis too weak to be supported by the intuitions that suggested it.

Even so, the mentation requirement on victimizability is still subject to counterexamples. Suppose a severe accident renders me totally unconscious for a month, after which I recover. Surely killing me while I am unconscious victimizes me, even though I am incapable of mentation during that time. It follows that Bassen's thesis fails. Apparently, attempts to restrict the value of a future-like-ours argument so that fetuses do not fall within its scope do not succeed.

V

In this essay, it has been argued that the correct ethic of the wrongness of killing can be extended to fetal life and used to show that there is a strong presumption that any abortion is morally impermissible. If the ethic of killing adopted here entails, however, that contraception is also seriously immoral, then there would appear to be a difficulty with the analysis of this essay.

But this analysis does not entail that contraception is wrong. Of course, contraception prevents the actualization of a possible future of value.

Hence, it follows from the claim that futures of value should be maximized that contraception is prima facie immoral. This obligation to maximize does not exist, however; furthermore, nothing in the ethics of killing in this paper entails that it does. The ethics of killing in this essay would entail that contraception is wrong only if something were denied a human future of value by contraception. Nothing at all is denied such a future by contraception, however.

Candidates for a subject of harm by contraception fall into four categories: (1) some sperm or other, (2) some ovum or other, (3) a sperm and an ovum separately, and (4) a sperm and an ovum together. Assigning the harm to some sperm is utterly arbitrary, for no reason can be given for making a sperm the subject of harm rather than an ovum. Assigning the harm to some ovum is utterly arbitrary, for no reason can be given for making an ovum the subject of harm rather than a sperm. One might attempt to avoid these problems by insisting that contraception deprives both the sperm and the ovum separately of a valuable future like ours. On this alternative, too many futures are lost. Contraception was supposed to be wrong, because it deprived us of one future of value, not two. One might attempt to avoid this problem by holding that contraception deprives the combination of sperm and ovum of a valuable future like ours. But here the definite article misleads. At the time of contraception, there are hundreds of millions of sperm, one (released) ovum and millions of possible combinations of all of these. There is no actual combination at all. Is the subject of the loss to be a merely possible combination? Which one? This alternative does not yield an actual subject of harm either. Accordingly, the immorality of contraception is not entailed by the loss of a future-like-ours argument simply because there is no nonarbitrarily identifiable subject of the loss in the case of contraception.

VI

The purpose of this essay has been to set out an argument for the serious presumptive wrongness of abortion subject to the assumption that the moral permissibility of abortion stands or falls on the moral status of the fetus. Since a fetus possesses a property, the possession of which in adult human beings is sufficient to make killing an adult human being wrong, abortion is wrong. This way of dealing with the problem of abortion seems superior to other approaches to the ethics of abortion, because it rests on an ethics of killing which is close to self-evident, because the crucial morally relevant property clearly applies to fetuses, and because the argument avoids the usual equivocations on 'human life', 'human being', or 'person'. The argument rests neither on religious claims nor on Papal dogma. It is not subject to the objection of "speciesism." Its soundness is compatible with the moral permissibility of euthanasia and contraception. It deals with our intuitions concerning young children.

Finally, this analysis can be viewed as resolving a standard problem—indeed, *the* standard problem—concerning the ethics of abortion. Clearly, it is wrong to kill adult human beings. Clearly, it is not wrong to end the life of some arbitrarily chosen single human cell. Fetuses seem to be like arbitrarily chosen human cells in some respects and like adult humans in other respects. The problem of the ethics of abortion is the problem of determining the fetal property that settles this moral controversy. The thesis of this essay is that the problem of the ethics of abortion, so understood, is solvable.

Notes

1. Feinberg, "Abortion," in *Matters of Life and Death: New Introductory Essays in Moral Philosophy.* Tom Regan, ed. (New York: Random House, 1986), pp. 256–293; Tooley, "Abortion and Infanticide," *Philosophy and Public Affairs,* II, 1 (1972):37–65, Tooley, *Abortion and Infanticide* (New York: Oxford, 1984); Warren, "On the Moral and Legal Status of Abortion," *The Monist,* I.VII, 1 (1973):43–61; Engelhardt, "The Ontology of Abortion," *Ethics,* I.XXXIV, 3 (1974):217–234; Sumner, *Abortion and Moral Theory* (Princeton: University Press, 1981); Noonan, "An Almost Absolute Value in History," in *The Morality of Abortion: Legal and Historical Perspectives,* Noonan, ed. (Cambridge: Harvard, 1970); and Devine, *The Ethics of Homicide* (Ithaca: Cornell, 1978).

2. For interesting discussions of this issue, see Warren Quinn, "Abortion: Identity and Loss," *Philosophy and Public Affairs,* XIII, 1 (1984):24–54; and Lawrence C. Becker, "Human Being: The Boundaries of the Concept," *Philosophy and Public Affairs,* IV, 4 (1975):334–359.

3. For example, see my "Ethics and The Elderly: Some Problems," in Stuart Spicker, Kathleen Woodward, and David Van Tassel, eds., *Aging and the Elderly: Humanistic Perspectives in Gerontology* (Atlantic Highlands, NJ: Humanities, 1978), pp. 341–355.

4. See Warren, *op. cit.,* and Tooley, "Abortion and Infanticide."

5. This seems to be the fatal flaw in Warren's treatment of this issue.

6. I have been most influenced on this matter by Jonathan Glover, *Causing Death and Saving Lives* (New York: Penguin, 1977), ch. 3; and Robert Young, "What Is So Wrong with Killing People?" *Philosophy,* I.IV, 210 (1979):515–528.

7. Feinberg, Tooley, Warren, and Engelhardt have all dealt with this problem.

8. "Duties to Animals and Spirits," in *Lectures on Ethics,* Louis Infeld, trans. (New York: Harper, 1963), p. 239.

9. I am indebted to Jack Bricke for raising this objection.

10. Presumably a preference utilitarian would press such an objection. Tooley once suggested that his account has such a theoretical underpinning. See his "Abortion and Infanticide," pp. 44/5.

11. Donald VanDeVeer seems to think this is self-evident. See his "Whither Baby Doe?" in *Matters of Life and Death,* p. 233.

12. "Must the Bearer of a Right Have the Concept of That to Which He Has a Right?" *Ethics,* XCV, 1 (1984):68–74.

13. See Tooley again in "Abortion and Infanticide," pp. 47–49.

14. "Present Sakes and Future Prospects: The Status of Early Abortion," *Philosophy and Public Affairs,* XI, 4 (1982):322–326.

15. Note carefully the reasons he gives on the bottom of p. 316.

Roe v. Wade: *A Study in Male Ideology*

Catharine MacKinnon

> In a society where women entered sexual intercourse willingly, where adequate contraception was a genuine social priority, there would be no "abortion issue." . . . Abortion is violence. . . . It is the offspring, and will continue to be the accuser of a more pervasive and prevalent violence, the violence of rapism.
>
> Adrienne Rich, *Of Woman Born*

This is a two-part feminist critique of *Roe v. Wade*. First I will situate abortion and the abortion right in the experience of women. The argument is that abortion is inextricable from sexuality, assuming that the feminist analysis of sexuality is our analysis of gender inequality.[1] I will then criticize the doctrinal choice to pursue the abortion right under the law of privacy. The argument is that privacy doctrine reaffirms what the feminist critique of sexuality criticizes: the public/private split. The political and ideological meaning of privacy as a legal doctrine is connected with the concrete consequences of the public/ private split for the lives of women. This analysis makes *Harris v. McRae*, in which public funding for abortions was held not required, appear consistent with the larger meaning of *Roe*.[2]

I will neglect two important explorations, which I bracket now. The first is, What are babies to men? On one level, men respond to women's right to abort as if confronting the possibility of their own potential nonexistence—

Reprinted with permission from *Abortion: Moral and Legal Perspectives,* eds. Jay Garfield and Patricia Hennessy (Amherst: University of Massachusetts Press, 1984), 45–54. Copyright © 1984 by The University of Massachusetts Press.

at *women's* hands, no less. On another level, men's issues of potency, of continuity as a compensation for mortality, of the thrust to embody themselves or their own image in the world, underlie their relation to babies (as well as to most everything else). To overlook these meanings of abortion to men as men, is to overlook political and strategic as well as fundamental theoretical issues, and is to misassess where much of the opposition to abortion is coming from. The second issue I bracket is one that, unlike the first, has been discussed extensively in the abortion debate: the moral rightness of abortion itself. My stance is that the abortion choice should be available and must be *women's*, but not because the fetus is not a form of life. In the usual argument, the abortion decision is made contingent on whether the fetus is a form of life. I cannot follow that. Why should not women make life or death decisions? This returns us to the first bracketed issue.

The issues I will explore have largely not been discussed in the terms I will use. What has happened instead, I think, is that women's embattled need to survive in a world hostile to our survival has precluded our exploring these issues as I am about to. That is, the perspective from which we have addressed abortion has been shaped and constrained by the very situation that the abortion issue requires us to address. We have not been able to risk thinking about these issues on our own terms because the terms have not been ours, either in sex, in life in general, or in court. The attempt to grasp women's situation on our own terms, from our own point of view, defines the feminist impulse. If doing that is risky, our situation also makes it risky not to. So, first feminism, then law.

Most women who seek abortions became pregnant while having sexual intercourse with men. Most did not mean or wish to conceive. In contrast to this fact of women's experience, the abortion debate has centered on separating control over sexuality from control over reproduction, and on separating both from gender. Liberals have supported the availability of the abortion choice as if the woman just happened on the fetus.[3] The political Right imagines that the intercourse which precedes conception is usually voluntary, only to urge abstinence, as if sex were up to women. At the same time, the Right defends male authority, specifically including a wife's duty to submit to sex. Continuing with this logic, many opponents of state funding of abortions, such as supporters of some versions of the Hyde Amendment, would permit funding of abortions when pregnancy results from rape or incest.[4] Thus, they make exceptions for those special occasions during which they presume women did not control sex. From all this I deduce that abortion's proponents and opponents share a tacit assumption that women significantly do control sex.

Feminist investigations suggest otherwise. Sexual intercourse, the most common cause of pregnancy, cannot simply be presumed co-equally determined. Feminism has found that women feel compelled to preserve the appearance—which, acted upon, becomes the reality—of male direction of sexual expression, as if it is male initiative itself that we want: it is that which turns us on. Men enforce this. It is much of what men want in a woman. It is what pornography eroticizes and prostitutes provide. Rape—that is, intercourse with force that is recognized as force—is adjudicated not according to the power or force that the man wields, but according to indices of intimacy between the parties. The more intimate you are with your accused rapist, the less likely a court is to find that what happened to you was rape. Often indices of intimacy include intercourse itself. If "no" can be taken as "yes," how free can "yes" be?

Under these conditions, women often do not use birth control because of its social meaning, a meaning we did not create. Using contraception means acknowledging and planning and taking direction of intercourse, accepting one's sexual availability, and appearing nonspontaneous. It means appearing available to male incursions. A good user of contraception is a bad girl. She can be presumed sexually available and, among other consequences, raped with relative impunity. (If you think this isn't true, you should consider rape cases in which the fact that a woman had a diaphragm in is taken as an indication that what happened to her was intercourse, not rape. "Why did you have your diaphragm in?") From studies of abortion clinics, women who repeatedly seek abortions (and now I'm looking at the repeat offenders high on the list of the Right's villains, their best case for opposing abortion as female irresponsibility),[5] when asked why, say something like, "The sex just happened." Like every night for two and a half years. I wonder if a woman can be presumed to control access to her sexuality if she feels unable to interrupt intercourse to insert a diaphragm; or worse, cannot even want to, aware that she risks a pregnancy she knows she does not want. Do you think she would stop the man for any other reason, such as, for instance, the real taboo—lack of desire? If not, how is sex, hence its consequences, meaningfully voluntary for women? Norms of sexual rhythm and romance that are felt to be interrupted by women's needs are constructed against women's interests. Sex doesn't look a whole lot like freedom when it appears normatively less costly for women to risk an undesired, often painful, traumatic, dangerous, sometimes illegal, and potentially life-threatening procedure, than it is to protect oneself in advance. Yet abortion policy has never been explicitly approached in the context of how women get pregnant; that is, as a consequence of intercourse under conditions of gender inequality; that is, as an issue of forced sex.

Now we come to the law. In 1973, *Roe v. Wade* found that a statute that made criminal all abortions except those to save the life of the mother violated the constitutional right to privacy.[6] The privacy right had been previously created as a constitutional principle in a case that decriminalized the prescription and use of contraceptives.[7] Note that courts use the privacy rubric to connect contraception with abortion in a way that parallels what I just did under the sexuality rubric. In *Roe,* that right to privacy was found "broad enough to encompass a woman's decision whether or not to terminate her pregnancy." In 1977, three justices observed, "In the abortion context, we have held that the right to privacy shields the woman from undue state intrusion in and external scrutiny of her very personal choice."[8] In 1981, the Supreme Court in *Harris v. McRae* decided that this right to privacy did not mean that federal Medicaid programs had to cover medically necessary abortions. According to the Court, the privacy of the woman's choice was not unconstitutionally burdened by the government supporting her decision to continue, but not her decision to end, a conception. In support of this conclusion, the Supreme Court stated that "although the government may not place obstacles in the path of a woman's exercise of her freedom of choice, it need not remove those not of its own creation."[9] It is apparently a very short step from that which the government has a duty *not* to intervene in, to that which it has *no* duty to intervene in.

If regarded as the outer edge of the limitations on government, I think the idea of privacy embodies a tension between precluding public exposure or governmental intrusion on the one hand, and autonomy in the sense of protecting personal self-action on the other. This is a tension, not just two facets of one whole right. This tension is resolved in the liberal state by identifying the threshold of the state with its permissible extent of penetration (a term I use advisedly) into a domain that is considered free by definition: the private sphere. By this move the state secures what has been termed "an inviolable personality" by insuring what has been called "autonomy or control over the intimacies of personal identity."[10] The state does this by centering its self-restraint on body and home, especially bedroom. By staying out of marriage and the family, prominently meaning sexuality—that is to say, heterosexuality—from contraception through pornography to the abortion decision, the law of privacy proposes to guarantee individual bodily integrity, personal exercise of moral intelligence, and freedom of intimacy.[11] What it actually does is translate traditional social values into the rhetoric of individual rights as a means of subordinating those rights to specific social imperatives.[12] In feminist terms, I am arguing that the logic of *Roe* consummated in *Harris* translates the ideology of the private sphere into the individual woman's legal right to privacy as a means of subordinating women's collective needs to the imperatives of male supremacy.

This is my retrospective on *Roe v. Wade*: reproduction is sexual, men control sexuality, and the state supports the interest of men as a group. *Roe* does not contradict this. So why was abortion legalized; why were women even imagined to have such a right as privacy? It is not an accusation of bad faith to answer that the interests of men as a social group converge with the definition of justice embodied in law in what I call the male point of view. The way the male point of view constructs a social event or legal need will be the way that social event or legal need is framed by state policy. For example, to the extent possession is the point of sex, illegal rape will be sex with a woman who is not yours unless the act makes her yours. If part of the kick of pornography involves eroticizing the putatively prohibited, illegal pornography—obscenity—will be prohibited enough to keep pornography desirable without ever making it truly illegitimate or unavailable. If, from the male standpoint, male is the implicit definition of human, maleness will be the implicit standard by which sex equality is measured in discrimination law. In parallel terms, abortion's availability frames, and is framed by, the conditions under which men, worked out between themselves, will grant legitimacy to women to control the reproductive consequences of intercourse.

Since Freud, the social problem posed by sexuality has been perceived as the problem of the innate desire for sexual pleasure being repressed by the constraints of civilization. Inequality arises as an issue in this context only in women's repressive socialization to passivity and coolness (so-called frigidity), in women's so-called desexualization, and in the disparate consequences of biology, that is, pregnancy. Who defines what is sexual, what sexuality therefore is, to whom what stimuli are erotic and why, and who defines the conditions under which sexuality is expressed—these issues are not even available for consideration. "Civilization's" answer to these questions instead fuses women's reproductivity with our attributed sexuality in its definition of what a woman is. We are defined as women by the uses to which men put us. In this context it becomes clear why the struggle for reproductive freedom has never included a woman's right to refuse sex. In this notion of sexual liberation, the equality issue has been framed as a struggle for women to have sex with men on the same terms as men: without consequences. In this sense the abortion right has been sought as freedom from the unequal reproductive consequences of sexual expression, with sexuality defined as centered on heterosexual genital intercourse. It has been as if biological organisms, rather than social relations, reproduce the species. But if your concern is not how more people can get more sex, if instead your concern is who defines sexuality—hence pleasure and violation—then the abortion right is situated within a very different problematic: the social and political problematic of the inequality of the sexes. As Susan Sontag said, "Sex itself is not liberating for women. Neither is more sex. . . . The question is, what sexuality shall women be liberated to enjoy?"[13] To be able to address this requires rethinking the problem of sexuality, from the repression of drives by civilization to the oppression of women by men.

Arguments for abortion under the rubric of feminism have rested upon the right to control one's own body—gender neutral. I think that argument has been appealing for the same reasons it is inadequate: Socially, women's bodies have not been ours; we have not controlled their meanings and destinies. Feminists tried to assert that control without risking the pursuit of the idea that something more might be at stake than our bodies, something closer to a net of relations in which we are (at present unescapedly) gendered.[14] Some feminists have noticed that our right to decide has become merged with an overwhelmingly male profession's right not to have his professional judgment second-guessed by the government.[15] But most abortion advocates argue in rigidly and rigorously gender-neutral terms.

Thus, for instance, because Judith Jarvis Thomson's celebrated abducted violinist had no obligation to be somebody else's life support system, women have no obligation to support a fetus.[16] Never mind that no woman who needs an abortion—no woman period—is valued, no potential a woman's life might hold is cherished, like a gender-neutral famous violinist's unencumbered possibilities. Not to mention that in that hypothetical, the underlying parallel to rape—the origin in force, in abduction, that gives the hypothetical its weight while confining its application to instances in which force is recognized as force—is seldom interrogated in the abortion context for its applicability to the normal case. And abortion policy is to apply to the normal case. So we need to talk about sex, specifically about intercourse in relation to rape in relation to conception. By avoiding this issue in the abortion context liberal feminists have obscured the unequal basis on which they are attempting to construct our personhood.

The meaning of abortion in the context of a sexual critique of gender inequality is its promise to women of sex with men on the same terms as promised to men—that is, "without consequences." Under conditions in which women do not control access to our sexuality, this facilitates women's heterosexual availability. In other words, under conditions of gender inequality, sexual liberation in this sense does not free women, it frees male sexual aggression. The availability of abortion thus removes the one remaining legitimized reason that women have had for refusing sex besides the headache. As Andrea Dworkin puts it, analyzing male ideology on abortion: "Getting laid was at stake."[17] The Playboy Foundation has supported abortion rights from day one; it continues to, even with shrinking disposable funds, on a level of priority comparable to its opposition to censorship.

Privacy doctrine is an ideal vehicle for this process. The democratic liberal ideal of the private holds that, so long as the public does not interfere, autonomous individuals interact freely and equally. Conceptually, this private is hermetic. It *means* that which is inaccessible to, unaccountable to, unconstructed by anything beyond itself. By definition, it is not part of or conditioned by anything systematic or outside of it. It is personal, intimate, autonomous, particular, individual, the original source and final outpost of the self, gender neutral. It is, in short, defined by everything that feminism reveals women have never been allowed to be or to have, and everything that women have been equated with and defined in terms of *men's* ability to have. It contradicts the liberal definition of the private to complain in public of inequality within it. In this view, no act of the state contributes to—hence should properly participate in—shaping its internal alignments or distributing its internal forces. Its inviolability by the state, framed as an individual right, presupposes that it is not already an arm of the state. In this scheme, intimacy is implicitly thought to guarantee symmetry of power. Injuries arise in violating the private sphere, not within and by and because of it.

In private, consent tends to be presumed. It is true that a showing of coercion voids this presumption. But the problem is getting anything private to be perceived as coercive. Why one would allow force in private—the "why doesn't she leave" question raised to battered women—is a question given its urgency by the social meaning of the private as a sphere of choice. But for women the measure of the intimacy has been the measure of the oppression. This is why feminism has had to explode the private. This is why feminism has seen the personal as the political. The private is public for those for whom the personal is political. In this sense, there is no private, either normatively or empirically. Feminism confronts the fact that women have no privacy to lose or to guarantee. We are not inviolable. Our sexuality is not only violable, it is—hence, we are—seen *in* and *as* our violation. To confront the fact that we have no privacy is to confront the intimate degradation of women as the public order.

In this light, a right to privacy looks like an injury got up as a gift. Freedom from public intervention coexists uneasily with any right which requires social preconditions to be meaningfully delivered. For example, if inequality is socially pervasive and enforced, equality will require intervention, not abdication, to be meaningful. But the right to privacy is not thought to require social change. It is not even thought to require any social preconditions, other than nonintervention by the public. The point for the abortion cases is not that indigency—which was the specific barrier to effective choice in *McRae*—is well within the public power to remedy, nor that the state is hardly exempt in issues of the distribution of wealth. The point is rather that *Roe v. Wade* presumes that government nonintervention into the private sphere promotes a woman's freedom of choice. When the alternative is jail, there is much to be said for this argument. But the *McRae* result sustains the meaning of privacy in *Roe*: women are guaranteed by the public no more than what we can get in private—that is, what we can extract through our intimate associations with men. Women with privileges get rights.

So women got abortion as a private privilege, not as a public right. We got control over reproduction that is controlled by "a man or The Man," an individual man or the doctors or the government. Abortion was not decriminalized, it was legalized. In *Roe*, the government set the stage for the conditions under which women gain access to this right. Virtually every ounce of control that women won out of legalization has gone directly into the hands of men—husbands, doctors, or fathers—or is now in the process of attempting to be reclaimed through regulation.[18] This, surely, must be what is meant by reform.

It is not inconsistent, then, that framed as a privacy right a woman's decision to abort would have no claim on public support and would genuinely not be seen as burdened by that deprivation. Privacy conceived as a right from public intervention and disclosure is the opposite of the relief that *McRae* sought for welfare women. State intervention would have provided a choice women did *not* have in private. The women in *McRae*, women whose sexual refusal has counted for particularly little, needed something to make their privacy effective.[19] The logic of the court's response resembles the logic by which women are supposed to consent to sex. Preclude the alternatives, then call the sole remaining option "her choice." The point is that the alternatives are precluded *prior to* the reach of the chosen legal doctrine. They are precluded by conditions of sex, race, and class—the very conditions the privacy frame not only leaves tacit, but which it exists to *guarantee*.

When the law of privacy restricts intrusions into intimacy, it bars change in control over that intimacy. The existing distribution of power and resources within the private sphere will be precisely what the law of privacy exists to protect. Just as pornography is legally protected as individual freedom of expression—without questioning whose freedom and whose expression and at whose expense—abstract privacy protects abstract autonomy, without inquiring into whose freedom of action is being sanctioned, at whose expense. It is probably not coincidence that the very things feminism regards as central to the subjection of women—the very place, the body; the very relations, heterosexual; the very activities, intercourse and reproduction; and the very feelings, intimate—form the core of privacy doctrine's coverage. From this perspective, the legal concept of privacy can and has shielded the place of battery, marital rape, and women's exploited labor; has preserved the central institutions whereby women are *deprived* of identity, autonomy, control and self-definition; and has protected the primary activity through which male supremacy is expressed and enforced.

To fail to recognize the meaning of the private in the ideology and reality of women's subordination by seeking protection behind a right *to* that privacy is to cut women off from collective verification and state support in the same act. I think this has a lot to do with why we can't organize women on the abortion issue. When women are segregated in private, separated from each other, one at a time, a right *to* that privacy isolates us at once from each other and from public recourse. This right to privacy is a right of men "to be let alone" to oppress women one at a time.[20] It embodies and reflects the private sphere's existing definition of womanhood. This instance of liberalism—applied to women as if we *are* persons, gender neutral—reinforces the division between public and private that is *not* gender neutral. It is at once an ideological division that lies about women's shared experience and mystifies the unity among the spheres of women's violation. It is a very material division that keeps the private beyond public redress and depoliticizes women's subjection within it. It keeps some men out of the bedrooms of other men.

Notes

1. See my article, "Feminism, Marxism, Method and the State," *Signs* 8 (1983): 635–58.

2. This is not to suggest that the decision should have gone the other way, or to propose individual hearings to determine coercion prior to allowing abortions. Nor is it to criticize Justice Blackmun, author of the majority opinion in *Roe*, who probably saw legalizing abortion as a way to help women out of a desperate situation, which it has done.

3. D. H. Regan, "Rewriting *Roe v. Wade*." 77 *Michigan Law Review* 1569 (1979), in which the Good Samaritan happens in the fetus.

4. As of 1973, ten states that made abortion a crime had exceptions for rape and incest; at least three had exceptions for rape only. Many of these exceptions were based on Model Penal Code Section 230.3 (Proposed Official Draft 1962), quoted in *Doe v. Bolton*, 410 U.S. 179, 205–7, App. B (1973), permitting abortion, *inter alia*, in cases of "rape, incest, or other felonious intercourse." References to states with incest and rape exceptions can be found in *Roe v. Wade*, 410 U.S. 113 n.37 (1973). Some versions of the Hyde Amendment, which prohibits use of public money to fund

abortions, have contained exceptions for cases of rape or incest. All require immediate reporting of the incident.

5. Kristin Luker, *Taking Chances: Abortion and the Decision Not to Contracept* (Berkeley and Los Angeles: University of California Press, 1976).

6. *Roe v. Wade,* 410 U.S. 113 (1973).

7. *Griswold v. Connecticut,* 381 U.S. 479 (1965).

8. *Eisenstadt v. Baird,* 405 U.S. 438 (1972).

9. *Harris v. McRae,* 448 U.S. 297 (1980).

10. T. Gerety, "Redefining Privacy," *Harvard Civil Rights Civil Liberties Law Review* 12 (1977): 233–96, at 236.

11. Kenneth I. Karst, "The Freedom of Intimate Association," *Yale Law Journal* 89 (1980): 624; "Developments—The Family," *Harvard Law Review* 93 (1980): 1157–1383; *Doe v. Commonwealth Atty,* 403 F. Supp. 1199 (E.D. Va. 1975), *aff'd without opinion,* 425 U.S. 901 (1976) but cf. *People v. Onofre,* 51 N.Y.2d 476 (1980), *cert. denied* 451 U.S. 987 (1981).

12. Tom Grey, "Eros, Civilization and the Burger Court," *Law and Contemporary Problems* 43 (1980): 83.

13. Susan Sontag, "The Third World of Women," *Partisan Review* 40 (1973): 188.

14. See Adrienne Rich, *Of Women Born: Motherhood As Experience and Institution* (New York: Bantam Books, 1977), ch. 3, "The Kingdom of the Fathers," esp. pp. 47, 48: "The child that I carry for nine months can be defined *neither* as me or as not-me" (emphasis in the original).

15. Kristin Booth Glen, "Abortion in the Courts: A Lay Women's Historical Guide to the New Disaster Area," *Feminist Studies* 4 (1978): 1.

16. Judith Jarvis Thomson, "A Defense of Abortion," *Philosophy and Public Affairs* 1 (1971): 47–66.

17. Andrea Dworkin, *Right Wing Women* (New York: Perigee, 1983). You must read this book. See also Friedrich Engels arguing on removing private housekeeping into social industry, *Origin of the Family, Private Property and the State* (New York: International Publishers, 1942).

18. *H. L. v. Matheson,* 450 U.S. 398 (1981); *Poe v. Gerstein; Bellotti v. Baird,* 443 U.S. 622 (1979); but cf. *Planned Parenthood of Central Missouri v. Danforth,* 428 U.S. 52 (1976).

19. See Dworkin, *Right Wing Women,* pp. 98–99.

20. S. Warren and L. Brandeis, "The Right to Privacy," *Harvard Law Review* 4 (1890); 190, p. 205; but note that the right of privacy under some *state* constitutions has been held to *include* funding for abortions: *Committee to Defend Reproductive Rights v. Meyers,* 29 Cal. 3d 252 (1981); *Moe v. Society of Admin. and Finance,* 417 N.E.2d 387 (Mass. 1981).

On the Moral and Legal Status of Abortion

Mary Anne Warren

We will be concerned with both the moral status of abortion, which for our purposes we may define as the act which a woman performs in voluntarily terminating, or allowing another person to terminate, her pregnancy, and the legal status which is appropriate for this act. I will argue that, while it is not possible to produce a satisfactory defense of a woman's right to obtain an abortion without showing that a fetus is not a human being, in the morally relevant sense of that term, we ought not to conclude that the difficulties involved in determining whether or not a fetus is human make it impossible to produce any satisfactory solution to the problem of the moral status of abortion. For it is possible to show that, on the basis of intuitions which we may expect even the opponents of abortion to share, a fetus is not a person, and hence not the sort of entity to which it is proper to ascribe full moral rights.

Of course, while some philosophers would deny the possibility of any such proof,[1] others will deny that there is any need for it, since the moral permissibility of abortion appears to them to be too obvious to require proof. But the inadequacy of this attitude should be evident from the fact that both the friends and the foes of abortion consider their position to be morally self-evident. Because pro-abortionists have never adequately come to grips with the conceptual issues surrounding abortion, most, if not all, of the arguments which they advance in opposition to laws restricting access to abortion fail to refute or even weaken the traditional anti-abortion argument, i.e., that a fetus is a human being, and therefore abortion is murder.

Reprinted from *The Monist*, vol. 57, no. 1 (1973), pp. 43–61. Copyright © 1973, *The Monist*, LaSalle, IL 61301. Used by permission of *The Monist*.

These arguments are typically of one of two sorts. Either they point to the terrible side effects of the restrictive laws, e.g., the deaths due to illegal abortions, and the fact that it is poor women who suffer the most as a result of these laws, or else they state that to deny a woman access to abortion is to deprive her of her right to control her own body. Unfortunately, however, the fact that restricting access to abortion has tragic side effects does not, in itself, show that the restrictions are unjustified, since murder is wrong regardless of the consequences of prohibiting it; and the appeal to the right to control one's body, which is generally construed as a property right, is at best a rather feeble argument for the permissibility of abortion. Mere ownership does not give me the right to kill innocent people whom I find on my property, and indeed I am apt to be held responsible if such people injure themselves while on my property. It is equally unclear that I have any moral right to expel an innocent person from my property when I know that doing so will result in his death.

Furthermore, it is probably inappropriate to describe a woman's body as her property, since it seems natural to hold that a person is something distinct from her property, but not from her body. Even those who would object to the identification of a person with his body, or with the conjunction of his body and his mind, must admit that it would be very odd to describe, say, breaking a leg, as damaging one's property, and much more appropriate to describe it as injuring oneself. Thus it is probably a mistake to argue that the right to obtain an abortion is in any way derived from the right to own and regulate property.

But however we wish to construe the right to abortion, we cannot hope to convince those who consider abortion a form of murder of the existence of any such right unless we are able to produce a clear and convincing refutation of the traditional anti-abortion argument, and this has not, to my knowledge, been done. With respect to the two most vital issues which that argument involves, i.e., the humanity of the fetus and its implication for the moral status of abortion, confusion has prevailed on both sides of the dispute.

Thus, both pro-abortionists and anti-abortionists have tended to abstract the question of whether abortion is wrong to that of whether it is wrong to destroy a fetus, just as though the rights of another person were not necessarily involved. This mistaken abstraction has led to the almost universal assumption that if a fetus is a human being, with a right to life, then it follows immediately that abortion is wrong (except perhaps when necessary to save the woman's life), and that it ought to be prohibited. It has also been generally assumed that unless the question about the status of the fetus is answered, the moral status of abortion cannot possibly be determined.

Two recent papers, one by B. A. Brody,[2] and one by Judith Thomson,[3] have attempted to settle the question of whether abortion ought to be prohibited apart from the question of whether or not the fetus is human. Brody examines the possibility that the following two statements are compatible: (1) that abortion is the taking of an innocent human, and therefore wrong; and (2) that nevertheless it ought not to be prohibited by law, at least under the present circumstances.[4] Not surprisingly, Brody finds it impossible to reconcile these two statements since, as he rightly argues, none of the unfortunate side effects of the prohibition of abortion is bad enough to justify legalizing the *wrongful* taking of human life. He is mistaken, however, in concluding that the incompatibility of (1) and (2), in itself, shows that "the legal problem about abortion cannot be resolved independently of the status of the fetus problem" [p. 369].

What Brody fails to realize is that (1) embodies the questionable assumption that if a fetus is a human being, then of course abortion is morally wrong, and that an attack on this assumption is more promising, as a way of reconciling the humanity of the fetus with the claim that laws prohibiting abortion are unjustified than is an attack on the assumption that if abortion is the wrongful killing of innocent human beings then it ought to be prohibited. He thus overlooks the possibility that a fetus may have a right to life and abortion still be morally permissible, in that the right of a woman to terminate an unwanted pregnancy might override the right of the fetus to be kept alive. The immorality of abortion is no more demonstrated by the humanity of the fetus, in itself, than the immorality of killing in self-defense is demonstrated by the fact that the assailant is a human being. Neither is it demonstrated by the *innocence* of the fetus, since there may be situations in which the killing of innocent human beings is justified.

It is perhaps not surprising that Brody fails to spot this assumption, since it has been accepted with little or no argument by nearly everyone who has written on the morality of abortion. John Noonan is correct in saying that "the fundamental question in the long history of abortion is, How do you determine the humanity of a being?"[5] He summarizes his own anti-abortion argument, which is a version of the official position of the Catholic Church, as follows:

> . . . it is wrong to kill humans, however poor, weak, defenseless, and lacking in opportunity to develop their potential they may be. It is therefore morally wrong to kill Biafrans. Similarly, it is morally wrong to kill embryos.[6]

Noonan bases his claim that fetuses are human upon what he calls the theologians' criterion of humanity: that whoever is conceived of human beings is human. But although he argues at length for the appropriateness of this criterion, he never questions the assumption that if a fetus is human then abortion is wrong for exactly the same reason that murder is wrong.

Judith Thomson is, in fact, the only writer I am aware of who has seriously questioned this assumption; she has argued that, even if we grant the anti-abortionist his claim that a fetus is a human being, with the same right to life as any other human being, we can still demonstrate that, in at least some and perhaps most cases, a woman is under no moral obligation to complete an unwanted pregnancy.[7] Her argument is worth examining, since if it holds up it may enable us to establish the moral permissibility of abortion without becoming involved in problems about what entitles an entity to be considered human, and accorded full moral rights. To be able to do this would be a great gain in the power and simplicity of the pro-abortion position, since, although I will argue that these problems can be solved at least as decisively as can any other moral problem, we should certainly be pleased to be able to avoid having to solve them as part of the justification of abortion.

On the other hand, even if Thomson's argument does not hold up, her insight, i.e., that it requires argument to show that if fetuses are human then abortion is properly classified as murder, is an extremely valuable one. The assumption she attacks is particularly invidious, for it amounts to the decision that it is appropriate, in deciding the moral status of abortion, to leave the rights of the pregnant woman out of consideration entirely, except possibly when her life is threatened. Obviously, this will not do; determining what moral rights, if any, a fetus possesses is only the first step in determining the moral status of abortion. Step two, which is at least equally essential, is finding a just solution to the conflict between whatever rights the fetus may have, and the rights of the woman who is unwillingly pregnant. While the historical error has been to pay far too little attention to the second step, Ms. Thomson's suggestion is that if we look at the second step first we may find that a woman has a right to obtain an abortion regardless of what rights the fetus has.

Our own inquiry will also have two stages. In Section I, we will consider whether or not it is possible to establish that abortion is morally permissible even on the assumption that a fetus is an entity with a full-fledged right to life. I will argue that in fact this cannot be established, at least not with the conclusiveness which is essential to our hopes of convincing those who are skeptical about the morality of abortion, and that we therefore cannot avoid dealing with the question of whether or not a fetus really does have the same right to life as a (more fully developed) human being.

In Section II, I will propose an answer to this question, namely, that a fetus cannot be considered a member of the moral community, the set of beings with full and equal moral rights, for the simple reason that it is not a person, and that it is personhood, and not genetic humanity, i.e., humanity as defined by Noonan, whatever its stage of development, satisfies none of the basic criteria of personhood, and is not even enough *like* a person to be accorded even some of the same rights on the basis of this resemblance. Nor, as we will see, is a fetus's *potential* personhood a threat to the morality of abortion, since, whatever the rights of potential people may be, they are invariably overridden in any conflict with the moral rights of actual people.

I

We turn now to Professor Thomson's case for the claim that even if a fetus has full moral rights, abortion is still morally permissible, at least sometimes, and for some reasons other than to save the woman's life. Her argument is based upon a clever, but I think faulty, analogy. She asks us to picture ourselves waking up one day, in bed with a famous violinist. Imagine that you have been kidnapped, and your bloodstream hooked up to that of the violinist, who happens to have an ailment which will certainly kill him unless he is permitted to share your kidneys for a period of nine months. No one else can save him, since you alone have the right type of blood. He will be unconscious all that time, and you will have to stay in bed with him, but after the nine months are over he may be unplugged, completely cured, that is provided that you have cooperated.

Now then, she continues, what are your obligations in this situation? The anti-abortionist, if he is consistent, will have to say that you are obligated to stay in bed with the violinist: for all people have a right to life, and violinists are people, and therefore it would be murder for you to disconnect yourself from him and let him die [p. 174]. But this is outrageous, and so there must be something wrong with the same argument when it is applied to abortion. It would certainly be commendable of you to agree to save the violinist, but it is absurd to suggest that your refusal to do so would be murder. His right to life does not obligate you to do whatever is required to keep him alive; nor does it justify anyone else in forcing you to do so. A law which required you to stay in bed with the violinist would clearly be an unjust law, since it is no proper function of the law to force unwilling people to make huge sacrifices for the sake of other people toward whom they have no such prior obligation.

Thomson concludes that, if this analogy is an apt one, then we can grant the anti-abortionist his claim that a fetus is a human being, and still hold that it is at least sometimes the case that a pregnant woman has the right to refuse to be a Good Samaritan towards the fetus, i.e., to obtain an abortion. For there is a great gap between the claim that x has a right to life, and the claim that y is obligated to do whatever is necessary to keep x alive, let alone that he ought to be forced to do so. It is y's duty to keep x alive only if he has somehow contracted a *special obligation* to do so; and a woman who is unwillingly pregnant, i.e., who has been raped, has done nothing which obligates her to make the enormous sacrifice which is necessary to preserve the conceptus.

This argument is initially quite plausible, and in the extreme case of pregnancy due to rape it is probably conclusive. Difficulties arise, however, when we try to specify more exactly the range of cases in which abortion is clearly justifiable even on the assumption that the fetus is human. Professor Thomson considers it a virtue of her argument that it does not enable us to conclude that abortion is always permissible. It would, she says, be "indecent" for a woman in her seventh month to obtain an abortion just to avoid having to postpone a trip to Europe. On the other hand, her argument enables us to see that "a sick and desperately frightened schoolgirl pregnant due to rape may *of course* choose abortion, and that any law which rules this out is an insane law" [p. 187]. So far, so good; but what are we to say about the woman who becomes pregnant not through rape but as a result of her own carelessness, or because of contraceptive failure, or who gets pregnant intentionally and then changes her mind about wanting a child? With respect to such cases, the violinist analogy is of much less use to the defender of the woman's right to obtain an abortion.

Indeed, the choice of a pregnancy due to rape, as an example of a case in which abortion is permissible even if a fetus is considered a human being, is extremely significant; for it is only in the case of pregnancy due to rape that the woman's situation is adequately analogous to the violinist case for our intuitions about the latter to transfer convincingly. The crucial difference between a pregnancy due to rape and the normal case of an unwanted pregnancy is that in the normal case we cannot claim that the woman is in no way responsible for her predicament; she could have remained chaste, or taken her pills more faithfully, or abstained on dangerous days, and so on. If, on the other hand, you are kidnapped by strangers, and hooked up to a strange violinist, then you are free of any shred of responsibility for the situation, on the basis of which it could be argued that you are obligated to keep the violinist alive. Only when her pregnancy is due to rape is a woman clearly just as nonresponsible.[8]

Consequently, there is room for the anti-abortionist to argue that in the normal case of unwanted pregnancy a woman has, by her own actions, assumed responsibility for the fetus. For if x behaves in a way which he could have avoided, and which he knows involves, let us say, a 1 percent chance of bringing into existence a human being, with a right to life, and does so knowing that if this should happen then that human being will perish unless x does certain things to keep him alive, then it is by no means clear that when it does happen x is free of any obligation to what he knew in advance would be required to keep that human being alive.

The plausibility of such an argument is enough to show that the Thomson analogy can provide a clear and persuasive defense of a woman's right to obtain an abortion only with respect to those cases in which the woman is in no way responsible for her pregnancy, e.g., where it is due to rape. In all other cases, we would almost certainly conclude that it was necessary to look carefully at the particular circumstances in order to determine the extent of the woman's responsibility, and hence the extent of her obligation. This is an extremely unsatisfactory outcome, from the viewpoint of the opponents of restrictive abortion laws, most of whom are convinced that a woman has a right to obtain an abortion regardless of how and why she got pregnant.

Of course a supporter of the violinist analogy might point out that it is absurd to suggest that forgetting her pill one day might be sufficient to obligate a woman to complete an unwanted pregnancy. And indeed it is absurd to suggest this. As we will see, the moral right to obtain an abortion is not in the least dependent upon the extent to which the woman is responsible for her pregnancy. But unfortunately, once we allow the assumption that a fetus has full moral rights, we cannot avoid taking this absurd suggestion seriously. Perhaps we can make this point more clear by altering the violinist story just enough to make it more analogous to a normal unwanted pregnancy and less to a pregnancy due to rape, and then seeing whether it is still obvious that you are not obligated to stay in bed with the fellow.

Suppose, then, that violinists are peculiarly prone to the sort of illness the only cure for which is the use of someone else's bloodstream for nine months, and that because of this there has been formed a society of music lovers who agree that whenever a violinist is stricken they will draw lots and the loser will, by some means, be made the one and only person capable of saving him. Now then, would you be obligated to cooperate in curing the violinist if you had voluntarily joined this society, knowing the possible consequences, and then your name had been drawn and you had been kidnapped? Admittedly, you did not promise ahead of time that you would, but you did deliberately place yourself in a position in which it might happen that a human life would be lost if you did not. Surely this is at least a *prima facie* reason for supposing that you have an obligation to stay in bed with the violinist. Suppose that you had gotten your name drawn deliberately; surely that would be quite a strong reason for thinking that you had such an obligation.

It might be suggested that there is one important disanalogy between the modified violinist case and the case of an unwanted pregnancy, which makes the woman's responsibility significantly less, namely, the fact that the fetus comes into existence as the result of the woman's actions. This fact might give her a right to refuse to keep it alive, whereas she would not have had this right had it existed previously, independently, and then as a result of her actions become dependent upon her for its survival.

My own intuition, however, is that x has no more right to bring into existence either deliberately or as a foreseeable result of actions he could have avoided, a being with full moral rights (y), and then refuse to do what he knew beforehand would be required to keep that being alive, than he has to enter into an agreement with an existing person, whereby he may be called upon to save that person's life, and then refuse to do so when so called upon. Thus, x's responsibility for y's existence does not seem to lessen his obligation to keep y alive, if he is also responsible for y's being in a situation in which only he can save him.

Whether or not this intuition is entirely correct, it brings us back once again to the conclusion that once we allow the assumption that a fetus has full moral rights it becomes an extremely complex and difficult question whether and when abortion is justifiable. Thus the Thomson analogy cannot help us produce a clear and persuasive proof of the moral permissibility of abortion. Nor will the opponents of the restrictive laws thank us for anything less; for their conviction (for the most part) is that abortion is obviously not a morally serious and extremely unfortunate, even though sometimes justified act, comparable to killing in self-defense or to letting the violinist die, but rather is closer to being a morally neutral act, like cutting one's hair.

The basis of this conviction, I believe, is the realization that a fetus is not a person, and thus does not have a full-fledged right to life. Perhaps the reason why this claim has been so inadequately defended is that it seems self-evident to those who accept it. And so it is, insofar as it follows from what I take to be perfectly obvious claims about the nature of personhood, and about the proper grounds for ascribing moral rights, claims which ought, indeed, to be obvious to both the friends and foes of abortion. Nevertheless, it is worth examining these claims, and showing how they demonstrate the moral innocuousness of abortion, since this apparently has not been adequately done before.

II

The question which we must answer in order to produce a satisfactory solution to the problem of the moral status of abortion is this: How are we to define the moral community, the set of beings with full and equal moral rights, such that we can decide whether a human fetus is a member of this community or not? What sort of entity, exactly, has the inalienable rights to life, liberty, and the pursuit of happiness? Jefferson attributed these rights to all men, and it may or may not be fair to suggest that he intended to attribute them only to men. Perhaps he ought to have attributed them to all human beings. If so, then we arrive, first, at Noonan's problem of deciding what makes a being human, and second, at the equally vital question which Noonan does not consider, namely, What reason is there for identifying the moral community with the set of all human beings, in whatever way we have chosen to define that term?

On the Definition of "Human"

One reason why this vital second question is so frequently overlooked in the debate over the moral status of abortion is that the term "human" has two distinct, but not often distinguished, senses. This fact results in a slide of meaning, which serves to conceal the fallaciousness of the traditional argument that since (1) it is wrong to kill innocent human beings, and (2) fetuses are innocent human beings, then (3) it is wrong to kill fetuses. For if "human" is used in the same sense in both (1) and (2) then, whichever of the two senses is meant, one of these premises is question-begging. And if it is used in two different senses then of course the conclusion doesn't follow.

Thus, (1) is a self-evident moral truth,[9] and avoids begging the question about abortion, only if "human being" is used to mean something like "a full-fledged member of the moral community." (It may or may not also be meant to refer exclusively to members of the species Homo sapiens.) We may call this the moral sense of "human." It is not to be confused with what we will call the genetic sense, i.e., the sense in which any member of the species is a human being, and no member of any other species could be. If (1) is acceptable only if the moral sense is intended, (2) is non-question-begging only if what is intended is the genetic sense.

In "Deciding Who Is Human," Noonan argues for the classification of fetuses with human beings by pointing to the presence of the full genetic code, and the potential capacity for rational thought. . . . It is clear that what he needs to show, for his version of the traditional argument to be valid, is that fetuses are human in the moral sense, the sense in which it is analytically true that all human beings have full moral rights. But, in the absence of any argument showing that whatever is genetically human is also morally human, and he gives none, nothing more than genetic humanity can be demonstrated by the presence of the human genetic code. And, as we will see, the potential capacity for rational thought can at most show that an entity has the potential for becoming human in the moral sense.

Defining the Moral Community

Can it be established that genetic humanity is sufficient for moral humanity? I think that there are very good reasons for not defining the moral community in this way. I would like to suggest an alternative way of defining the moral community, which I will argue for only to the extent of explaining why it is, or should be, self-evident. The suggestion is simply that the moral community consists of all and only *people,* rather than all and only human beings;[10] and probably the best way of demonstrating its self-evidence is by considering the concept of personhood, to see what sorts of entities are and are not persons, and what the decision that a being is or is not a person implies about its moral rights.

What characteristics entitle an entity to be considered a person? This is obviously not the place to attempt a complete analysis of the concept of personhood, but we do not need such a fully adequate analysis just to determine whether and why a fetus is or isn't a person. All we need is a rough and approximate list of the most basic criteria of personhood, and some idea of which, or how many, of these an entity must satisfy in order to properly be considered a person.

In searching for such criteria, it is useful to look beyond the set of people with whom we are acquainted, and ask how we would decide whether a totally alien being was a person or not. (For we have no right to assume that genetic humanity is necessary for personhood.) Imagine a space traveler who lands on an unknown planet and encounters a race of beings utterly unlike any he has ever seen or heard of. If he wants to be sure of behaving morally toward these beings, he has to somehow decide whether they are people, and hence have full moral rights, or whether they are the sort of thing which he need not feel guilty about treating as, for example, a source of food.

How should he go about making this decision? If he has some anthropological background, he might look for such things as religion, art, and the manufacturing of tools, weapons, or shelters, since these factors have been used to distinguish our human from our prehuman ancestors, in what seems to be closer to the moral than the genetic sense of "human." And no doubt he would be right to consider the presence of such factors as good evidence that the alien beings were people, and morally human. It would, however, be overly anthropocentric of him to take the absence of these things as adequate evidence that they were not, since we can imagine people who have progressed beyond, or evolved without ever developing, these cultural characteristics.

I suggest that the traits which are most central to the concept of personhood, or humanity in the moral sense, are, very roughly, the following:

1. consciousness (of objects and events external and/or internal to the being), and in particular the capacity to feel pain;

2. reasoning (the developed capacity to solve new and relatively complex problems);

3. self-motivated activity (activity which is relatively independent of either genetic or direct external control);

4. the capacity to communicate, by whatever means, messages of an indefinite variety of types, that is, not just with an indefinite number of possible contents, but on indefinitely many possible topics;

5. the presence of self-concepts, and self-awareness, either individual or racial, or both.

Admittedly, there are apt to be a great many problems involved in formulating precise definitions of these criteria, let alone in developing universally valid behavioral criteria for deciding when they apply. But I will assume that both we and our explorer know approximately what (1)–(5) mean, and that he is also able to determine whether or not they apply. How, then, should he use his findings to decide whether or not the alien beings are people? We needn't suppose that an entity must have all of these attributes to be properly considered a person; (1) and (2) alone may well be sufficient for personhood, and quite probably (1)–(3) are sufficient. Neither do we need to insist that any one of these criteria is necessary for personhood, although once again (1) and (2) look like fairly good candidates for **necessary conditions**, as does (3), if "activity" is construed so as to include the activity of reasoning.

All we need to claim, to demonstrate that a fetus is not a person, is that any being which satisfies none of (1)–(5) is certainly not a person. I consider this claim to be so obvious that I think anyone who denied it, and claimed that a being which satisfied none of (1)–(5) was a person all the same, would thereby demonstrate that he had no notion at all of what a person is— perhaps because he had confused the concept of a person with that of genetic humanity. If the opponents of abortion were to deny the appropriateness of these five criteria, I do not know what further arguments would convince them. We would probably have to admit that our conceptual schemes were indeed irreconcilably different, and that our dispute could not be settled objectively.

I do not expect this to happen, however, since I think that the concept of a person is one which is very nearly universal (to people), and that it is common to both pro-abortionists and anti-abortionists, even though neither group has fully realized the relevance of this concept to the resolution of their dispute. Furthermore, I think that on reflection even the anti-abortionists ought to agree not only that (1)–(5) are central to the concept of personhood, but also that it is a part of this concept that all and only people have full moral rights. The concept of a person is in part a moral concept; once we have admitted that x is a person we have recognized, even if we have not agreed to respect, x's right to be treated as a member of the moral community. It is true that the claim that x is a human being is more commonly voiced as part of an appeal to treat x decently than is the claim that x is a person, but this is either because "human being" is here used in the sense which implies personhood, or because the genetic and moral senses of "human" have been confused.

Now if (1)–(5) are indeed the primary criteria of personhood, then it is clear that genetic humanity is neither necessary nor sufficient for establishing that an entity is a person. Some human beings are not people, and there may well be people who are not human beings. A man or woman whose consciousness has been permanently obliterated but who remains alive is a human being which is no longer a person; defective human beings, with no appreciable mental capacity, are not and presumably never will be people; and a fetus is a human being which is not yet a person, and which therefore cannot coherently be said to have full moral rights. Citizens of the next century should be prepared to recognize highly advanced, self-aware robots or computers, should such be developed, and intelligent inhabitants of other worlds, should such be found, as people in the fullest sense, and to respect their moral rights. But to ascribe full moral rights to an entity which is not a person is as absurd as to ascribe moral obligations and responsibilities to such an entity.

Fetal Development and the Right to Life

Two problems arise in the application of these suggestions for the definition of the moral community to the determination of the precise moral status of a human fetus. Given that the paradigm example of a person is a normal adult human being, then (1) How like this paradigm, in particular how far advanced since conception, does a human being need to be before it begins to have a right to life by virtue, not of being fully a person as of yet, but of being like a person? and (2) To what extent, if any, does the fact that a fetus has the potential for becoming a person endow it with some of the same rights? Each of these questions requires some comment.

In answering the first question, we need not attempt a detailed consideration of the moral rights of organisms which are not developed enough, aware enough, intelligent enough, etc., to be considered people, but which resemble people in some respects. It does seem reasonable to suggest that the more like a person, in the relevant respects, a being is, the stronger is the case for regarding it as having a right to life, and indeed the stronger its right to life is. Thus we ought to take seriously the suggestion that, insofar as "the human individual develops biologically in a continuous fashion . . . the rights of a human person might develop in the same way."[11] But we must keep in mind that the attributes which are relevant in determining whether or not an entity is enough like a person to be regarded as having some of the same moral rights are no different from those which are relevant to determining whether or not it is fully a person—i.e., are no different from (1)–(5)—and that being genetically human, or having recognizably human facial and other physical features, or detectable brain activity, or the capacity to survive outside the uterus, are simply not among these relevant attributes.

Thus it is clear that even though a seven- or eight-month fetus has features which make it apt to arouse in us almost the same powerful protective instinct as is commonly aroused by a small infant, nevertheless it is not significantly more person-like than is a very small embryo. It is somewhat more person-like; it can apparently feel and respond to pain, and it may even have a rudimentary form of consciousness, insofar as its brain is quite active. Nevertheless, it seems safe to say that it is not fully conscious, in the way that an infant of a few months is, and that it cannot reason, or communicate messages of indefinitely many sorts, does not engage in self-motivated activity, and has no self-awareness. Thus, in the relevant respects, a fetus, even a fully developed one, is considerably less person-like than is the average mature mammal, indeed the average fish. And I think that a rational person must conclude that if the right to life of a fetus is to be based upon its resemblance to a person, then it cannot be said to have any more right to life than, let us say, a newborn guppy (which also seems to be capable of feeling pain), and that a right of that magnitude could never override a woman's right to obtain an abortion, at any stage of her pregnancy.

There may, of course, be other arguments in favor of placing legal limits upon the stage of pregnancy in which an abortion may be performed. Given the relative safety of the new techniques of artificially inducing labor during the third trimester, the danger to the woman's life or health is no longer such an argument. Neither is the fact that people tend to respond to the thought of abortion in the later stages of pregnancy with emotional repulsion, since mere emotional responses cannot take the place of moral reasoning in determining what ought to be permitted. Nor, finally, is the frequently heard argument that legalizing abortion, especially late in the pregnancy, may erode the level of respect for human life, leading, perhaps, to an increase in unjustified euthanasia and other crimes. For this threat, if it is a threat, can be better met by educating people to the kinds of moral distinctions which we are making here than by limiting access to abortion (which limitation may, in its disregard for the rights of women, be just as damaging to the level of respect for human rights).

Thus, since the fact that even a fully developed fetus is not person-like enough to have any significant right to life on the basis of its person-likeness shows that no legal restrictions upon the stage of pregnancy in which an abortion may be performed can be justified on the grounds that we should protect the rights of the older fetus; and since there is no other apparent justification for such restrictions, we may conclude that they are entirely unjustified. Whether or not it would be *indecent* (whatever that means) for a woman in her seventh month to obtain an abortion just to avoid having to postpone a trip to Europe, it would not, in itself, be *immoral,* and therefore it ought to be permitted.

Potential Personhood and the Right to Life

We have seen that a fetus does not resemble a person in any way which can support the claim that it has even some of the same rights. But what about its *potential,* the fact that if nurtured and allowed to develop naturally it will very probably become a person? Doesn't that alone give it at least some right to life? It is hard to deny that the fact that an entity is a potential person is a strong *prima facie* reason for not destroying it; but we need not conclude from this that a potential person has a right to life, by virtue of that potential. It may be that our feeling that it is better, other things being equal, not to destroy a potential person is better explained by the fact that potential people are still (felt to be) an invaluable resource, not to be lightly squandered. Surely, if every speck of dust were a potential person, we would be much less apt to conclude that every potential person has a right to become actual.

Still, we do not need to insist that a potential person has no right to life whatever. There may well be something immoral, and not just imprudent, about wantonly destroying potential people, when doing so isn't necessary to protect anyone's rights. But even if a potential person does have some *prima facie right* to life, such a right could not possibly outweigh the right of a woman to obtain an abortion, since the rights of any actual person invariably outweigh those of any potential person, whenever the two conflict. Since this may not be immediately obvious in the case of a human fetus, let us look at another case.

Suppose that our space explorer falls into the hands of an alien culture, whose scientists decide to create a few hundred thousand or more human beings, by breaking his body into its component cells, and using these to create fully developed human beings, with, of course, his genetic code. We may imagine that each of these newly created men will have all of the original man's abilities, skills, knowledge, and so on, and also have an individual self-concept, in short that each of them will be a bona fide (though hardly unique) person. Imagine that the whole project will take only seconds, and that its chances of success are extremely high, and that our explorer knows all of this, and also knows that these people will be treated fairly. I maintain that in such a situation he would have every right to escape if he could, and thus to deprive all of these potential people of their potential lives; for his right to life outweighs all of theirs together, in spite of the fact that they are all genetically human, all innocent, and all have a very high probability of becoming people very soon, if only he refrains from acting.

Indeed, I think he would have a right to escape even if it were not his life which the alien scientists planned to take, but only a year of his freedom, or, indeed, only a day. Nor would he be obligated to stay if he had gotten captured (thus bringing all these people-potentials into existence) because of his own carelessness, or even if he had done so deliberately, knowing the consequences. Regardless of how he got captured, he is not morally obligated to remain in captivity for *any* period of time for the sake of permitting any number of potential people to come into actuality, so great is the margin by which one actual person's right to liberty outweighs whatever right to life even a hundred thousand potential people have. And it seems reasonable to conclude that the rights of a woman will outweigh by a similar margin whatever right to life a fetus may have by virtue of its potential personhood.

Thus, neither a fetus's resemblance to a person, nor its potential for becoming a person provides any basis whatever for the claim that it has any significant right to life. Consequently, a woman's right to protect her health, happiness, freedom, and even her life,[12] by terminating an unwanted pregnancy, will always override whatever right to life it may be appropriate to ascribe to a fetus, even a fully developed one. And thus, in the absence of any overwhelming social need for every possible child, the laws which restrict the right to obtain an abortion, or limit the period of pregnancy during which an abortion may be performed, are a wholly unjustified violation of a woman's most basic moral and constitutional rights.[13]

Postscript on Infanticide

Since the publication of this article, many people have written to point out that my argument appears to justify not only abortion but infanticide as well. For a new-born infant is not significantly more person-like than an advanced fetus, and consequently it would seem that if the destruction of the latter is permissible so too must be that of the former. Inasmuch as most people, regardless of how they feel about the morality of abortion, consider infanticide murder, this might appear to be a serious flaw in my argument.

Now, if I am right in holding that it is only people who have a full-fledged right to life, and who can be murdered, and if the criteria of personhood are as I have described them, then it obviously follows that killing a newborn infant isn't murder. It does *not* follow, however, that infanticide is permissible, for two reasons. In the first place, it would be wrong, at least in this country and this period of history, and other things being equal, to kill a new-born infant, because even if its parents do not want it and would not suffer from its destruction, there are other people who would like to have it, and would, in all probability, be deprived of a great deal of pleasure by its destruction. Thus, infanticide is wrong for reasons analogous to those which make it wrong wantonly to destroy natural resources, or great works of art.

Secondly, most people, at least in this country, value infants, and would much prefer that they be preserved, even if foster parents are not immediately available. Most of us would rather be taxed to support orphanages than allow unwanted infants to be destroyed. So long as there are people who want an infant preserved, and who are willing and able to provide the means of caring for it, under reasonably humane conditions, it is *ceteris paribus,* wrong to destroy it.

But, it might be replied, if this argument shows that infanticide is wrong, at least at this time and in this country, doesn't it also show that abortion is wrong? After all, many people value fetuses, and are disturbed by their destruction, and would much prefer that they be preserved, even at some cost to themselves. Furthermore, as a potential source of pleasure to some foster family, a fetus is just as valuable as an infant. There is, however, a crucial difference between the two cases: so long as the fetus is unborn, its preservation contrary to the wishes of the pregnant woman, violates her rights to freedom, happiness, and self-determination. Her rights override the rights of those who would like the fetus preserved, just as if someone's life or limb is threatened by a wild animal, his right to protect himself by destroying the wild animal overrides the rights of those who would prefer that the animal not be harmed.

The minute the infant is born, however, its preservation no longer violates any of its mother's rights, even if she wants it destroyed, because she is free to put it up for adoption. Consequently, while the moment of birth does not mark any sharp discontinuity in the degree to which an infant possesses the right to life, it does mark the end of its mother's right to determine its fate. Indeed, if abortion could be performed without killing the fetus, she would never possess the right to have the fetus destroyed, for the same reasons that she has no right to have an infant destroyed.

On the other hand, it follows from my argument that when an un-wanted or defective infant is born into a society which cannot afford and/or is not willing to care for it, then its destruction is permissible. This conclusion will, no doubt, strike many people as heartless and immoral; but remember that the very existence of people who feel this way, and who are willing and able to provide care for unwanted infants, is reason enough to conclude that they should be preserved.

Notes

1. For example, Roger Wertheimer, who in "Understanding the Abortion Argument," *Philosophy and Public Affairs,* 1, no. 1 (Fall, 1971), argues that the problem of the moral status of abortion is insoluble, in that the dispute over the status of the fetus is not a question of fact at all, but only a question of how one responds to the facts.

2. B. A. Brody, "Abortion and the Law," *The Journal of Philosophy,* 68, no. 12 (June 17, 1971) 357–69.

3. Judith Thomson, "A Defense of Abortion," *Philosophy and Public Affairs,* 1, no. 1 (Fall, 1971).

4. I have abbreviated these statements somewhat, but not in a way which affects the argument.

5. John Noonan, "Abortion and the Catholic Church: A Summary History," *Natural Law Forum,* 12 (1967), 125.

6. John Noonan, "Deciding Who Is Human," *Natural Law Forum,* 13 (1968), 134.

7. "A Defense of Abortion."

8. We may safely ignore the fact that she might have avoided getting raped, e.g., by carrying a gun, since by similar means you might likewise have avoided getting kidnapped, and in neither case does the victim's failure to take all possible precautions against a highly unlikely event (as opposed to reasonable precautions against a rather likely event) mean that she is morally responsible for what happens.

9. Of course, the principle that it is (always) wrong to kill innocent human beings is in need of many modifications, e.g., that it may be permissible to do so to save a greater number of other innocent human beings, but we may safely ignore these complications here.

10. From here on, we will use "human" to mean genetically human, since the moral sense seems closely connected to, and perhaps derived from, the assumption that genetic humanity is sufficient for membership in the moral community.

11. Thomas L. Hayes, "A Biological View," *Commonweal*, 85 (March 17, 1967), 677–78: quoted by Daniel Callahan, in *Abortion, Law, Choice, and Morality* (London: Macmillan & Co., 1970).

12. That is, insofar as the death rate, for the woman, is higher for childbirth than for early abortion.

13. My thanks to the following people, who were kind enough to read and criticize an earlier version of this paper: Herbert Cold, Gene Glass, Anne Lauterbach, Judith Thomson, Mary Mothersill, and Timothy Binkley.

Excerpts from the 1973 Supreme Court Decision in Roe v. Wade

Majority Opinion
(Written by Mr. Justice Harry A. Blackmun)

. . . A recent review of the common law precedents argues that even post-quickening abortion was never established as a common law crime. This is of some importance because while most American courts ruled, in holding or in dictum, that abortion of an unquickened fetus was not criminal under their received common law, others followed Coke in stating that abortion of a quick fetus was a "misprison," a term they translated to mean "misdemeanor." That their reliance on Coke on this aspect of the law was uncritical and, apparently in all reported cases, dictum (due probably to the paucity of common law prosecutions for post-quickening abortion), makes it now appear doubtful that abortion was ever firmly established as a common law crime even with respect to the destruction of a quick fetus. It is . . . apparent that at common law, at the time of the adoption of our Constitution, and throughout the major portion of the 19th century, abortion was viewed with less disfavor than under most American statutes currently in effect. Phrasing it another way, a woman enjoyed a substantially broader right to terminate a pregnancy than she does in most States today. At least with respect to the early stage of pregnancy, and very possibly without such a limitation, the opportunity to make this choice was present in this country well into the 19th century. Even later, the law continued for some time to treat less punitively an abortion procured in early pregnancy. . . .

Three reasons have been advanced to explain historically the enactment of criminal abortion laws in the 19th century and to justify their continued existence.

Reprinted from the Majority and Dissenting Opinions in *Roe v. Wade*.
United States Supreme Court. 410 U.S. 113 (1973).

It has been argued occasionally that these laws were the product of a Victorian social concern to discourage illicit sexual conduct. Texas, however, does not advance this justification in the present case, and it appears that no court or commentator has taken the argument seriously. . . .

A second reason is concerned with abortion as a medical procedure. When most criminal abortion laws were first enacted, the procedure was a hazardous one for the woman. This was particularly true prior to the development of antisepsis. Antiseptic techniques, of course, were based on discoveries by Lister, Pasteur, and others first announced in 1867, but were not generally accepted and employed until about the turn of the century. Abortion mortality was high. Even after 1900, and perhaps until as late as the development of antibiotics in the 1940's, standard modern techniques such as dilatation and curettage were not nearly so safe as they are today. Thus it has been argued that a State's real concern in enacting a criminal abortion law was to protect the pregnant woman, that is, to restrain her from submitting to a procedure that placed her life in serious jeopardy.

Modern medical techniques have altered this situation. Appellants and various *amici* refer to medical data indicating that abortion in early pregnancy, that is, prior to the end of first trimester, although not without its risk, is now relatively safe. Mortality rates for women undergoing early abortions, where the procedure is legal, appear to be as low as or lower than the rates for normal childbirth. Consequently, any interest of the State in protecting the woman from an inherently hazardous procedure, except when it would be equally dangerous for her to forgo it, has largely disappeared. Of course, important state interests in the area of health and medical standards do remain. The State has a legitimate interest in seeing to it that abortion, like any other medical procedure, is performed under circumstances that insure maximum safety for the patient. This interest obviously extends at least to the performing physician and his staff, to the facilities involved, to the availability of after-care, and to adequate provision for any complication or emergency that might arise. The prevalence of high mortality rates at illegal "abortion mills" strengthens, rather than weakens, the State's interest in regulating the conditions under which abortions are performed. Moreover, the risk to the woman increases as her pregnancy continues. Thus the State retains a definite interest in protecting the woman's own health and safety when an abortion is performed at a late stage of pregnancy.

The third reason is the State's interest—some phrase it in terms of duty—in protecting prenatal life. Some of the argument for this justification rests on the theory that a new human life is present from the moment of conception. The State's interest and general obligation to protect life then extends, it is argued, to prenatal life. Only when the life of the pregnant mother herself is at stake, balanced against the life she carries within her, should the interest of the embryo or fetus not prevail. Logically, of course, a legitimate state interest in this area need not stand or fall on acceptance of the belief that life begins at conception or at some other point prior to live birth. In assessing the State's interest, recognition may be given to the less rigid claim that as long as at least *potential* life is involved, the State may assert interests beyond the protection of the pregnant woman alone.

Parties challenging state abortion laws have sharply disputed in some courts the contention that a purpose of these laws, when enacted, was to protect prenatal life. Pointing to the absence of legislative history to support the contention, they claim that most state laws were designed solely to protect the woman. Because medical advances have lessened this concern, at least with respect to abortion in early pregnancy, they argue that with respect to such abortions the laws can no longer be justified by any state interest. There is some scholarly support for this view of original purpose. The few state courts called upon to interpret their laws in the late 19th and early 20th centuries did focus on the State's interest in protecting the woman's health rather than in preserving the embryo and fetus. . . .

The Constitution does not explicitly mention any right of privacy. In a line of decisions, however, going back perhaps as far as *Union Pacific R. Co. v. Botsford* (1891), the Court has recognized that a right of personal privacy, or a guarantee of certain areas or zones of privacy, does exist under the Constitution. In varying contexts the Court or individual Justices have indeed found at least the roots of that right in the First Amendment, . . . in the Fourth and Fifth Amendments . . . in the penumbras of the Bill of Rights . . . in the Ninth Amendment . . . or in the concept of liberty guaranteed by the first section of the Fourteenth Amendment. . . . These decisions make it clear that only personal rights that can be deemed "fundamental" or "implicit in the concept of ordered liberty," . . . are included in this guarantee of personal privacy. They also make it clear that the right has some extension to activities relating to marriage, . . . procreation, . . . contraception, . . . family relationships, . . . and child rearing and education.

This right of privacy, whether it be founded in the Fourteenth Amendment's concept of personal liberty and restrictions upon State action, as we feel it is, or, as the District Court determined, in the Ninth Amendment's reservation of rights to the people, is broad enough to encompass a woman's decision whether or not to terminate her pregnancy. . . .

. . . [A]ppellants and some *amici* argue that the woman's right is absolute and that she is entitled to terminate her pregnancy at whatever time, in whatever way, and for whatever reason she alone chooses. With this we do not agree. Appellants' arguments that Texas either has no valid interest at all in regulating the abortion decision, or no interest strong enough to support any limitation upon the woman's sole determination, is unpersuasive. The Court's decisions recognizing a right of privacy also acknowledge that some State regulation in areas protected by that right is appropriate. As noted above, a State may properly assert important interests in safeguarding health, in maintaining medical standards, and in protecting potential life. At some point in pregnancy, these respective interests become sufficiently compelling to sustain regulation of the factors that govern the abortion decision. The privacy right involved, therefore, cannot be said to be absolute. . . .

We therefore conclude that the right of personal privacy includes the abortion decision, but that this right is not unqualified and must be considered against important State interests in regulation.

We note that those federal and state courts that have recently considered abortion law challenges have reached the same conclusion. . . .

Although the results are divided, most of these courts have agreed that the right of privacy, however based, is broad enough to cover the abortion decision; that the right, nonetheless, is not absolute and is subject to some limitations; and that at some point the state interests as to protection of health, medical standards, and prenatal life, become dominant. We agree with this approach. . . .

The appellee and certain *amici* argue that the fetus is a "person" within the language and meaning of the Fourteenth Amendment. In support of this they outline at length and in detail the well-known facts of fetal development. If this suggestion of personhood is established, the appellant's case, of course, collapses, for the fetus' right to life is then guaranteed specifically by the Amendment. The appellant conceded as much on reargument. On the other hand, the appellee conceded on reargument that no case could be cited that holds that a fetus is a person within the meaning of the Fourteenth Amendment. . . .

All this, together with our observation, *supra*, that throughout the major portion of the 19th century prevailing legal abortion practices were far freer than they are today, persuades us that the word "person," as used in the Fourteenth Amendment, does not include the unborn. . . . Indeed, our decision in *United States v. Vuitch* (1971) inferentially is to the same effect, for we there would not have indulged in statutory interpretation favorable to abortion in specified circumstances if the necessary consequence was the termination of life entitled to Fourteenth Amendment protection.

. . . As we have intimated above, it is reasonable and appropriate for a State to decide that at some point in time another interest, that of health of the mother or that of potential human life, becomes significantly involved. The woman's privacy is no longer sole and any right of privacy she possesses must be measured accordingly.

Texas urges that, apart from the Fourteenth Amendment, life begins at conception and is present throughout pregnancy, and that, therefore, the State has a compelling interest in protecting that life from and after conception. We need not resolve the difficult question of when life begins. When those trained in the respective disciplines of medicine, philosophy, and theology are unable to arrive at any consensus, the judiciary, at this point in the development of man's knowledge, is not in a position to speculate as to the answer.

It should be sufficient to note briefly the wide divergence of thinking on this most sensitive and difficult question. There has always been strong support for the view that life does not begin until live birth. This was the belief of the Stoics. It appears to be the predominant, though not the unanimous, attitude of the Jewish faith. It may be taken to represent also the position of a large segment of the Protestant community, insofar as that can be ascertained;

organized groups that have taken a formal position on the abortion issue have generally regarded abortion as a matter for the conscience of the individual and her family. As we have noted, the common law found greater significance in quickening. Physicians and their scientific colleagues have regarded that event with less interest and have tended to focus either upon conception or upon live birth or upon the interim point at which the fetus becomes "viable," that is, potentially able to live outside the mother's womb, albeit with artificial aid. Viability is usually placed at about seven months (28 weeks) but may occur earlier, even at 24 weeks. . . .

In areas other than criminal abortion the law has been reluctant to endorse any theory that life, as we recognize it, begins before live birth or to accord legal rights to the unborn except in narrowly defined situations and except when the rights are contingent upon live birth. . . . In short, the unborn have never been recognized in the law as persons in the whole sense.

In view of all this, we do not agree that, by adopting one theory of life, Texas may override the rights of the pregnant woman that are at stake. We repeat, however, that the State does have an important and legitimate interest in preserving and protecting the health of the pregnant woman, whether she be a resident of the State or a nonresident who seeks medical consultation and treatment there, and that it has still *another* important and legitimate interest in protecting the potentiality of human life. These interests are separate and distinct. Each grows in substantiality as the woman approaches term and, at a point during pregnancy, each becomes "compelling."

With respect to the State's important and legitimate interest in the health of the mother, the "compelling" point, in the light of present medical knowledge, is at approximately the end of the first trimester. This is so because of the now established medical fact . . . that until the end of the first trimester mortality in abortion is less than mortality in normal childbirth. It follows that, from and after this point, a State may regulate the abortion procedure to the extent that the regulation reasonably relates to the preservation and protection of maternal health. Examples of permissible state regulation in this area are requirements as to the qualifications of the person who is to perform the abortion; as to the licensure of that person; as to the facility in which the procedure is to be performed, that is, whether it must be a hospital or may be a clinic or some other place of less-than-hospital status; as to the licensing of the facility; and the like.

This means, on the other hand, that, for the period of pregnancy prior to this "compelling" point, the attending physician, in consultation with his patient, is free to determine, without regulation by the State, that in his medical judgment the patient's pregnancy should be terminated. If that decision is reached, the judgment may be effectuated by an abortion free of interference by the State.

With respect to the State's important and legitimate interest in potential life, the "compelling" point is at viability. This is so because the fetus then presumably has the capability of meaningful life outside the mother's womb. State regulation protective of fetal life after viability thus has both logical and biological justifications. If the State is interested in protecting fetal life after viability, it may go so far as to proscribe abortion during that period except when it is necessary to preserve the life or health of the mother. . . .

To summarize and repeat:

1. A state criminal abortion statute of the current Texas type, that excepts from criminality only a *life saving* procedure on behalf of the mother, without regard to pregnancy stage and without recognition of the other interests involved, is violative of the Due Process Clause of the Fourteenth Amendment.

    a. For the stage prior to approximately the end of the first trimester, the abortion decision and its effectuation must be left to the medical judgment of the pregnant woman's attending physician.

    b. For the stage subsequent to approximately the end of the first trimester, the State, in promoting its interest in the health of the mother, may, if it chooses, regulate the abortion procedure in ways that are reasonably related to maternal health.

    c. For the stage subsequent to viability the State, in promoting its interest in the potentiality of human life, may, if it chooses, regulate, and even proscribe, abortion except where it is necessary, in appropriate medical judgment, for the preservation of the life or health of the mother.

2. The State may define the term "physician," as it has been employed [here], to mean only a physician currently licensed by the State, and may proscribe any abortion by a person who is not a physician as so defined.

    . . . The decision leaves the State free to place increasing restrictions on abortion as the period of pregnancy lengthens, so long as those restrictions are tailored to the recognized state interests. The decision vindicates the right of the physician to administer medical treatment according to his professional judgment up to the points where important state interests provide compelling justifications for intervention. Up to those points the abortion decision in all its aspects is inherently, and primarily, a medical decision, and basic responsibility for it must rest with the physician. If an individual practitioner abuses the privilege of exercising proper medical judgment, the usual remedies, judicial and intraprofessional, are available. . . .

Minority Opinion (Written by Mr. Justice Byron R. White)

At the heart of the controversy in these cases are those recurring pregnancies that pose no danger whatsoever to the life or health of the mother but are nevertheless unwanted for any one or more of a variety of reasons—convenience, family planning, economics, dislike of children, the embarrassment of illegitimacy, etc. The common claim before us is that for any one of such reasons, or for no reason at all, and without asserting or claiming any threat to life or health, any woman is entitled to an abortion at her request if she is able to find a medical advisor willing to undertake the procedure.

The Court for the most part sustains this position: During the period prior to the time the fetus becomes viable, the Constitution of the United States values the convenience, whim or caprice of the putative mother more than the life or potential life of the fetus; the Constitution, therefore, guarantees the right to an abortion as against any state law or policy seeking to protect the fetus from an abortion not prompted by more compelling reasons of the mother.

With all due respect, I dissent. I find nothing in the language or history of the Constitution to support the Court's judgment. . . . As an exercise of raw judicial power, the Court perhaps has authority to do what it does today; but in my view its judgment is an improvident and extravagant exercise of the power of judicial review which the Constitution extends to this Court.

The Court apparently values the convenience of the pregnant mother more than the continued existence and development of the life or potential life which she carries. . . .

It is my view, therefore, that the Texas statute is not constitutionally infirm because it denies abortions to those who seek to serve only their convenience rather than to protect their life or health. . . .

Excerpts from the 1989 Supreme Court Decision in Webster v. Reproductive Health Services

Majority Opinion
(Written by Chief Justice William H. Rehnquist)

This appeal concerns the constitutionality of a Missouri statute regulating the performance of abortions. The United States Court of Appeals for the Eighth Circuit struck down several provisions of the statute on the ground that they violated this Court's decision in *Roe v. Wade* (1973) and cases following it. We noted probable jurisdiction and now reverse.

I

In June 1986, the Governor of Missouri signed into law Missouri Senate Committee Substitute for House Bill No. 1596 (hereinafter Act or statute), which amended existing state law concerning unborn children and abortions. The Act consisted of 20 provisions, 5 of which are now before the Court. The first provision, or preamble, contains "findings" by the state legislature that "[t]he life of each human being begins at conception," and that "unborn children have protectable interests in life, health, and well-being." The Act further requires that all Missouri laws be interpreted to provide unborn children with

Reprinted from the Opinion of Chief Justice William H. Rehnquist in *Webster v. Reproductive Health Services*. United States Supreme Court. 109 S. Ct. 3040 (1989).

the same rights enjoyed by other persons, subject to the Federal Constitution and this Court's precedents. Among its other provisions, the Act requires that, prior to performing an abortion on any woman whom a physician has reason to believe is 20 or more weeks pregnant, the physician ascertain whether the fetus is viable by performing "such medical examinations and tests as are necessary to make a finding of the gestational age, weight, and lung maturity of the unborn child." The Act also prohibits the use of public employees and facilities to perform or assist abortions not necessary to save the mother's life, and it prohibits the use of public funds, employees, or facilities for the purpose of "encouraging or counseling" a woman to have an abortion not necessary to save her life.

In July 1986, five health professionals employed by the State and two nonprofit corporations brought this class action in the United States District Court for the Western District of Missouri to challenge the constitutionality of the Missouri statute. Plaintiffs, appellees in this Court, sought declaratory and injunctive relief on the ground that certain statutory provisions violated the First, Fourth, Ninth, and Fourteenth Amendments to the Federal Constitution. . . .

Plaintiffs filed this suit "on their own behalf and on behalf of the entire class consisting of facilities and Missouri licensed physicians or other health care professionals offering abortion services or pregnancy counseling and on behalf of the entire class of pregnant females seeking abortion services or pregnancy counseling within the State of Missouri." The two nonprofit corporations are Reproductive Health Services, which offers family planning and gynecological services to the public, including abortion services up to 22 weeks "gestational age," and Planned Parenthood of Kansas City, which provides abortion services up to 14 weeks gestational age. . . .

Several weeks after the complaint was filed, the District Court temporarily restrained enforcement of several provisions of the Act. . . .

The Court of Appeals for the Eighth Circuit affirmed, with one exception not relevant to this appeal. The Court of Appeals determined that Missouri's declaration that life begins at conception was "simply an impermissible state adoption of a theory of when life begins to justify its abortion regulations." Relying on *Colautti v. Franklin* (1979), it further held that the requirement that physicians perform viability tests was an unconstitutional legislative intrusion on a matter of medical skill and judgment. The Court of Appeals invalidated Missouri's prohibition on the use of public facilities and employees to perform or assist abortions not necessary to save the mother's life. It distinguished our decisions in *Harris v. McRae* (1980) and *Maher v. Roe* (1977), on the ground that "'[t]here is a fundamental difference between providing direct funding to effect the abortion decision and allowing staff physicians to perform abortions at an existing publicly owned hospital.'" The Court of Appeals struck down the provision prohibiting the use of public funds for "encouraging or counseling" women to have nontherapeutic abortions, for the reason that this provision was both overly vague and inconsistent with the right to an abortion enunciated in *Roe v. Wade*. . . .

II

Decision of this case requires us to address four sections of the Missouri Act: (a) the preamble; (b) the prohibition on the use of public facilities or employees to perform abortions; (c) the prohibition on public funding of abortion counseling; and (d) the requirement that physicians conduct viability tests prior to performing abortions. We address these *seriatim.*

A

The Act's preamble, as noted, sets forth "findings" by the Missouri legislature that "[t]he life of each human being begins at conception," and that "[u]nborn children have protectable interests in life, health, and well-being." The Act then mandates that state laws be interpreted to provide unborn children with "all the rights, privileges, and immunities available to other persons, citizens, and residents of this state," subject to the Constitution and this Court's precedents. In invalidating the preamble, the Court of Appeals relied on this Court's dictum that "'a State may not adopt one theory of when life begins to justify its regulation of abortions.'" It rejected Missouri's claim that the preamble was "abortion-neutral," and "merely determine[d] when life begins in a nonabortion context, a traditional state prerogative." The court thought that "[t]he only plausible inference" from the fact that "every remaining section of the bill save one regulates the performance of abortions" was that "the state intended its abortion regulations to be understood against the backdrop of its theory of life."

    The State contends that the preamble itself is precatory and imposes no substantive restrictions on abortion. . . .

    . . . Certainly the preamble does not by its terms regulate abortion or any other aspect of appellees' medical practice. The Court has emphasized that *Roe v. Wade* "implies no limitation on the authority of a State to make a value judgment favoring childbirth over abortion." The preamble can be read simply to express that sort of value judgment.

    We think the extent to which the preamble's language might be used to interpret other state statutes or regulations is something that only the courts of Missouri can definitively decide. . . .

    It will be time enough for federal courts to address the meaning of the preamble should it be applied to restrict the activities of appellees in some concrete way. . . . We therefore need not pass on the constitutionality of the Act's preamble.

B

Section 188.210 provides that "[i]t shall be unlawful for any public employee within the scope of his employment to perform or assist an abortion, not necessary to save the life of the mother," while §188.215 makes it "unlawful for any public facility to be used for the purpose of performing or assisting an abortion not necessary to save the life of the mother." The Court of Appeals held that these provisions contravened this Court's abortion decisions. We take the contrary view.

As we said earlier this Term . . . , "our cases have recognized that the Due Process Clauses generally confer no affirmative right to governmental aid, even where such aid may be necessary to secure life, liberty, or property interests of which the government itself may not deprive the individual." In *Maher v. Roe, supra,* the Court upheld a Connecticut welfare regulation under which Medicaid recipients received payments for medical services related to childbirth, but not for nontherapeutic abortions. The Court rejected the claim that this unequal subsidization of childbirth and abortion was impermissible under *Roe v. Wade.* As the Court put it:

> "The Connecticut regulation before us is different in kind from the laws invalidated in our previous abortion decisions. The Connecticut regulation places no obstacles—absolute or otherwise—in the pregnant woman's path to an abortion. An indigent woman who desires an abortion suffers no disadvantage as a consequence of Connecticut's decision to fund childbirth; she continues as before to be dependent on private sources for the service she desires. The State may have made childbirth a more attractive alternative, thereby influencing the woman's decision, but it has imposed no restriction on access to abortions that was not already there. The indigency that may make it difficult—and in some cases, perhaps, impossible—for some women to have abortions is neither created nor in any way affected by the Connecticut regulation."

Relying on *Maher,* the Court in *Poelker v. Doe* (1977) held that the city of St. Louis committed "no constitutional violation . . . in electing, as a policy choice, to provide publicly financed hospital services for childbirth without providing corresponding services for nontherapeutic abortions."

More recently, in *Harris v. McRae* (1980), the Court upheld "the most restrictive version of the Hyde Amendment," which withheld from States federal funds under the Medicaid program to reimburse the costs of abortions, "'except where the life of the mother would be endangered if the fetus were carried to term.'" As in *Maher* and *Poelker,* the Court required only a showing that Congress' authorization of "reimbursement for medically necessary services generally, but not for certain medically necessary abortions" was rationally related to the legitimate governmental goal of encouraging childbirth.

The Court of Appeals distinguished these cases on the ground that "[t]o prevent access to a public facility does more than demonstrate a political choice in favor of childbirth; it clearly narrows and in some cases forecloses the availability of abortion to women." The court reasoned that the ban on the use of public facilities "could prevent a woman's chosen doctor from performing an abortion because of his unprivileged status at other hospitals or because a private hospital adopted a similar anti-abortion stance." It also thought that "[s]uch a rule could increase the cost of obtaining an abortion and delay the timing of it as well."

We think that this analysis is much like that which we rejected in *Maher, Poelker,* and *McRae.* As in those cases, the State's decision here to use public facilities and staff to encourage childbirth over abortion "places no governmental obstacle in the path of a woman who chooses to terminate her pregnancy." Just as Congress' refusal to fund abortions in *McRae* left "an indigent woman with at least the same range of choice in deciding whether to obtain a medically necessary abortion as she would have had if Congress had chosen to subsidize no health care costs at all," Missouri's refusal to allow public employees to perform abortions in public hospitals leaves a pregnant woman with the same choices as if the State had chosen not to operate any public hospitals at all. The challenged provisions only restrict a woman's ability to obtain an abortion to the extent that she chooses to use a physician affiliated with a public hospital. This circumstance is more easily remedied, and thus considerably less burdensome, than indigency, which "may make it difficult—and in some cases, perhaps, impossible—for some women to have abortions" without public funding. Having held that the State's refusal to fund abortions does not violate *Roe v. Wade,* it strains logic to reach a contrary result for the use of public facilities and employees. If the State may "make a value judgment favoring childbirth over abortion and . . . implement that judgment by the allocation of public funds," surely it may do so through the allocation of other public resources, such as hospitals and medical staff. . . .

. . . Thus we uphold the Act's restrictions on the use of public employees and facilities for the performance or assistance of nontherapeutic abortions.

C

The Missouri Act contains three provisions relating to "encouraging or counseling a woman to have an abortion not necessary to save her life." Section 188.205 states that no public funds can be used for this purpose; § 188.210 states that public employees cannot, within the scope of their employment, engage in such speech; and § 188.215 forbids such speech in public facilities. The Court of Appeals did not consider § 188.205 separately from §§ 188.210 and 188.215. It held that all three of these provisions were unconstitutionally vague, and that "the ban on using public funds, employees, and facilities to encourage or counsel a woman to have an abortion is an unacceptable infringement of the woman's fourteenth amendment right to choose an abortion after receiving the medical information necessary to exercise the right knowingly and intelligently."

Missouri has chosen only to appeal the Court of Appeals' invalidation of the public funding provision, § 188.205. A threshold question is whether this provision reaches primary conduct, or whether it is simply an instruction to the State's fiscal officers not to allocate funds for abortion counseling. We accept, for purposes of decision, the State's claim that § 188.205 "is not directed at the conduct of any physician or health care provider, private or public," but "is directed solely at those persons responsible for expending public funds."

Appellees contend that they are not "adversely" affected under the State's interpretation of § 188.205, and therefore that there is no longer a case or controversy before us on this question. . . . A majority of the Court agrees with appellees that the controversy over § 188.205 is now moot. . . .

D

Section 188.029 of the Missouri Act provides:

> "Before a physician performs an abortion on a woman he has reason to believe is carrying an unborn child of twenty or more weeks gestational age, the physician shall first determine if the unborn child is viable by using and exercising that degree of care, skill, and proficiency commonly exercised by the ordinarily skillful, careful, and prudent physician engaged in similar practice under the same or similar conditions. In making this determination of viability, the physician shall perform or cause to be performed such medical examinations and tests as are necessary to make a finding of the gestational age, weight, and lung maturity of the unborn child and shall enter such findings and determination of viability in the medical record of the mother."

As with the preamble, the parties disagree over the meaning of this statutory provision. The State emphasizes the language of the first sentence, which speaks in terms of the physician's determination of viability being made by the standards of ordinary skill in the medical profession. Appellees stress the language of the second sentence, which prescribes such "tests as are necessary" to make a finding of gestational age, fetal weight, and lung maturity.

The Court of Appeals read § 188.029 as requiring that after 20 weeks "doctors *must* perform tests to find gestational age, fetal weight and lung maturity." The court indicated that the tests needed to determine fetal weight at 20 weeks are "unreliable and inaccurate" and would add $125 to $250 to the cost of an abortion. It also stated that "amniocentesis, the only method available to determine lung maturity, is contrary to accepted medical practice until 28–30 weeks of gestation, expensive, and imposes significant health risks for both the pregnant woman and the fetus."

We must first determine the meaning of § 188.029 under Missouri law. Our usual practice is to defer to the lower court's construction of a state statute, but we believe the Court of Appeals has "fallen into plain error" in this case. "'In expounding a statute, we must not be guided by a single sentence or member of a sentence, but look to the provisions of the whole law, and to its object and policy.'" The Court of Appeals' interpretation also runs "afoul of the well-established principle that statutes will be interpreted to avoid constitutional difficulties."

We think the viability-testing provision makes sense only if the second sentence is read to require only those tests that are useful to making subsidiary findings as to viability. If we construe this provision to require a physician to perform those tests needed to make the three specified findings *in all circumstances,* including when the physician's reasonable professional judgment indicates that the tests would be irrelevant to determining viability or even dangerous to the mother and the fetus, the second sentence of § 188.029 would conflict with the first sentence's *requirement* that a physician apply his reasonable professional skill and judgment. It would also be incongruous to read this provision, especially the word "necessary," to require the performance of tests irrelevant to the expressed statutory purpose of determining viability. It thus seems clear to us that the Court of Appeals' construction of § 188.029 violates well-accepted canons of statutory interpretation used in the Missouri courts. . . .

The viability-testing provision of the Missouri Act is concerned with promoting the State's interest in potential human life rather than in maternal health. Section 188.029 creates what is essentially a presumption of viability at 20 weeks, which the physician must rebut with tests indicating that the fetus is not viable prior to performing an abortion. It also directs the physician's determination as to viability by specifying consideration, if feasible, of gestational age, fetal weight, and lung capacity. The District Court found that "the medical evidence is uncontradicted that a 20-week fetus is *not* viable," and that "23½ to 24 weeks gestation is the earliest point in pregnancy where a reasonable possibility of viability exists." But it also found that there may be a 4-week error in estimating gestational age, which supports testing at 20 weeks.

In *Roe v. Wade,* the Court recognized that the State has "important and legitimate" interests in protecting maternal health and in the potentiality of human life. During the second trimester, the State "may, if it chooses, regulate the abortion procedure in ways that are reasonably related to maternal health." After viability, when the State's interest in potential human life was held to become compelling, the State "may, if it chooses, regulate, and even proscribe, abortion except where it is necessary, in appropriate medical judgment, for the preservation of the life or health of the mother."

In *Colautti v. Franklin, supra,* upon which appellees rely, the Court held that a Pennsylvania statute regulating the standard of care to be used by a physician performing an abortion of a possibly viable fetus was void for vagueness. But in the course of reaching that conclusion, the Court reaffirmed its earlier statement in *Planned Parenthood of Central Missouri v. Danforth* (1976), that "'the determination of whether a particular fetus is viable is, and must be, a matter for the judgement of the responsible attending physician.'" The dissent ignores the statement in *Colautti* that "neither the legislature nor the courts may proclaim one of the elements entering into the ascertainment of viability—be it weeks of gestation or fetal weight or any other single factor—as the determinant of when the State has a compelling interest in the life or health of the fetus." To the extent that § 188.029 regulates the method for determining viability, it undoubtedly does superimpose state regulation on the medical determination of whether a particular fetus is viable. The Court of Appeals and the District Court thought it unconstitutional for this reason. To the extent that the viability tests increase the cost of what are in fact second-trimester abortions, their validity may also be questioned under *Akron v. Akron Center for Reproductive Health* (1983), where the Court held that a requirement that second trimester abortions must be performed in hospitals was invalid because it substantially increased the expense of those procedures.

We think that the doubt cast upon the Missouri statute by these cases is not so much a flaw in the statute as it is a reflection of the fact that the rigid trimester analysis of the course of a pregnancy enunciated in *Roe* has resulted in subsequent cases like *Colautti* and *Akron* making constitutional law in this area a virtual Procrustean bed. Statutes specifying elements of informed consent to be provided abortion patients, for example, were invalidated if they were thought to "structur[e] . . . the dialogue between the woman and her physician." *Thornburgh v. American College of Obstetricians and Gynecologists* (1986). As the dissenters in *Thornburgh* pointed out, such a statute would have been sustained under any traditional standard of judicial review, or for any other surgical procedure except abortion.

Stare decisis is a cornerstone of our legal system, but it has less power in constitutional cases, where, save for constitutional amendments, this Court is the only body able to make needed changes. We have not refrained from reconsideration of a prior construction of the Constitution that has proved "unsound in principle and unworkable in practice." We think the *Roe* trimester framework falls into that category.

In the first place, the rigid *Roe* framework is hardly consistent with the notion of a Constitution cast in general terms, as ours is, and usually speaking in general principles, as ours does. The key elements of the *Roe* framework—trimesters and viability—are not found in the text of the Constitution or in any place else one would expect to find a constitutional principle. Since the bounds of the inquiry are essentially indeterminate, the result has been a web of legal rules that have become increasingly intricate, resembling a code of regulations rather than a body of constitutional doctrine. As JUSTICE WHITE has put it, the trimester framework has left this Court to serve as the country's "*ex officio* medical board with powers to approve or disapprove medical and operative practices and standards throughout the United States."

In the second place, we do not see why the State's interest in protecting potential, human life should come into existence only at the point of viability, and that there should therefore be a rigid line allowing state regulation after viability but prohibiting it before viability. The dissenters in *Thornburgh*, writing in the context of the *Roe* trimester analysis, would have recognized this fact by positing against the "fundamental right" recognized in *Roe* the

State's "compelling interest" in protecting potential human life throughout pregnancy. . . .

The tests that § 188.029 requires the physician to perform are designed to determine viability. The State here has chosen viability as the point at which its interest in potential human life must be safeguarded. It is true that the tests in question increase the expense of abortion, and regulate the discretion of the physician in determining the viability of the fetus. Since the tests will undoubtedly show in many cases that the fetus is not viable, the tests will have been performed for what were in fact second-trimester abortions. But we are satisfied that the requirement of these tests permissibly furthers the State's interest in protecting potential human life, and we therefore believe § 188.029 to be constitutional.

The dissent takes us to task for our failure to join in a "great issues" debate as to whether the Constitution includes an "unenumerated" general right to privacy as recognized in cases such as *Griswold v. Connecticut* (1965) and *Roe*. But *Griswold v. Connecticut*, unlike *Roe*, did not purport to adopt a whole framework, complete with detailed rules and distinctions, to govern the cases in which the asserted liberty interest would apply. As such, it was far different from the opinion, if not the holding, of *Roe v. Wade*, which sought to establish a constitutional framework for judging state regulation of abortion during the entire term of pregnancy. That framework sought to deal with areas of medical practice traditionally subject to state regulation, and it sought to balance once and for all by reference only to the calendar the claims of the State to protect the fetus as a form of human life against the claims of a woman to decide for herself whether or not to abort a fetus she was carrying. The experience of the Court in applying *Roe v. Wade* in later cases suggests to us that there is wisdom in not unnecessarily attempting to elaborate the abstract differences between a "fundamental right" to abortion, as the Court described it in *Akron*, a "limited fundamental constitutional right," which JUSTICE BLACKMUN'S dissent today treats *Roe* as having established, or a liberty interest protected by the Due Process Clause, which we believe it to be. The Missouri testing requirement here is reasonably designed to ensure that abortions are not performed where the fetus is viable—an end which all concede is legitimate—and that is sufficient to sustain its constitutionality.

The dissent also accuses us, *inter alia*, of cowardice and illegitimacy in dealing with "the most politically divisive domestic legal issue of our time." There is no doubt that our holding today will allow some governmental regulation of abortion that would have been prohibited under the language of cases such as *Colautti v. Franklin* and *Akron v. Akron Center for Reproductive Health, Inc., supra*. But the goal of constitutional adjudication is surely not to remove inexorably "politically divisive" issues from the ambit of the legislative process, whereby the people through their elected representatives deal with matters of concern to them. The goal of constitutional adjudication is to hold true the balance between that which the Constitution puts beyond the reach of the democratic process and that which it does not. We think we have done that today. The dissent's suggestion that legislative bodies, in a Nation where more than half of our population is women, will treat our decision today as an invitation to enact abortion regulation reminiscent of the dark ages not only misreads our views but does scant justice to those who serve in such bodies and the people who elect them.

III

Both appellants and the United States as *Amicus Curiae* have urged that we overrule our decision in *Roe v. Wade.* The facts of the present case, however, differ from those at issue in *Roe.* Here, Missouri has determined that viability is the point at which its interest in potential human life must be safeguarded. In *Roe,* on the other hand, the Texas statute criminalized the performance of *all* abortions, except when the mother's life was at stake. This case therefore affords us no occasion to revisit the holding of *Roe,* which was that the Texas statute unconstitutionally infringed the right to an abortion derived from the Due Process Clause, and we leave it undisturbed. To the extent indicated in our opinion, we would modify and narrow *Roe* and succeeding cases.

Because none of the challenged provisions of the Missouri Act properly before us conflict with the Constitution, the judgment of the Court of Appeals is *Reversed.*